LORD OF THE IMPOSSIBLE

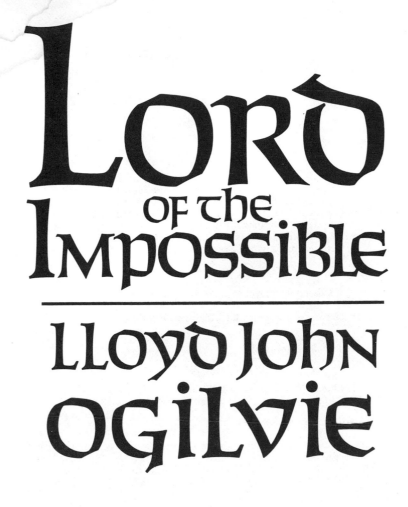

# LORD
## OF THE
# IMPOSSIBLE

# LLOYD JOHN
# OGILVIE

ABINGDON PRESS
NASHVILLE

LORD OF THE IMPOSSIBLE

*This book is printed on recycled, acid-free paper.*

**Library of Congress Cataloging-in-Publication Data**

OGILVIE, LLOYD JOHN.
Lord of the impossible.

**ISBN 0-687-22710-0**

1. Bible. O.T.—Biography I. Title.
BS571.037      1984      221.9′22 [B]      84-333

TO
EILEEN ROACH OGILVIE
Daughter-in-Law
Sister in Christ
Friend in Faith
For Whom Impossibilities Are a Prelude
to God's Amazing Possibilities

# Contents

# Preface

Strange thing about heroes. They seldom set out to be heroic. Conviction mingled with courage enabled them to do the spectacular things history later calls heroism. They had to do it. The dynamic men and women we hail as our biblical heroes were driven by a creative compulsion. A mysterious encounter with God spurred them on to attempt the impossible. It was in the dangerous interface between what they were and what God called them to be and do that they discovered the secret of his strength. Faith! Greatness was realized through the gift of faith.

Faith is risky. It isn't real faith without a risk. A willingness to risk was all that God asked of them. The greater the risk, the greater the power of faith given them. And those who dared to risk in attempting the impossible found the liberating truth that we all desperately need for life's awesome challenges. They discovered that the Creator and Sustainer of the universe is the Lord of the impossible!

In each stage of the unfolding drama of Israel's history there is a pivotal character, a person through whom God sought to move his people forward in the realization of being his called and chosen people. The Bible is very honest about its heroes. They were fallible, humanly inadequate people who discovered that God's work done by his power produces his results.

In this book I want to help readers meet the Lord of the impossible through these people. I have selected a few out of the hundreds of faithful and obedient heroes of faith, with the aim of seeing them in the context of the time in which they lived and learning what the Lord taught his people through them.

My goal has been to give more than a series of personality profiles. Rather, I have wanted to confront the hurts and hopes we face today through these characters. I have taken an expository—textual—topical approach. Each chapter is an exposition of the most salient portion of Scripture about each character in order to expose what God was trying to communicate about his nature and what that means for us today. We will focus on problems facing us today which were also confronted and lived through by these Old Testament personalities.

In preparation for a contemporary treatment of the lives of these heroes, I asked my Hollywood congregation and the viewers of our television program, "Let God Love You," to share with me the greatest challenges they face in living their faith. These challenges were organized into categories and kept in mind as I searched for biblical passages which exposed the supernatural power of the Lord of the impossible.

An in-depth, comprehensive study of how God called and equipped people to do what they could not do alone reveals the power available to us today. The Lord constantly wants to surprise us with what he can do if we dare to risk, to accept his gift of faith, and to leave the results to him.

Each chapter leads to Calvary and the ultimate intervention of the Lord of the impossible. The Lord of Abraham, Jacob, Joseph, Moses, Joshua, Gideon, Ruth, the great kings, and incisive prophets was the Lord of the incarnation, the cross, an empty tomb, and the birth of the new Israel at Pentecost. Meeting the Old Testament heroes is discovering the New Testament Savior in a new way. Whatever they discovered of the supernatural is only a prelude to the ultimate revelation of the Lord of the impossible when he lived among us. However great these men and women became by God's intervention, it is only a shadow of the new creation available to us.

The most difficult challenge in writing this book has been to limit the number of characters. The choice had to be made between a brief treatment of many or a deeper study of a few representative types. In spanning the hundreds of years from Abraham to Ezekiel, many of my favorite heroes had to be omitted. My concern was to focus on the Lord of the impossible and his intervening power available today. That became the final test of who among the pioneers of adventuresome faith would be included.

As with all my previous books, this book is an effort to speak to the deepest needs and concerns of people today. My commitment to listen to people and then to God as he speaks through the Bible is reflected in the style and intent of this writing. It is my privilege to be a part of a growing fellowship of people in America who long to live the abundant life in Christ with freedom, joy, and hope. Their quest to live life more fully has spurred me on to be both practical and personal in what I have written.

We all face what we perceive are impossibilities. Life has its culs-de-sac of problems and perplexities which seem to offer no way out. Difficult people and awesome opportunities confront us all. When life challenges us and we say, "Why, that's impossible," we need to make the liberating assurance of God's angel our motto, "With God, nothing is impossible." Meeting the Lord of the impossible in down-to-earth, gutsy, vulnerable people on the pages of the Old Testament has renewed my own "all things are possible with God" desire to dare to risk. My prayer is that this renewal also will happen to you.

I want to express my gratitude to my administrative assistant, Jeri Gonzalez, for her typing of the manuscript in preparation for publication. Her own friendship with God and her experience of him as the Lord of the impossible has made the project a source of many stimulating conversations.

And now to you, my reader, fellow-adventurer, and partner in faith, I commit this book in the hope that it will help you dare to believe that "the things which are impossible with men are possible with God."

LORD OF THE IMPOSSIBLE

# CHAPTER ONE

# Nothing Is Impossible

## ——*Abraham*——

What are you attempting that you cannot accomplish without an intervention from the Lord? That's a question I've asked others and myself for years. Most of us live our lives within the narrow limits of what we can do on our own strength and talents. We keep life carefully constricted inside the boundaries of what we are sure we can handle by ourselves. In reality, we don't need God. Our fear of risk keeps us away from anything we cannot control or do with our own ability.

At the same time we are surrounded with problems, challenges, and opportunities. We tackle the things that can't be avoided. Our vision of what can happen is usually calculated on what we are able to do with our own resources and experience. When we do ask for God's help, our prayers are often for his power to do what we think is best. He is gracious to respond, and our Christianity settles into the set of self-determined possibilities.

I shared these thoughts with my congregation one Sunday morning. Then at the end of the service, we took a prolonged time for prayer. Each of us was asked to think about his or her life on several levels. We were guided in our prayers to reflect on the unlimited power of God. What would we dare to attempt if we were sure that the Lord would intervene to help us? What had we avoided by saying, "Why that's impossible"? Where had we stepped back from involvement in something that we couldn't do by ourselves? We were asked to picture the impossible person, the difficult relationship, limitation, illness, crisis, or assignment that we had kept at arms length because we wanted to keep life safe and free of risk. Then we dared to ask God to give us a picture of how we would live if we were sure that he would unleash the same power revealed in the lives of our biblical heroes, in the resurrection, and in the Book of Acts.

To blast the cap off our limited perception of what is possible, we read John 14:12-14. "Most assuredly, I say to you, he who believes in Me, the works that I do he will do also; and greater works than these he will do, because I go to My Father. And whatever you ask in My name, that I will do, that the Father may be glorified in the Son. If you ask anything in My name, I will do it" (NKJV).

The atmosphere in the sanctuary was electric after that! Had the same power to love, forgive, heal, reconcile, and take up our cross of obedience been given to us? Yes! And more than that, we have been called to do the thing Jesus of Nazareth could not do when he spoke this promise prior to the crucifixion, resurrection, and Pentecost—introduce people to him as the living, victorious Lord! To whom in our lives do we need to risk time and costly caring to communicate Jesus' love? What opportunities for service in the social sickness of our community are we carefully avoiding? What goals for our families, our work, our church does the Lord want us to risk our security to attempt?

After this incisive inventory, the people were asked to place their open hands before them. In the hands, we placed the person, situation, problem, or action on which our prayers focused. What had the Lord guided us to be, do, or attempt which was impossible without his intervention and power? Then when everybody was ready, they were asked to lift those impossibilities in expectant surrender. Looking out over the congregation, I saw hands go up, slowly at first, and then with vigor, until almost every person sat with arms uplifted, hands open, releasing the God-guided and focused impossibilities to him. The closing hymn shook the rafters.

Even more exciting than the service was the change that took place in the people and in our church. The letters and conversations in the weeks that followed recounted amazing things. Many people said they had never asked God for a vision of his will which would be impossible for them to do without his help. But now, through their new vision of attempting the impossible, God had given healing, supernatural strength, reconciled relationships which had been strained for years, renewal of marriages, job changes, personal evangelism, and mission projects in the community. A miniature Pentecost had started as people dared to risk doing what only the Lord of the impossible could do through them. These people have found that the Lord provides and guides them in the impossibilities.

In order to replenish the flow of the Lord's power each week, the lay elders of the church gather in the chancel to be available to pray with people at the conclusion of the worship services. Many who are in small groups shared their impossibilities with their covenant sisters and brothers. They have become committed cheerleaders to spur on their fellow-adventurers.

When church members sense a call to step out in costly discipleship, suddenly the whole church program takes on new meaning and purpose. The worship, education, and fellowship activities become part of the equipping of people for ministry.

The longer I live in the adventure of faith and share deeply with others what they are discovering about God, the more I have been led to a liberating conviction: that the Lord loves us and cares more about our concerns than we do. He is the Lord of radical interventions. On time, and in time, he invades our problems and perplexities with supernatural power. There are times when he actually leads us into challenges and opportunities in order to astound us with what he is able to do with our impossibilities.

What is it for you? Have you ever asked God to help you dare to risk attempting something he's revealed he wants you to be or do? That's crucial. God performs the impossible through a radical intervention in what he has guided. Keep that focus in your mind. All that I want to say in this book will make more sense if we keep our God-guided impossibility before us as we consider the characters of the Old Testament. Then, we can learn from them what they discovered about the Lord of the impossible in their circumstances. They will help us realize his power in ours.

Oswald Chambers in *My Utmost for His Highest* (Dodd Mead & Co.) put it this way. Our impossibilities "provide a platform for the display of His almighty grace and power. He will not only deliver us, but in doing so, He will give us a lesson we will never forget; and to which we will return with joyous reflection. We will never be able to thank God enough for having done exactly what He did."

That was the exciting discovery Abraham made in his growing friendship with God. The audacious accolade of the Bible about this adventuresome pioneer is, "Abraham Thy friend forever" (II Chron. 20:7 NASB). God's own affirmation through the prophet Isaiah was an assurance of that: "Abraham My friend" (Isa. 41:8 NASB). The apostle James' summary of the unfolding drama of that friendship was, " 'And Abraham believed God, and it was reckoned to him as righteousness,' and he was called a friend of God" (James 2:23 NASB).

Friendship with God did not come easily for Abraham. It took repeated evidences of the Lord's intervention to bring him to that abiding conviction. All that he went through was preparation for him to be able to believe and say, "The Lord will provide." Through it all, he became a hero of faith who towers over all other heroes of the Old Testament. The secret of his life is the gift of faith the Lord gave him. He is distinguished for the risks he dared to take and the succession of radical interventions the Lord displayed in his life.

Abraham's heroic life can be divided into three acts: his call to faith, his realization of the gift of faith, and his ultimate test of that faith. Act three is our major focus, but the penultimate events of acts one and two are absolutely necessary to understand in order to appreciate Abraham's bold, "the Lord will provide" conviction in the most harrowing experience of his friendship with God.

*The call to faith* came to Abram, as he was then called, first as the son of Terah among the Semitic people who had migrated to and settled in the highly advanced culture of Ur in northern Mesopotamia. A multiplicity of gods and idol worship pervaded the Sumerian polytheism of the area and time. A problem, we will observe, that was manifested repeatedly in this early stage of the history of the people of God. For a time these good Semites syncretized their God of creation, the flood, and Noah with the local gods, particularly the moon god. The evidence of that blending is shown in Terah's name, which in Hebrew is related to the word "moon." That may be the reason that the Lord had to extricate him and his family out of the prosperous and sophisticated culture. He created a restlessness in Terah and motivated him to take his son Abram, his son's wife Sarai, and Lot, Abram's nephew, out of Ur and follow a mysterious inner guidance to move toward the land of Canaan. They traveled along the Euphrates Valley as far as Haran.

It was there, some years later, that the same God who first guided Terah to move from Ur, appeared in a direct revelation to Abram. What he said must have put both awe and panic in Abram's soul. The Lord had great plans for Abram. It would take a lifetime of friendship with God before Abram realized that God would provide for each step of the way. "Go forth from your country, / And from your relatives, / And from your father's house, / To a land which I will show you" (Gen. 12:1 NASB). The Hebrew verb can be translated "go for yourself." The risks the Lord challenges us to take are always for our good, however frightening they may seem at first. The Lord continued: "And I will make you a great nation, / And I will bless you, / And make your name great; / And so you shall be a blessing; / And I will bless those who bless you, / And the one who curses you I will curse. / And in you all the families of the earth shall be blessed" (Gen. 12:2-3 NASB).

Quite a promise! Acting on it required risk. Abram had nothing to go on except the promise of God. But he went forth with what little guidance he had. In the years ahead he learned the absolute faithfulness and enduring friendship of God. He needed all those years to grow in that friendship—to trust it—experiencing its reality in times when he did not trust.

After Terah died, Abram left the security of Haran, and proceeded into Canaan. The altars he built along the way were symbolic of his growing faith in God which enabled him to take new risks. However, when a famine hit the land of Canaan, he went even farther south into Egypt. While there Abram showed his other side—the fearful side that resisted risk, that did not trust. As he and Sarai entered Egypt, he told her to say that she was his sister—a lie based on lack of trust in God's promise. Sarai was beautiful and Abram feared that the Egyptians would take her and kill him. None other than the Pharaoh himself was attracted to her. He took her to his home and honored Abram, whom he assumed was Sarai's brother. But the Lord had other plans. He sent plagues on the Pharaoh and his household until the truth was

told. Abram almost thwarted the plan of God to make him the
father of a great people. He and Sarai barely escaped with their
lives.

*The realization of faith,* act two of the drama of Abram, soon to
become Abraham, came when the Lord led him out of Egypt into
Canaan. The Lord appeared to him at his first major camp and
reminded him of the blessing which could be seen in Abram's
increasing livestock and in his silver and gold. Added to that, the
Lord showed him the land which was to be his and his
descendants. "Now lift up your eyes and look from the place
where you are, northward and southward and eastward and
westward; for all the land which you see, I will give it to you and
your descendants forever. And I will make your descendants as
the dust of the earth; so that if anyone can number the dust of the
earth, then your descendants can also be numbered" (Gen.
13:14-16 NASB).

Then the Lord told Abram to do a strange thing. "Arise, walk
about the land through its length and breadth; for I will give it to
you" (Gen. 13:17 NASB). In order to build in Abram the
confidence of a risktaker, the Lord had to help him claim the
reality of the seemingly impossible. He not only gave him a vision,
but he also made him walk through that vision until he made it
really his own.

God does the same thing with you and me. First he gives us the
impossible dream, then he helps us envision what it will be like to
possess our possession, and then through our imagination he
helps us persistently image the reality. What is the dream for you?

Abram built an altar to thank the Lord and to show that he
believed. What can we do to show the same Lord of the impossible
that we believe in him today?

Act two comes to a close with repeated evidence of the Lord's
blessing on Abram. Not only did he defeat the king of Sodom in
battle, but Melchizedek, king of Salem and a priest of the Lord,
met Abram after the battle with a victory celebration of bread and
wine. Most significantly he blessed Abram: "Blessed be Abram of
God Most High, / Possessor of heaven and earth; / And blessed
be God most High, / Who has delivered your enemies into your
hand" (Gen. 14:19-20 NASB). It must have been very comforting
to Abram to hear from another human being the same promise he

had heard repeatedly from God. The bond of friendship between God and Abram was growing firm and strong.

Good thing. For in act three we see the greatest test of that friendship. Abram was in a quandary. The promise of God had been given that he would have innumerable descendants, but Sarai was still childless. How could he be the father of multitudes without a son? Since he had no offspring, would one of the lads born in his household be heir? No. Instead, the Lord made Abram what seemed to be an impossible promise. He and Sarai would have a son. Abram found that very difficult to believe. He was a hundred years old and Sarai was ninety! It was then that the Lord provided a gift, one which he generously offers to everyone who dares to risk—the gift of faith. He showed Abram the stars in the heavens and told him to count them. "So shall your descendants be."

What follows in Genesis 15:6 is one of the most crucial verses in the Old Testament. "Then he [Abram] believed in the Lord; and He reckoned it to him as righteousness" (NASB). God gave Abram the only thing that can please him and make us right with him. What God requires he longs to release in us. It is by faith alone—not works or goodness of our own—that a right relationship with God is established and maintained. This later became the critical issue for both the early church and the Reformation. How are we made right with God? By faith alone. And what God wants from us, he implants within us. *Faith is a gift.*

Abram needed a constant replenishment of that gift as he grappled with the humanly impossible promise of a son. The Lord had provided in the past, but how could his ninety-year-old wife have a child? After this most propitious promise, Sarai insisted that Abram impregnate Hagar, her Egyptian maid. Once again our hero is exposed as finding it difficult to believe God's awesome promise. "And Abram listened to the voice of Sarai" (Gen. 16:2*b* NASB). A sad mistake! It sent both Abram and Sarai down an equivocating eddy out of the stream of God's direct will for some time.

Ishmael was born of the unblessed relationship of Abram and Hagar. As we shall discover repeatedly in the unfolding revelation of the Lord of the impossible, some of our choice heroes had to cope with second best because they would not wait patiently for

God's best. But, as we shall also discover, the Lord never forgets or gives up on those he has chosen, or goes back on his promises.

The Lord takes Abram back to "zero planning" again. Once again he makes his promise as the Lord of the impossible. This time he gives both Abram and Sarai new names. Abram is to be Abraham, the father of multitudes, and Sarai is to be Sarah, a mother of nations. Added to the vision focused in new names, the Lord uses a definitive name for himself to give Abraham new courage: El Shaddai, God Almighty, the One who has all power. As if all this were not enough, the mighty El Shaddai then offered a covenant, a promise and agreement, that he would bless Abraham and his descendents forever. The firstfruit evidence of this would be a male child to be called Isaac.

And Abraham's response? He laughed! Later, so did Sarah when she learned of the impossible promise. That hurt their Friend. He wanted them to laugh *with* him in sheer delight and glee over what he would do, not *at* him or his promise. No wonder he pressed the point. There is humor in the heart of God which calls forth in us the laughter of surprise, not the laughter of scoffing. Wrestle with God until you can grasp his promises, but never laugh at him! He's too good a Friend for that . . .

When Isaac was born, Sarah had learned her lesson. She said in grateful praise, "God has made laughter for me; everyone who hears will laugh *with* me. . . . Who would have said to Abraham that Sarah would nurse children? Yet I have borne him a son in his old age" (Gen. 21:6-7 NASB, italics mine). Who but God, the Lord of the impossible!

Isaac grew to be a fine, cherished lad. Abraham and Sarah loved him deeply, not only because they finally had an offspring, but because now they knew that the covenant the Lord had made would be fulfilled. Isaac became Abraham's pride and joy—a sense of significance and a hope for the future. The boy became his life!

Now get inside Abraham's heart so you can empathize with the panic he must have felt when the Lord asked the impossible of him in the *test of his faith*. We can feel the stabs of anguish with each word of the Lord's command. "Take now your son, your only son, whom you love, Isaac, and go to the land of Moriah; and offer him there as a burnt offering on one of the mountains of which I tell you" (Gen. 22:2 NASB). What did it mean? Abraham ached with inexplicable pain. "Why, God, why?" he must have cried, his feelings torn asunder. "My son, God? How shall your covenant come true that I shall be the father of multitudes without Isaac?" No request could have been worse. Nothing could have seemed more abhorrent.

I have tried to ponder these questions from inside Abraham's soul. I have sat at the Dome of the Rock in Jerusalem beneath which is Mount Moriah and wondered why God asked this of Abraham. Some have suggested that Abraham thought up the idea himself in keeping with the child-sacrifices of the Moabites. It was considered the ultimate expression of obedience to the gods of the people. But God had been too good a friend to Abraham for him to think of needing to placate him with a pagan sacrifice. And further, if this command of God had been the figment of Abraham's self-justification, what of all the other times God spoke to him? No, the command to offer Isaac was real—an ultimate test of Abraham's faith that God would provide a way out.

What was at issue was the fact that Isaac was God's gift not Abraham's possession. Could it be that like most of us, he had allowed his pride in Isaac to dull his praise to God who had entrusted the lad to him? It is a subtle, slippery transition from "all that I have and am is a gift of God" to "all that I have and am is mine—belongs to me and God—and in that order."

All of us fall into that kind of self-gratifying pride all the time. It's what *we* do for God with our strength that becomes important to us. We forget that we could not breathe a breath or think a thought or accomplish anything if it were not for God's moment by moment blessing.

I think of the times of crisis when I have had to relinquish control of my family, or profession, or future, and be called back to the realization that they are not mine, but a trust, a gift from God. Sickness, difficulties, disappointments have shocked me alive again to the fact that I cannot clutch tenaciously the entrusted gifts of life. Over the years of friendship with God I have been brought to a surrender, a crucial letting go, of what I foolishly thought was mine because of my right or hard work.

The issue is: Who or what is your Isaac? Who in your life competes with God for first place? What do you have or what have you accomplished that competes with God for the meaning of your life? It is often when a crisis comes that we realize that God does not have our ultimate loyalty or energy in daily living. False gods are not just idols in the fields or temples of an ancient, pagan time; they are living in our homes, deposited in our portfolio, fastened to the titles on our office doors, invested in the goals and plans of our self-generated lordship of our own destinies.

But we must go even deeper to discern what God was doing in asking Abraham to go through this excruciating ordeal. Faith is risk. It is a belief that God will provide, unswerving confidence that he will give us exactly what we need at the right moment to see us through. That's what God gave to Abraham. The thundering truth of this story for us is that God gave Abraham more than a challenge; he gave him faith in the knowledge that he would not contradict his covenant. God got to the bottom of Abraham and introduced him to the rock-bottom security of the Rock of Ages.

In your heart and mind's eye climb Moriah with Abraham and Isaac. The lad enjoyed being with his father and was delighted to go with him to make a sacrifice. But catch the note of passing concern about where the lamb is for the sacrifice, which turns to panic as they trudge farther up the mountain. "My father!" he said. "Behold, the fire and the wood, but where is the lamb for the burnt offering?" (Gen. 22:7 NASB). Isaac trusted his father. But Abraham trusted God even more. He responded with pathos. "God will provide for Himself the lamb for the burnt offering, my son" (Gen. 22:8 NASB). And they walked on, Isaac's real question unanswered. Surely he knew about child sacrifice practiced in that area. "Could it be? Not Abraham, my father!"

Dare to imagine what passed between father and son when they reached the top of Moriah, and Abraham silently, almost compulsively, built the altar, arranged the wood, and then began to bind his son. Feel Abraham's heart when his eyes met the incredulous eyes of his son. And then the fatal moment came. Abraham took out his knife to slay his son before the fire was lighted. Just at the moment he was about to thrust the knife in Isaac's chest, the Lord called, "Abraham, Abraham!"

Not a moment too soon; not a moment too late. The words were perfectly timed! And then God said, "Do not stretch out your hand against the lad, and do nothing to him; for now I know that you fear God, since you have not withheld your son, your only son, from Me" (Gen. 22:12 NASB). Abraham had taken the ultimate risk and God was faithful to his promise.

Rembrandt's painting of this traumatic intervention depicts the salient truth. As Abraham is about to thrust the knife, he looks up in response to God's intercepting call. The knife is actually flying out of his hand into the air, as if he had been waiting for the voice and when he heard it he flung the knife away with a triumphant, "I knew you'd come! I knew you'd provide a way!" Rembrandt has captured a mixture of awe, amazement, and assurance on Abraham's face. I am moved when I reflect that Rembrandt used the same model for Abraham's face as he used for the father in his painting of the return of the prodigal son. The loving heart of God is evident in both.

After the moment of the radical intervention, Abraham looked up and saw behind him in the thicket a ram caught by its horns. God did provide! Here was the substitionary sacrifice. We've felt Abraham's anguish; now let your imagination capture his joy. He offered the ram in place of his son, and called the place, YHWH-jireh, which means, the Lord will provide. The words became a metaphor of the intervening majesty of God. They have been repeated by succeeding generations during difficulties and have been put on the placards carried before armies and processions.

This familiar story in Genesis 22 flashes like a diamond, displaying new rays of truth each time we hold it up for reflection. We never tire of it, not only because of the gripping drama, but because it speaks to our deepest need to trust God for the gift of faith in times of risking, and touches our longing to be reassured of the timely interventions of God.

Most of all, we are called back to another mount a short distance from Mount Moriah—Mount Calvary. There God did what was truly impossible. He gave his own Son as a sacrifice for the sins of all people, in all ages. What he did not require of Abraham with Isaac, he required of himself with Jesus Christ, that we might know that we are ultimately loved and forgiven.

An awesome chill swept over me the day I walked from the side of Moriah, the Dome of the Rock, to the Garden Tomb and then around from the open tomb, to the jagged rock that bears the shape of the skull of Golgotha. Visits to ancient tels and historic sites can be sentimental, but not if what happened at them is relived in our hearts and minds. God is the same—yesterday, today, and tomorrow. He is the Lord of the impossible—Moriah and Calvary. There was a cross in the heart of God when he intervened with Abraham and dealt with the syndrome of sin through the once-for-all sacrifice of Jesus Christ on the cross. And the same cross-shaped heart beats for you and me right now. He loves us to the uttermost and he came himself that we might know that we are his beloved, cherished people.

There are three crucial things that we have learned from Abraham about the Lord of the impossible. They are all closely intertwined as part of one great assurance to help us in living now and forever.

The first is that *the Lord created you and me to be his friends.* That conviction lacks neither reverence nor awe. In fact it engenders both. He came in Jesus Christ to call us into a profound friendship and revealed the lengths he would go in indefatigable love on the cross. In the confidence of that friendship we can seek his guidance, dare to risk, and know his abiding presence with us. When we look into the face of God in Christ we see his incredible affirmation and acceptance, unending support and undying love. And as we gaze, lost in wonder and gratitude, we hear him remind us that his friendship is not dependent on our adequacy or perfection. "Greater love has no man than this, that one lay down his life for his friends. You are my friends if you do what I command you. No longer do I call you slaves, for the slave servant does not know what his master is doing; but I have called you friends" (John 15:13-15 NASB). Put your name in the place of Abraham's and hear the Lord say, "Abraham, My friend!"

The second thing Abraham has taught us in that *the essence of faith is risk.* We can dare to risk, knowing that the Lord loves our Isaac more than we do. That was Abraham's startling discovery. In the focus of both Moriah and Calvary, we can see our Isaac in an entirely different perspective. God is for us and not against us. He does not want a religious sacrifice of our Isaac but an unreserved surrender of our willful control of whomever or whatever has become our Isaac. Think of the people who become the extension of your ego—whose success brings you false pride or whose failure breaks your heart. Or consider the thing you cherish most—health, reputation, position, or plans for the future. And then reflect on opportunities which may have become obsessions. Your job, some cause, the church, or a responsibility may have become the passion of your life. Whatever or whoever bridges the gap between our fondest dreams and our longing for fulfillment becomes our Isaac. The adventure of friendship with God is surrendering our control of what we were never meant to control. We commit what is not ours in order to gain what we cannot lose. Abraham gave God his Isaac, his future, and his destiny as the father of multitudes. In return the Lord gave Isaac as a gift and assurance that he loved the boy and believed in Abraham's future more than Abraham did.

The same can happen to you and me. But not without the third thing we've learned from Abraham. The liberating legacy the great hero of faith has left us is *the sure conviction that the Lord will provide*. He really believed that God would intervene. He could not have endured the excruciating ordeal unless he knew that. When we entrust our Isaac to the Lord, we can be sure he will provide a way through and out of our difficulties. We can face anything because in Jesus Christ he has done that sublimely on the cross. The Lord of radical intervention has taken the total burden of our sin, failure, and rebellion. Christ is the ram in the thicket, the Lamb of God who takes away the sin of the world. Not only did God step in to take our sin upon himself, he raised Jesus from the dead as our victorious Lord over death and evil. Now we live by hope that at the right time he will resurrect all the impossibilities which we've surrendered to him. We don't have to sacrifice ourselves or our Isaac to win his favor. He has taken both off our hands. Now we are free to live expectantly, anticipating the same intervening power in all that we have committed to him.

And what can we do in response? Give him complete control of our life, our Isaac, our future. And as an expression of our unreserved faith, dare to risk the impossible as he guides. Fly the banner "The Lord will provide!" on the ramparts of our heart. And he will—be sure of that.

# CHAPTER TWO

# The Willful Wrestler

## —*Jacob*—

We all need it desperately. It is the one great need we all share in common. We were born for it and there is no lasting joy without it. What oxygen is for the lungs and protein for the body, that is what it is for our souls. It is the only source of spiritual security and psychological health, the basis of self-esteem and confidence. With it we become winsome and free; without it we are willful and fearful. It is the one thing people most need from us, but the one thing we cannot give until we have received it. When it is not engendered in us by our parents, because it was denied them, we will spend the rest of our lives demanding it or trying to earn it from others. And yet, no human being can satisfy our aching desire for it. It is life's most precious possession.

What is this longed-for possession, this dynamic power? *The blessing.* Each of us needs to be blessed, to feel blessed, and in turn to become a communicator of blessing to others.

The word *blessing* is one of the most misused and misunderstood words in our language. It is more than prosperity or possessions, success or achievement. From ancient biblical times until now, the blessing of God is the assurance that we belong to him, that he is delighted in us, and that he has singled us out as the target of his unqualified love. To be a blessed person is to know, feel, and relish God's affirmation and assurance, acceptance, and approval. It is the experience of being chosen and cherished, valued and enjoyed. A blessed person can say, in the words of Karl Barth, "God is for me!" and mean it with four propitious emphases: *God* is for me! God *is* for me! God is *for* me! and God is for *me!*

This chapter is for those who need to feel that blessing who find it difficult to allow God to bless them, and who are often stingy with their blessing for others around them. It is for people like you and me. The riddle of life is that we resist what we need and want most of all. So many people feel unblessed in this deeper dimension of what it means to be blessed. Something in us has closed off the cornucopia of God's blessing. Many who have gifts of talents, opportunities, and material success still feel unblessed.

Why is this? The mysterious syndrome of life is that if we do not feel blessed, we negate being blessed. If parents and significant others in our growing years have withheld blessing, denied us affirmation, approval, and the assurance of being special, we will find it difficult to allow God to bless us. This is the reason so many who have an intellectual comprehension of the faith and a firm belief in God, do not feel his love for them or sense an intimate, personal relationship with him. If the blessing of affirmation has been humanly denied, it is difficult to be divinely received.

My thesis is this. People who feel unblessed become strong-willed. The more unblessed a person feels, the more he or she inadvertently develops a willfulness to maintain control and keep from being hurt. The blessed are just the opposite. People who feel affirmed and loved are flexible, receptive, willing. But the unblessed become willful wrestlers. They strive for the blessing from others, expressed in approval and esteem, but they often resist, and usually question, overtures of blessing from people and, most of all, from God. Striving and resisting become a survival tactic.

The will is a very vital part of our nature. It is a gift of God for the implementation of intellectual convictions and emotional feeling. The will puts into action our decisions, what we want, and what we think is best. With it we run our lives. Willfulness is a distortion of this volitional gift. It is demanding our way, manipulating others to get it, becoming intractable. Willful people must be in charge. They become competitive and combative. Their question in every situation, "Who's in charge here?" carries the implication that they want to be in charge and will do anything that is necessary to assure that they are.

A willful wrestler must eventually go to the mat with God. He will engage us in a wrestle to the finish until we can say, "Your will be done." He will pin us down until we finally ask for the blessing that he is far more ready to give than we are to ask for. He will not cross the picket line of our willfulness. But he will arrange the circumstances of life to bring us to the point where we recognize that our need for affirmation of our value and worth is only a diminutive desire in comparison to the divinely implanted hunger only he can satisfy. That's exactly what he did for Jacob.

Jacob, the unblessed, insecure, restless, strong-willed son of Isaac, provides us a startling look in the mirror. The willful wrestler in me reaches out to the willful wrestler in you and together we reach back to our patron patriarch. The Bible is very honest about Jacob's struggle to be blessed. Good thing. An in-depth study of him helps us identify our struggles and see what God can do with them. Jacob's life forms a classic profile of a person whose unblessed childhood caused a willfulness that made it difficult for him to allow God to bless him. He lived on a collision course heading toward the time when his will collided with the will of God over who would be lord of his life. What I like to call history's greatest wrestling match took place late one night at Jabbok, a ford of the River Jordan, when, at a time of immense crisis in Jacob's life, the Lord entered the ring with him for a wrestle to the finish. The implications for us today can be appreciated only if we consider carefully what brought Jacob to this crucial event, what happened in it, and what resulted in his life from it. The story of Jacob is a gripping before-and-after drama of what it means to feel unblessed, what happens when we allow God to bless us, and the blessing we can be to others once we feel blessed.

Jacob and his twin brother Esau were born to Abraham's son Isaac and his wife Rebekah. Esau was born first, and Jacob second, but only moments apart, for Jacob came out of the womb with his hand holding Esau's heel. That's where he got his name. Jacob means "one who takes by the heel," "heel catcher," or "supplanter." From the beginning Esau was his father's favorite. He grew up to be a hunter, a man of the field. His father's son. Like Isaac he loved the thrill of the hunt, the freedom of adventure, the taste of game. Jacob was Rebekah's favorite. The Scripture tells us he was a peaceful man, living in tents. I've often wondered if Esau was free in his spirit to wander emulating his father's interests because Isaac had taken time to show him affirmation, while Jacob hung around home longing to receive it. The sibling rivalry between the sons was rooted in the battle of wills in the parents. The reason Isaac and Rebekah didn't love both boys equally was because they didn't love each other sufficiently. The psychological ambience of the family was competition for dominance. In a family where a husband and wife are in contest, the whole family loses. One parent's preference of one child over the other is usually rooted in a very unstable marriage.

The issue at stake in Isaac's family was which of the sons would have the birthright—the right of primogeniture. In biblical times, the firstborn was given the right to assume his father's place, property, and authority as the ruling member of the family at the time of his father's death. But of equal spiritual importance was a father's blessing on all his children. This was the precious gift of approval, affirmation, and the seal of the father's love, giving each child a sense of identity and significance throughout his life. That's what Jacob did not receive but wrestled for most of his life. Rebekah's passionate wish for her son, however, was not just that he feel blessed, but that he have the birthright instead of Esau. She inbred her compulsion in Jacob so that he joined her in conniving to get the birthright when what he really wanted was Isaac's blessing. Esau cared little for the birthright because he felt he had Isaac's blessing already.

This is shown by an event in the brothers' ongoing rivalry. One day Esau came in from the fields famished after a hard day's work. Jacob was cooking stew and with youthful impetuosity Esau demanded some of it—saying he would die if he didn't eat immediately! Our statement, "I'm so hungry I could die," matches his feeling.

Jacob wanted the birthright so much he could die! "First sell me your birthright," he exclaimed to Esau. Esau's nonchalant attitude toward the birthright is indicated by his response. "Behold, I am about to die; of what use is a birthright to me?" So Esau sold the birthright and got a dish of stew. The exchange reveals the willful nature of Jacob and his manipulative efforts to find security and self-esteem.

The plot intensified some time later when Isaac sensed he was dying. He called Esau into his tent and asked him to go on a hunt and find game for a savory dish. "Bring it to me that I may eat, so that my soul may bless you before I die" (Gen. 27:4 NASB). The birthright son went off into the field to accomplish the task for his father. But Rebekah had been listening through the thin walls of the tent. The moment she had been waiting for had arrived! Quickly she ran to Jacob, told him to kill a choice kid from the flock, prepare the savory dish his father desired, and receive the blessing and birthright intended for Esau. Jacob protested that Esau was a hairy man and his own skin was smooth. His father would touch him and know immediately that he was not Esau. Rebekah had a ready plan for that also. There was urgency bordering on frenzy in her voice as she ordered Jacob to dress in Esau's clothes, put goat skins on his neck and hands so that Isaac would be deceived.

The two pulled off the deception. Isaac was served a sumptuous meal and after his suspicions were distracted by Jacob's costume of pretense, he blessed him and gave him the birthright. The content of the precious blessing helps us understand why it was such a prize.

> "Now may God give you the dew of heaven,
> And of the fatness of the earth,
> And an abundance of grain and new wine;
> May peoples serve you,
> And nations bow down to you;
> Be master of your brothers,
> And may your mother's sons bow down to you.
> Cursed be those who curse you,
> And blessed be those who bless you." (Gen. 27:28-29 NASB)

Quite a blessing! We look back at it and realize that it contains the affirmation every child seeks. We wonder why the same blessing could not have been given to both sons. That was not the custom and tradition then. But the vestige of preference has caused and continues to cause competition between children in families. The "he loves you more than me" syndrome is still around.

When Esau returned home he discovered what his mother and brother had done against him, and begged for some blessing from Isaac. "Do you have only one blessing, my father? Bless me, even me also, O my father," he cried with the anguish of rejection. We find it difficult to understand the severity of Isaac's depreciation of Esau's destiny. Was it flaming anger over being deceived by his wife that made him so intractable? And yet what he predicted for Esau came true.

> "Behold, away from the fertility of the earth
>   Shall be your dwelling,
> And away from the dew of heaven from above.
> And by your sword you shall live,
> And your brother you shall serve;
> But it shall come about when you become restless,
> That you shall break. . . ." (Gen. 27:39-40 NASB)

And so a terrible grudge became the riverbed for the flow of competition, hatred, and jealousy between Jacob and Esau. Esau made plans to kill his brother as soon as Isaac was dead.

God had to remove Jacob out of that complicated web of conflict of wills in order to get him to a place where he would allow himself to be blessed. It is fascinating to see how God used conniving Rebekah's fear that Jacob might marry one of the local women, coupled with her anguish over what Esau might do to him. Her idea (was it hers?) was to send Jacob to her brother, Laban. Apparently she sold the plan to Isaac for he sent Jacob off with his "blessing" to Paddan-aram where Laban lived. In most decisions like that in the Old Testament, what looks like a logical human choice is really the deeper plan of the Lord.

Jacob set out for Laban's land feeling as unblessed as he always had. He was defeated and embittered. Though Isaac had blessed him, he knew that it was a stolen blessing. It had not satisfied his longing for affirmation. Like any love which is forced from another, it leaves both taker and taken empty. Jacob was launched into manhood devoid of feeling his father's delight in him for himself, and with the realization that he had been a pawn in his mother's strong-willed checkmate of his father. He left home starved of the crucial character nutrients that build self-confidence and esteem. All he had was the memory of what he had done to Esau and what both his parents had failed to do for his inner security. The result was a cunning, manipulative man, hardened in his determination to live by his own grit and guile. He became an "if anything is to be done I must do it for myself" kind of person—a take-charge, self-reliant man. Surely Isaac and Rebekah had told him about the God of Abraham, his grandfather, and all the promises which should be his as Abraham's descendant, but the psychological conditioning of the family was a brash contradiction that made it difficult for Jacob to trust. He had an intellectual belief in God, but a callousness protected his unblessed, sensitive heart. The wound in Jacob's psyche now was layered with the scar tissue of determined willfulness.

The Jacob syndrome. People in every generation since have suffered with it in varying degrees. It is obvious in some; in others it is carefully hidden, but manifested in subtle ways; in still others it crops out in bravado behavior. I am no longer surprised when, in an unguarded moment of intimate honesty, some outwardly confident and seemingly self-assured person tells me about being denied parental affirmation in childhood or being rejected by others in his or her growing years. This has resulted in a subsequent, lifelong struggle for approval. Parents, the family, and the heroes and heroines of impressionable years of our growth have the power to give or withhold the blessing of affirmation. When it is withheld, or inadvertently unexpressed because of the unblessed insecurity of the potential giver, we slip into adulthood with an acquired duality. A polished surface sustained by a strong will; an inner yearning for approbation and reassurance. We wander through life looking for a surrogate father, mother, older brother or sister, or some authority figure to tell us, finally, that we are okay.

This past summer, during my travels in the Middle East in preparation for this writing, I met a brilliant professor from Chicago. He was spending his summer in search of some meaning and purpose in life. Our paths crossed several times in archaeological sites in Egypt and Israel. One afternoon, we struck up what turned out to be a long and profound conversation. He was Irish Roman Catholic by background. Little matter. He might well have been Scotch Presbyterian or Fundamentalist or Pentecostal. I've heard his same sad story from all of them—and many more. Strange how travelers talk about personal feelings with other travelers they believe, and often hope, they will never see again.

The man could not remember ever having either his father or mother tell him that he or she loved him. His father had died when he needed him most and his mother to this day hides behind the equivocation, "I'm just not one to talk about my feelings." The young scholar has a distinguished record both in his education and now as a teacher. But none of the accomplishments have been equal to the emptiness inside.

I guess he had to tell someone about his last visit to his invalid mother before beginning his pilgrimage. He had pleaded with her to tell him she loved him. She finally eked out, "Why must you insist on that? I've always loved you. My actions should have told you!" Then she proceeded to give this accomplished man of the world a scolding fit for a schoolboy about how he should live his life and how he was neglecting her. What little assurance she had given was erased by her attitude. The man was hurting. He needed to be blessed.

The nationally syndicated television ministry we have at Hollywood Presbyterian Church brings in hundreds of letters from viewers each week. So many are explicit or implicit expressions of the insecurity of being unsure of God, other people, themselves. One woman is not unlike this man I just described. She is intelligent, attractive, and very capable. Everyone thinks of her that way except one person. Herself. Her father had not given her the healthy affirmation every young girl needs to begin to feel the joy of being a woman. Her mother was a fidgety complex of repressions and fears. Sunday school had been a refortification of parental discipline, and the church an institutional religion of don'ts. After college the woman married a fine, warmhearted man who had deep feelings of love which she found difficult to trust and receive. Now after a succession of babies and domestic distraction, for the first time the woman has an opportunity to find out who she is.

A chance flipping of the television dial brought our program into the quiet of her home one day when she was alone. The message of that program was about God's unqualified love for us in Jesus Christ. The invitation to respond by writing to me gave her a chance to express feelings buried for years. The seven-page letter was not from a crank, a neurotic, or a compulsive complainer. Rather, a lovely person wrote to ask what to do when you don't feel lovely, when all of the inner feelings about yourself preclude the possibility of letting God or anybody else love you. What would you have written in response? What from your own life would you have given her as the secret of self-esteem? How could she find a truly satisfying experience of being a blessed person?

I have shared the two stories of real people not because they are exceptional, but because they are so typical of how many people feel. They are everywhere. Perhaps one is inside your own skin suffering with the Jacob syndrome.

The Lord had great plans for Jacob, and as soon as he got him away from Isaac's qualified acceptance and the vice of Rebekah's dominance, he began to shape the man he had destined him to be. The Lord knew that it was his blessing for which Jacob longed the most.

On his way to Paddan-aram, one night Jacob had a dream about a ladder set on the earth, but reaching up to heaven with the angels of God ascending and descending on it. The message was clear: the glory of God came down to Jacob and he was lifted up into the Lord's presence, ushered into the splendor of the glory of God. That's what the willful young man needed: the fullness of God to fill his unblessed emptiness. In the dream the Lord assured him of a greater birthright—to be the recipient of the promises given to Abraham and Isaac.

> "I am the Lord, the God of your father Abraham and the God of Isaac; the land on which you lie, I will give it to you and your descendants. Your descendants shall also be like the dust of the earth, and you shall spread out to the west and to the east and to the north and to the south; and in you and in your descendants shall all the families of the earth be blessed. And behold, I am with you, and will keep you wherever you go, and will bring you back to this land; for I will not leave you until I have done what I have promised you." (Gen. 28:13-15 NASB)

Jacob's reaction when he awoke tells us a great deal about why the Lord had to get him out of the clutches of Rebekah and the blessed-unblessed status he had with Isaac. He was afraid. "Surely the Lord is in this place, and I did not know it. . . . How

awesome is this place! This is none other than the house of God,
and this is the gate of heaven" (Gen. 28:16-17 NASB). Jacob did
not expect to meet the Lord under the stars there at Luz.
Apparently he had little or no faith of his own back home. He
didn't know he needed it until he had to face life alone with raw
courage. The Lord, for whom all things are possible, always has to
get the strong-willed, clever people to a place of lonely facing of
the impossible so he can reveal his power.

Jacob was profoundly moved by his dream. He built an altar
calling it Bethel, meaning "house of God." As he reflected on the
amazing promise God had given him, he made a vow to give a
tenth of all that the Lord would give him. Surely he had gotten the
idea of the tithe from Abraham, through his father Isaac. Jacob
was feeling the first stirrings of what it was like to feel blessed.

We see signs of that when he reached Laban. His uncle was
a rogue of rogues! Rebekah had come by her conniving
naturally—it was a family trait. If we thought she was manipulative, Laban was worse. But Jacob worked hard and honestly for
him. He fell in love with Laban's daughter, Rachel. True to form,
Laban did not offer wages, but asked Jacob to strike a bargain.
Jacob offered to work seven years for Rachel's hand. Laban
accepted, but didn't like the idea of having Rachel, the younger,
married before her older sister, Leah. He agreed to the offer but
with a trick up his sleeve. Jacob worked hard for Rachel. "Jacob
served seven years for Rachel and they seemed to him but a few
days because of his love for her" (Gen. 29:20 NASB). A new
quality of man was emerging. God often intrudes on life with a
frightening example of the kind of person we tend to be so that we
can change and alter the course of our life. Laban and Jacob were
cut from the same cloth, but God had something much different in
mind for the wardrobing of Jacob's character.

When the seven years were up, Jacob demanded his beloved
Rachel. Laban gave a wedding feast and late at night sent Leah
to Jacob's tent as his wife instead of Rachel. The feast must have
had more than enough libation to dull Jacob's perception,
for he did not know until morning that it was Leah and not
Rachel with whom he had consummated marriage. Strange irony—
reminiscent of a deed of deception he had accomplished when he
falsified his identity with his near-blind father for the birthright.
Life does have its costly boomerangs!

Jacob was enraged. Laban the rogue had outmaneuvered Jacob the manipulator. Laban persuaded him into working another week before he could marry Rachel, working another seven years to keep her, and six years beyond that! These thirteen years were prosperous and productive, but not without conflict between the women in his life. Rachel and Leah had a continuing battle over Jacob's affections. This was particularly difficult for Rachel, because she was barren through the first years of her marriage, while Leah bore him six sons and a daughter. This prompted Rachel to have two children vicariously through her maid whom she gave to Jacob. Not to be outdone, Leah, at a time when she had temporarily stopped bearing, gave Jacob her maid for two more sons. That makes ten sons. Finally, Joseph was born to Rachel and became the cherished son of his father. Jacob gave Joseph all that he had been denied by Isaac and almost ruined the lad, as we shall see in the next chapter. Eventually Rachel died giving birth to her second son, Benjamin.

When the twenty years were completed at long last, Jacob was restless. There was unfinished business in his soul. He could not forget what he had done to Esau, and he longed to return home. It was not easy to get away from Laban, who by this time had discovered that it was the Lord's blessing on Jacob which had brought him such great prosperity. Laban was not willing to give that up without a battle. Again he tried to outwit Jacob. Their agreement was that Jacob was to have all the speckled and spotted sheep and every black lamb, and every speckled and spotted goat. Laban, true to form, worked another double cross. He took all the sheep and goats he had just agreed were Jacob's and hid them three day's journey away. So Jacob had to start all over again, but this time with something more than his guile pitted against Laban's. The Lord was with him, and Jacob knew it. When he mated the sheep, speckled and black sheep were born. These he mated with the strong stock he separated from Laban. When he told Rachel what had happened, he gave God the glory. Willful Jacob was learning that with God all things are possible. He was ready to respond when the Lord told him to return to the land of his fathers and assured him that he would be with him.

And so, Jacob, his wives and children, cattle and flocks and camels, secretly left Laban's land in great prosperity and strength. When Laban caught up with him, a negotiated truce between the men was possible only because of another intervention of the Lord. Laban was warned by God to deal fairly with Jacob and let him go. It was not wit or will that won that battle. Indeed, the Lord was with Jacob. God was getting him ready for a very decisive encounter, not just with Esau, but with himself. As we shall see with so many of the great men and women we will consider subsequently, a breaking of self-will in each was a part of making the person God intended. Jacob would not have been ready for what God had in store for him on his journey home if he had not endured the trials and been forced to realize that the Lord—not his grit, guts, or guile—made possible the triumphs.

Free of Laban, Jacob could now get on with the task at hand, one he dreaded. The panic he felt at the thought of meeting Esau was prompted by the memories of what he had done to his brother and all the feelings of being unblessed he had had as a child. The old manipulator rose to the surface again. Momentarily he fell back on his old ways rather than raw trust in the God who had revealed himself so capable of handling the impossible. Jacob sent messengers on ahead to assure Esau that he had great flocks and herds to share.

Spiritual transformation is slow in any of us. There was an old and a new person battling within willful Jacob. The elaborate lengths he went to in preparing a spectacular gift for Esau indicate that Jacob was still dependent on manipulation rather than on God. He said to his peace envoys, "After this manner you shall speak to Esau when you find him . . . 'Behold, your *servant* Jacob also is behind us.' " Then he exposed his solicitous strategy, "I will appease him with the present that goes before me. Then afterward I will see his face; perhaps he will accept me" (Gen. 32:19-20 NASB, italics mine). There it is again. Acceptance. Jacob had needed that from Esau all of his life. What he did not realize was that only God could give that precious gift. When we accept God's gift of acceptance, we finally get free of demanding it or manipulating people to assure its flow. And that's exactly what happened to Jacob during the night before he met Esau.

What is it like to wrestle with God? It is a struggle with the past and a battle over who will be in charge of the future. The Lord wants to make us willing to be made willing to seek and do his will by his strength for his results. A combination of fear, guilt, and a life of manipulative guile resisted God's presence and power in

Jacob's life. Do you know what that's like? Have you ever relived the past with each failure marching before your mind's eye? Have you ever been awakened in panic in the middle of the night and gone to the mat with the Lord with restless worry? Then you know, as I do, what it's like to have the Lord battle for control of your will until you allow him to forgive the past and take charge of the future.

Genesis 32:24-32 records vividly this battle for Jacob's soul. The Scripture says that a man wrestled with Jacob all night long. Some expositors have suggested that Jacob's battle within himself was so great that it was manifested in a dream of wrestling with a "man." But Jacob's own testimony and the name he gave to the Jabbok ford gives us the real truth. He called the place Peniel, which means "the face of God," and he said, "I have seen God face to face, yet my life has been preserved." In reality, his new life was just beginning. As the crucial night of encounter ended, Jacob was crippled in the socket of his thigh. G. Campbell Morgan has succinctly entitled the experience "Crippled to Crown," an apt description. Jacob would not let the Lord go until he blessed him. That was his greatest need from childhood. The Lord's response was to give him a new name. No longer Jacob, the supplanter, but now Israel, meaning "God strives." That's the issue for the new man emerging in the old Jacob. God had and would always strive with, for, and on behalf of him and his descendants.

We are amazed that Jacob, now Israel, asks for the name of the One with whom he has wrestled. "Please tell me your name." The Lord's response was a question to end all Israel's questions. "Why is it that you ask My name?" Why, indeed! After all the times God had intervened for him and spoken to him, he should have known. But willfulness has not only a short fuse, but a short memory. And Jacob wanted to be sure. He knew that this was the crucial encounter of his life and did not want it to pass, leaving him unblessed again. God was the only one Jacob could not manipulate. He gave the blessing for which Jacob longed because it is his nature to bless. Jacob did nothing to deserve or earn it. In fact, all through his life up to that propitious night, he had done about everything he could to negate it. Now he had a limp that would remind him that God not only touched the socket of his thigh, but the secret places of his heart.

When morning came it was the beginning of a new life. We meet a totally new Jacob, now called Israel. After that night, his new name reminded him that God had striven with him and now would strive for him. The willful manipulator had become willing to be molded by the eternal Father. From that time on we feel compassion, gentleness, openness, receptivity in Israel. He didn't have to work at being loved any longer. He was blessed.

After the wrestling match was finished and the sun had lifted the veil of night, Israel looked up and saw Esau coming. The Scripture makes no mention of a spasm of panic in Israel this time. The wrestling with the Lord had accomplished a transformation. Israel had allowed God to bless him and then was free to receive from Esau. It is a tender scene. Esau, with remarkable grace, ran to Israel and fell on his neck, kissing him, and tears flowed from both. Then Israel said something which is the expression of a blessed heart, "I see your face as one sees the face of God, and you have received me favorably" (Gen. 33:10 NASB).

What does all this mean to you and me? Three crucial things. First, all our efforts to earn and receive blessing from others will never fill the God-shaped emptiness in us—*only God's affirmation can build lasting assurance.* The same God who strove with Jacob and made him Israel is the God who came himself to bless the world in Jesus Christ. He lived, taught, died, was raised up, and returned at Pentecost through the Holy Spirit, with indwelling power so that we might be a part of the new Israel, the Lord's own blessed, loved, and forgiven people.

The second thing Jacob has to teach us is that if we persist, *God will give us a new name* which describes the new person he intends for us to be. What characteristic is the opposite of what you were before allowing the Lord to bless you? If the long night of wrestling with God is still before you, picture the person you want to be if you were ultimately secure in God's acceptance and affirmation. Then let the Lord give you a new name. For me, a person whose boyhood insecurities developed a willful determination to win by human effort and manipulation, my new name would be "Lloyd, the defenseless, affirmed." I do not need to be defensive any more. What about you?

Last, *an affirmed person becomes an affirmer.* We break the human cycle of hoarded love and become lavish lovers of the unblessed of the world. And since the psychological background of most people has left them in desperate need of affirmation, we can care for them, earning the right to tell them about the only blessing which satisfies and lasts. Here is an inventory to determine the extent to which you have allowed God to bless you.

1. Do you have a deep, abiding sense of being cherished by God as his special person?
2. Have you accepted his gift of forgiving, liberating love in Christ our Lord?
3. Do you have an assurance that there is nothing that you can do to make God stop loving you?
4. Have you evaluated the pluses and minuses of your childhood and accepted what parents and significant others did or did not do for you?
5. Can you let go of the past, let God bless you now and in the future?
6. Are you willing to allow that blessing of God's affirmation make you an affirmer, one blessed to be a blessing?
7. Can you yield your will to allow God to make you willing to be willing to do his will as an affirmer?
8. Will you ask God whom he has placed on your agenda to be blessed by you?
9. Are you willing to give yourself away to those people—giving time, energy, and resources to help them be sure of your love and God's grace?
10. Will you accept God's new name for you—focusing your new purpose and power to become the person you were meant to be?

If you have said yes to these questions, you are no longer a willful wrestler striving against God, but an Israel for whom God will strive, bless, and continue blessing through all of life—now and forever.

# CHAPTER THREE

# Let God Be God

## —*Joseph*—

It is unsettling to contemplate how life makes some people grim and others gracious. Two people can walk through the same valley of discouraging circumstances. One emerges with resentment, the other with resiliency. Tragedy can be the making of some and the breaking of others. Some grow; others shrivel. Why?

What happens to our dreams can make us grim or gracious. We all have plans, hopes, expectations for our lives. They seldom turn out exactly as we had anticipated. And yet for some, setbacks in the accomplishment of their dreams are taken in stride with the confidence that God is working out a greater plan. Others are immobilized by defeat, engulfed in bitter self-incrimination or blame for life's inequalities and the people around them. The question is, What do you do when circumstances seem to contradict your fondest dreams for your life? Or as one woman asked in exasperation, "What do you do when life goes bump?"

Here's how it happens to some of us. God calls us to be dreamers. He desires to give us a vision of what life can be. Then through our prolonged prayer he offers us a special calling that perfectly matches the talents he has given us and the special spiritual gifts he will entrust to us. A picture of our destiny forms in our minds. His call sounds in our souls. We make a commitment to high adventure following the Master. And then, circumstances roll in on us like a fog which separates us from the brightness and warmth of the sun. What happened? Has God reversed his guidance? Was our dream only self-aggrandizement?

One of the most challenging and difficult lessons in the school of faith-obedience is that the God who gives the dream also prepares the dreamer to realize the dream. What we go through as we move toward our God-given goals is perfectly planned to make great people capable of handling a great dream. That's the salient truth the story of Joseph has to teach us.

Give yourself a gift. Read Genesis, chapters thirty-seven through fifty. Meet one of the most remarkable dreamers of the Old Testament. The gracious man we meet at the end of the account could not have appreciated or appropriated his dream without the valleys of vicissitudes he'd been through. As we follow Joseph's pilgrimage carefully, five powerful guidelines for disappointed dreamers emerge.

The first is—*let God be God of your dreams*. We first meet Joseph as a lad of seventeen. He was the favorite son of Jacob. The patriarch raised the young man with a feeling of being special, cherished. Jacob gave Joseph a sense of destiny. The roots of Joseph's faith were firmly planted by what he had learned of his father's encounters with God. But Jacob's experience in childhood affected the way he raised Joseph. As is often the case, what has been denied a father is lavished on the son. Jacob's struggle for the blessing of Isaac made him oversolicitous in blessing Joseph. The result was rivalry with his brothers. Joseph was self-confident with assurance bordering on arrogance. Jacob put an exclamation point to his favoritism by giving Joseph a long coat in which he strutted about with peacock pride. (Tradition has mistranslated the Hebrew, calling it a coat of many colors. Sunday school pageants notwithstanding, the Hebrew means, "a coat that reaches the extremities.") It symbolized aristocracy and exemption from hard labor. Colored or long, the coat was an anethema and inflamed his brothers' jealousy.

Neither Joseph nor his brothers were prepared for the dream that he had one night. He and his family were binding sheaves in the field. Suddenly one sheaf arose and stood upright and all the other sheaves gathered around it and bowed down to it. The single sheaf was Joseph! As if that were not enough, the dream was followed by another with the same impact. The sun, moon, and eleven stars bowed down to the dreamer himself. That's a heady dream for a lad of seventeen. His father's affirmation, minus the rigors of discipline and hard work, had ill-prepared him to handle the dream. He did not have the humility to quietly ponder it in his heart. Instead, he blurted it out to the whole family. Jacob rebuked Joseph, but the damage to his brothers' uneasy egos had been done. The die of a dreadful deed was cast.

It happened in the valley of Dothan. Joseph had been sent by Jacob to observe his brothers at work pasturing the flocks. When they saw Joseph coming, the anger and jealousy of the years erupted. "Here comes this dreamer!" they said with disdain. "Now then, come and let us kill him and throw him into one of the pits; and we will say, 'A wild beast devoured him.' Then let us see what will become of his dreams!" (Gen. 37:19-20 NASB).

Only Reuben's intervention (who put the thought in his mind?) saved Joseph. "Shed no blood. Throw him into this pit that is in the wilderness, but do not lay hands on him" (Gen. 37:22 NASB). So they tore the beautiful, full-length robe off him and threw him in a wide bottomed, narrow-necked pit. While Joseph screamed, begging for help, the brothers sat down and ate bread. Nothing, save murder itself, could have expressed their feelings more eloquently. A meal of celebration marking the demise of a brother!

But God had other plans. A caravan of Ishmaelites traveling from Gilead to Egypt came by while the brothers were eating. The strange, serendipitous strategy of God! Now Judah sided with Reuben's caution. "What profit is it for us to kill our brother and cover up his blood? Come and let us sell him to the Ismaelites and not lay our hands on him; for he is our brother, our own flesh" (Gen. 37:26-27 NASB). Joseph was sold for twenty shekels of silver and was carried off kicking and screaming to Egypt while his brothers took his abhorred tunic, dipped it in goat's blood, and went to Jacob with the lie that his beloved son was dead.

How do you like that for a set of circumstances to contradict a dream? Get inside Joseph's mind as he is carried away, strapped to a camel's back. Feel what he felt as he crouched cautiously around the Ishmaelites' campfire at night. Live through the lonesome nights and weary days with the perspective of a frightened, lonely, homesick seventeen-year-old lad. And yet, the first step of the preparation of the dreamer for his dream had begun. God was up to a great thing in Joseph. The arrogance had to be replaced with character, the self-assurance with dependence and trust in God alone. Nothing would happen to Joseph which the Lord would not use to make him a usable instrument.

To let God be God of our dreams is to acknowledge him as the source of the vision for our life. Praise and not pride is the essence. All that we have and are is his gift. Our sense of calling is not for leverage or superiority. It is for responsibility and quiet obedience. When God gives a hope and an expectation, it must be given back to him for his timing and plan. Joseph misinterpreted his dream. He was to be blessed so he could be a blessing. After the transmission of the dream, there had to follow the transformation of the dreamer. That would never have happened in the complex web of favoritism and sibling rivalry in his Canaanite home. God closes and opens doors. He knows what he is doing.

Something happened to Joseph on the way to Egypt. He could not have become the man of faith he became without it. All the willfulness he had inherited from Jacob was being broken. Strange, how each generation must learn for itself. The one thing Jacob had not been able to share was that in wrestling with the Lord, the Lord always wins.

That leads to the second part of Joseph's story and to the next truth we can learn from him—*Let God be God when circumstances seem to contradict your dream.* Joseph was sold to Potiphar, the captain of the Pharaoh's bodyguard. Though young, he rose to power and prosperity and was in charge of the Egyptian officer's entire household. The story could have ended at this point; if Joseph's family had known, they might have bowed down to his position. But once again, circumstances seemed to go against the dreamer; he was thrown into prison on a false charge. Yet the account tells us a great deal about what was happening to Joseph's faith. He rejected the sexual overtures of Potiphar's wife because of his loyalty to Potiphar and his allegiance to God. "How then could I do this great evil, and sin against God?" (Gen. 39:9*b* NASB). How very different from the self-indulgent lad we observed a few years before. The Lord was the center and security of his life. A childhood faith had grown to manly integrity and authenticity. No circumstance could contradict that. But his God-centered morality was costly. It landed him in jail. Psalm 105:18 tells us that he was placed in irons. But God used this experience to put iron in his soul. Joseph learned that we do not find God in circumstances, we bring him to our circumstances. The grace of God is greater than the grief of life.

We must honestly confront a heresy which beguiles and befuddles many of us. The heresy is: the more we grow in God's grace, the easier things become. So often when we meet trials, our first thought is that God is punishing us. Or we suppose that if we prayed more circumstances would not frustrate our dreams. This is inconsistent with the lives of the great men and women of the Old Testament, the life and message of Jesus Christ, and the saints, martyrs, and faithful followers of the Master. We need to be a lot tougher in our thinking. Our prayer must not be for easy lives, but for God-empowered lives which become great by his grace. True, there are some difficulties which are the result of rebellion and disobedience. If we confess our disobedience, then we can get on to the soul-sized issues which will enlarge our hearts until they are open and inclusive enough to contain God's Spirit.

The times I have grown the most and been further shaped into the person God intends me to be, are the times of challenges and reversals which demanded raw dependence. When I felt most alone, I found a Friend who never forgets or forsakes. A recent example of this for me was the time I was launching a national television ministry. Last spring the financial needs were so great that the future of the ministry was in jeopardy. One night I was so worried I could not sleep. Pride kept me from making the needs known to my viewers. I did not want to beg for contributions or make people feel that sending their gifts was a qualification of the friendship we share through the program. And yet, without a significant inflow of funds, I could not go on. "What can I do, Lord?" I asked repeatedly during the long night of wrestling with the problem. "You must trust me and tell your viewers the urgent need," the Lord seemed to respond. "I will put it in their hearts to respond."

Up to that point the television ministry was something I was trying to do for the Lord. Now I realized that it was his ministry and not mine. I had to relinquish its future. The old saying, "The Lord gives and takes away," was being reversed. In this case, the Lord seemed to take away and give back. In the weeks which followed that surrender of the future of the ministry, I swallowed my pride and asked for people's help. The response was overwhelming. Not only was the future of the program secured, but funds came in to enable a great expansion. The turning point occurred and as a result of national syndication of the program was made possible.

After that crisis, I felt a new freedom as I spoke on the program. The panic was gone. In its place was a firm confidence, not in my ability to keep it going, but in the Lord's provision. He had greater plans than I dared to envision. I had to let go.

I've known the same experience in marriage. Some years ago when my wife and I hit a plateau of bland mediocrity in our relationship, I discovered that the breakdown in communication was a result of my own insecurity manifested in patterns of control. Here again, the breakthrough to a new life together came when I cried out, "Lord, help me! I can't do it by myself. Change my marriage by showing me the husband you need me to be for my wife." That was the beginning of a healing in me which resulted in a new life of happiness and romance in my marriage.

The same thing has happened repeatedly in difficult relationships and problems that I've encountered as a leader. When crises strike, as they do for all of us, I have been driven back to the Lord for his corrective and comfort. When I go to him and spread out the difficulties, he patiently shows me what I must do to change and then steps in to open the way to resolution of problems for which there seemed to be no human solution.

To be sure, my life has had resting places of gratitude along the way, respites in the battles of life for rest and rejuvenation. But the waiting times, after I have surrendered the excruciating problems life dished out, have been the growing times. How about you?

The goal of greatness in the Spirit is the result of trust and anticipation. When we believe, really, that the Lord is in charge, we can relax quietly in the present and look forward expectantly to God's plans working through what is happening to and around us right now.

There is a repeated phrase which punctuates the account of the trials of Joseph. "But the Lord was with Joseph." Replace Joseph's name for your own. The Lord is with you and me. We can take anything with that knowledge. Mark Twain in his colorful way spoke of the unswerving regularity of irregularity. Don't wait for life to settle down to bland regularity before you believe that God is with you. You'll have a long wait and miss the truth that getting to your dream isn't half the adventure; it is the adventure!

Joseph's leadership skills plus his impelling, God-filled character and personality attracted the jailer. Once again he rose to power, this time as head of the whole jail! God does have a sense of humor, doesn't he?

If Joseph had not been put in prison, he would not have met the Pharaoh's disaffected cupbearer and baker. We talk about contradicting circumstances. What about those divinely arranged to press us on to the dream the Lord has given us? The cupbearer and the baker both had dreams. The strategic one for God's arrangement of circumstances was the dream of the cupbearer. He had a dream of a vine with three branches producing grapes. He took the Pharaoh's cup, squeezed the grapes into it, and served the Pharaoh the wine. Joseph, the dreamer of God, was ready with an interpretation: three days and the cupbearer would be released and would once again serve the Pharaoh. It happened. Now the cupbearer was in a crucial place to remember the mysterious, gifted Hebrew he had met in prison when, two years later, the Pharoah had a dream that was to be strategic in God's plans for Egypt, Joseph, and eventually the birth of the Hebrew nation.

The Pharaoh dreamed of seven lean and seven fat cows. The lean cows devoured the fat cows. This was followed by another dream of seven good and full ears that grew on a single stalk followed by seven withered ears scorched by the east wind. "What did this mean?" the Pharaoh wanted to know. The dreams defied the interpretive powers of the ruler's magicians. God's cue! The cupbearer remembered Joseph and told the Pharaoh. When given audience, Joseph was quick to inform him that he did not have powers of dream interpretation, but served a powerful God. Joseph had learned a hard lesson through suffering. What we see before the Pharaoh is a God-dependent man who had allowed God to be the Lord of his own dreams. The arrogance of years before was gone, replaced by the humility that only suffering could have produced.

You remember his interpretation of Pharaoh's dream. Ahead for Egypt were seven prosperous years to be followed by seven lean years. The sublime sagacity given to Joseph by God is utilized to give the Pharaoh very crucial advice. In the seven years of prosperity, prepare for the lean years. Fill the granaries and be ready. The Pharaoh was so taken by Joseph's insight and his practical application that he made him prime minister, vice regent of all Egypt, second in power only to him! In reality, not second at all—the Lord of the universe was first in Joseph's life.

I'd like to underline what I think God is trying to communicate to us at this point in the story of Joseph. He not only gives us a dream and prepares us to be capable of living that dream; he also gives others dreams that fit into ours and moves us forward toward the accomplishment of our dreams. God is Lord of circumstances *and* people, and is ready to deploy one person's need for the fulfillment of his purposes in another. Think of the people who have come along just at the right time to help us. Some were friends, others antagonists. But God used them all! He is the dynamic deployer of people through whom he moves us on to the next phase of realizing his dream for us.

That brings us to our third major discovery out of a study of Joseph's life—*let God be God in the successes of life.* The growing greatness of Joseph in fellowship with God is revealed not only by how he endured difficulties, but in how he handled success. At no time in the account of his masterful leadership of Egypt do we sense that he used his power for his own aggrandizement or privilege. He served God by serving Egypt as his divinely appointed task. He built granaries and prepared for the famine. In so doing, he was able to save Egypt and all the surrounding territory from ultimate damage in the seven lean years.

God entrusts spiritual success to those who will give him the glory. We should not abhor success any more than difficulties. There are times of triumph as well as turbulence in the Christian life. We can thank God for both. Effectiveness in the Christian life, recognition, and advancement in leadership are our occasion for deeper trust and praise.

God had prepared a man and now was ready to use him in His strategy of creating a chosen people. He had to get Jacob and his family into Egypt not only to save them from the famine, but to build them into a nation prepared for the promised land and the distinctiveness of being God's people.

The famine which struck Egypt also devoured Canaan. Jacob eventually was forced to send his sons to Egypt for grain. Fearing harm might befall them, he kept back his youngest son, Benjamin, the only remaining son of his beloved wife Rachel. That brings us to the next chapter in the unfolding drama of Joseph's dream and to another insight—*let God be God over the failures of others who have frustrated your dreams.*

When the brothers made their first trip to Egypt to buy food, they did not recognize Joseph. It had been more than twenty years since they had seen him, and besides he was dressed as an Egyptian. Imagine the mixture of feelings Joseph had when he saw his brothers—the very men who in hatred and jealousy had sold him to the Ishmaelites! He had the power to execute them on the spot, torture them to admission of their crime, shock them by immediately revealing his identity. Instead he expresses immense graciousness. But not without some intrigue and humor thrown in. What Joseph put his brothers through before exposing who he was is consistent with some very basic and profound spiritual laws of relationships and reconciliation. When we let God be God of other people's sins against us, we must mediate forgiveness in a way that it can be accepted and appropriated. That's not easy, as we shall see in the way Joseph dealt with his family. There had to be acknowledgment of wrong before the forgiveness in Joseph's heart could be offered and accepted. That process hurt him more than his brothers.

Accusing them of being spies, Joseph put his brothers on the defensive right from the beginning. They protested their innocence and mouthed the oft-repeated lie about his death. Their story must have broken Joseph's heart. They were too frightened to catch the deeper pathos in his voice when he asked, "Is your father still alive?" "Your servants are twelve brothers in all," they said, "the sons of one man in the land of Canaan; and behold, the one brother, the youngest is with our father today, and one is no more." No more! Joseph must have been tempted to rip aside his disguise and face his brothers with the truth. But it was not the time yet.

"It is as I said to you, you are spies," he told them, "by this you will be tested: by the life of the Pharaoh, you shall not go from this place unless your youngest brother comes here!" After putting them in prison for three days, he went to them and swore by God (that must have had a strange and familiar ring to his brothers' ears!) that he would keep one of them in prison and allow the others to return to bring the youngest brother back to Egypt.

The challenge had the impact Joseph intended: the calloused

repression of hidden guilt covered over with layers of lies through the years was ripped open. The brothers were forced to talk with one another about their sin against Joseph. Strange how crisis in a new situation brings back unresolved guilt. As he listened to their self-incriminations, Joseph turned his face and wept. And yet, he did not expose his true identity. He would not heal a deep wound lightly by too-ready and glib offers of forgiveness. Ponder that. Joseph held fast, kept Simeon, and sent the nine brothers on their way to Canaan, their sacks full of grain and, by his secret order unknown to the brothers, the money they had paid for it. When they opened a sack on the way home, the money fell out. Note again the manifestation of guilt. Instead of delight, they trembled and asked, "What is this that God has done to us?"

Jacob was grief-stricken by the news that Simeon had been kept as a hostage and refused to comply with the demand that Benjamin be returned to Egypt. But the famine worsened and gave him little choice. Finally, he sent the brothers back to Egypt, with Benjamin. The issue at stake for Jacob was the awful possibility of losing all his heirs to Egypt. What would become of the promises made to Abraham and Isaac? What he did not know was that the promise was being fulfilled in his grief-filled relinquishment of all his sons to return to Egypt.

Joseph had softened his strategy by the time the brothers met him again. He greeted them warmly and was moved to tears at the sight of his full brother, Benjamin. Simeon was released from prison and a great feast was served. Genesis 43:32-34 catches the drama Joseph staged. Joseph's place was at a separate table with the Egyptians. The table for his brothers was carefully arranged by birth order with the firstborn birthright son in the place of honor down to Benjamin as the youngest. No wonder the brothers looked at one another with astonishment. Only someone knowledgeable of the family could have arranged that! Who was this mysterious vice-regent of Egypt? But still it was not the moment of self-disclosure. The brothers were not ready.

Once again Joseph sent them back, and again he arranged for another encounter on their way home. His own silver cup was hidden in Benjamin's sack. After the brothers were well on their way, he sent his house servants to stop them and accuse them of taking the silver cup. The brothers pled innocence. When the sacks were searched, sure enough, the cup was found in

Benjamin's sack. They tore their clothes—an ancient Hebrew act of total desperation and indignation. They were nearing the breaking point.

When they were brought back to Joseph, they fell on their faces. They rehearsed the whole ambiguous relationship they had had with him as vice-regent. Judah made the impassioned appeal not to have Bejamin blamed and kept in Egypt. It would be more than his poor father, Jacob, could stand if they returned without Benjamin. Judah would stay in his place. It was the description of Jacob's grief and the gallant offer of Judah that finally broke Joseph's heart wide open. The evidence of love for father and brother so lacking when he knew them was what he was waiting for.

Now Joseph sent everyone except his brothers from the room. Then all the repressed love and loneliness for his family surfaced in tears and cries so loud that the whole household of the Egyptians heard it. Few exclamations in Scripture contain the pathos of Joseph's cry to his brothers: "I am Joseph! Is my father still alive?" (Gen. 45:3 NASB). When they were dismayed beyond words to respond, Joseph had his brothers come close to him so that they could see, indeed, that the vice-regent was the brother they had sold into slavery.

Seeing their guilt-stricken faces, Joseph implored them not to be grieved or angry with themselves, but to see that God had used the evil they had done. Mark his words: "God sent me before you to preserve for you a remnant in the earth, and to keep you alive by a great deliverance. Now, therefore, it was not you who sent me here but God" (Gen. 45:7-8a NASB). When the brothers were ready, Joseph gave the forgiveness he had had pent up in his heart, but it was given in the awesome awareness that God uses the worst to bring about the best.

This time the brothers were sent off fully supplied with provisions. Their mission was to bring Jacob and their families to Egypt. If Joseph's healing encounter with his brothers was filled with pathos, his reunion with his father has to be one of the most tender and joyous meetings in the Old Testament. The Scripture vividly portrays him racing his chariot to see his father. When the two met, Joseph embraced Jacob "and wept on his neck for a long time." Joseph had been through unbelievable anguish waiting for that moment. He trusted God when it seemed to be an impossibility. The Lord of the impossible had the final word.

After Jacob died, the brothers came to Joseph with their father's dying instruction that they should seek Joseph's forgiveness. It had been offered already, but wise old Jacob knew that the brothers had to articulate their confession. Good thing. It occasioned a response from Joseph which has echoed down through the ages as one of the finest explanations of God's providence ever spoken. Joseph's dream that his brothers would bow down to him was only the exterior wrapping of the deeper promise that he would be used as a strategic instrument for the blessing of his family and the accomplishment of God's plan.

So with us. We need to look deeper into the dreams and visions of our life. What we feel called to be and do is part of a greater plan which cannot fail. Then we can deal tenderly and forgivingly with others. Everything that Joseph had been through made him able to say, " 'Do not be afraid, for am I in God's place? And as for you, you meant evil against me, but God meant it for good in order to bring about this present result, to preserve many people alive. So therefore, do not be afraid; I will provide for you and your little ones.' So he comforted them and spoke kindly to them" (Gen. 50:19-21 NASB).

Joseph was able to make that statement in retrospect. If we, too, can look back and say it about what has happened to us, then it can become our motto and mission in the present frustration and problems we are facing. It becomes a vibrant basis of hope for the future. Life, people, circumstances will press on us what seems to be evil, but God will use it for good to bring us closer to his dream for us.

Joseph's story leaves us with an inventory to take, a time of honest introspection to dare. Have the struggles of life brought you and me to Joseph's quality of trust in the providence of God? Further, has that conviction made us forgiving, gracious people? When we realize how tenderly God has dealt with us in moving us forward to our dream, can we do less for others? He used the cross to give us an ultimate hope, that beyond our earthly goals and dreams, we have an eternal destiny. And from that cross of ultimate, providential, intervening grace—a greater one than Joseph said, "Father, forgive them for they know not what they do."

One last insight ties together all the previous insights—*Let God be God of the future as he works out his greater purpose in history.* When Joseph was dying, he made an awesome statement that thunders his unswerving trust in God. "I am about to die, but God will surely take care of you, and bring you up from this land to the land which He promised on oath to Abraham, to Isaac and to Jacob. . . . God will surely take care of you, and you shall carry my bones up from here" (Gen. 50:24-25 NASB). In his dying, Joseph was as confident of God's care as he had been all through the troublesome years of his life. His personal dream was now part of God's plan for the eventual birth of Israel as a nation.

Joseph could die knowing that nothing could reverse the irrevocable, immutable, forward-moving strategy of God. He could let go of his concern about the future because he had learned that God is utterly reliable. The sixty-six people Jacob brought with him to Egypt, plus Joseph, his wife and his two sons, made seventy. Four hundred and thirty years later, Israel would leave Egypt in the Exodus with over two million. God had a plan.

Joseph is remembered as one of history's greatest men because he let God be the God of his dreams. He became a better person through it all rather than a bitter person because of it all. And what of us? Is life making us grim—or gracious? The test is whether we can say with Joseph, "Listen life; hear me, my friends; hear me, those who think you are enemies; what seems like evil at the time, God means for good. I'm going to keep my dream!"

CHAPTER FOUR

# The Lord Never Forgets

## —*Moses, God's Man*—

When we think we have no next move, God is about to make his big move. So often what we consider the worst is but the last stage of preparation for the best. Our sense of hopelessness is the prelude to the birth of genuine hopefulness. What seems like the end is only a phase of a new beginning.

That's the gripping message of the opening chapter of Exodus. At the very time the Hebrews were ready to give up, God was preparing Moses. The last two sentences of Exodus 2 serve as an exclamation point following the excruciating details of Israel's suffering in bondage in Egypt, and Moses' birth, growth, and identification with his people. "So God heard their groaning; and God remembered His covenant with Abraham, Isaac, and Jacob. And God saw the sons of Israel, and God took notice of them" (Exod. 2:24-25 NASB).

The Lord never forgets. Circumstances may point to the limited human conclusion that he has forgotten us. It may seem that he has had a lapse of memory about our personal plight or about the perplexities of his people as a whole. But this story tells us that at the very moment we despair, God is arranging a strategy of extrication. Always beyond our perception of the possible, exceeding the reach of our wildest expectation, God is at work. The same God who made a covenant with his friend Abraham, who wrestled with willful Jacob in order to bless him, who graced Joseph with the gift of faith to trust him so that he could become better rather than bitter, is also the extricating Lord of Moses and the Exodus. God had not forgotten his people in Egypt. When they thought they were finished, the Lord was preparing both their deliverance and a deliverer who would become the mightiest man of the Old Testament.

The people of Israel had been in Egypt for over four hundred years when Moses was born. After the death of Joseph, their status radically changed from that of honored and privileged guests in Egypt to one of bondage and servitude. The Pharaoh who had entrusted such great dignity and power to Joseph was succeeded by less magnanimous rulers who feared the growing number of the Hebrew people, as they were now called. The concern was that in the event of war the Hebrews would side with the enemy and defeat the Egyptians. Grave measures were taken to limit the growth of the numbers of the Hebrews. Midwives were commanded to kill the newborn male babies. When this proved unsuccessful, orders were given to search out the Hebrew male children and throw them into the Nile. At the same time, the labor of making bricks for the ever-expanding grandeur of temples and cities was increased. Added to that was the cruel command that the straw which had been provided for the Hebrews, they now had to gather themselves. Life became intolerable. Each new Pharaoh increased the demand. Fiendishly cruel taskmasters were appointed to afflict the people. But the more they were afflicted, the more the Hebrew people multiplied. And at the height of the increasingly impossible suffering, a male child was born to a couple of the house of Levi who was to become the mighty prophet of the Lord of the impossible!

We are so familiar with the account of Moses' birth and growth that we can miss the wonderful truth of how God prepares *us* for what he has prepared for us. The story of how his mother outwitted the Pharaoh in saving the child is filled with intrigue and a touch of humor. She managed to keep him hidden for three terror-filled months. Imagine her apprehension at the sound of each approaching footstep. At any moment, the beautiful child could be wrenched from her arms and slain before her eyes!

Soon the task of concealing him became too dangerous. I believe the Lord gave her the brilliant plan of putting him in a wicker basket covered with tar and pitch and setting it in the Nile at the very place she knew the daughter of the Pharaoh would come to bathe. You know what happened. The princess found the child, was moved to save his life, and decided to take him to her palace. But who would nurse him? Here's the humor. Miriam, the baby's sister, was standing nearby with a ready solution. Why not call one of the Hebrew women to nurse the child? The Pharaoh's daughter agreed. And who was called? The child's own mother. I think God smiled that day! He was working out his plan. The child was named Moses which means "drawn out of the water." An appropriate name for one whom God eventually would use to draw his people out of the high tides of persecution and suffering. While the people moaned, God was moving!

In Pharaoh's household Moses was given the best of two worlds. He was nursed and inbred with his Hebrew heritage at his own mother's breast and knee. His adopted mother gave him the finest training in Egyptian culture and education. Since the succession to the throne often went through the oldest daughter of the Pharaoh, he was groomed to succeed the Pharaoh. That meant that he was provided the academic, military, and leadership education which would prepare him to rule all of Egypt. The sumptuous splendor of Egypt was at his command as the privileged son of the Pharaoh's daughter. But all this preparation would be used for a greater purpose!

In order to appreciate the Egypt in which Moses was raised, I spent a period of time one summer sailing on the Nile. Prolonged stops to visit the ancient temples of Luxor, Karnak, the Valley of the Kings, Kom Ombo, Aswan, and others gave me a sense of the splendor of Moses' Egypt. I was struck with the mythology of the gods of ancient Egypt and the emphasis on the worship of Ra, the sun-god. The rites of coronation of the Pharaohs depicted on the walls of the temples further impressed me with the position of power which was waiting for the adopted son of Pharaoh's daughter. As I stood gawking at the magnificent pillars of the temples and the gigantic obelisks, I remarked to my scholarly guide that the construction and erection must have needed thousands of workers. He evaded the implications of my remark. Many of the temples were constructed during the four hundred or more years of the Hebrew slavery in Egypt. That would span the time from the sixteenth to the thirteenth centuries and would include the building projects of Hatshepsut in the fifteenth century and Ramses II in the thirteenth century. Perhaps the Hebrews were pressed into hard labor making more than bricks!

All of this investigation heightened my awareness of the breadth of Moses' training and education. It also provided an immense empathy for the turbulence that must have brewed within him as the Spirit of God began to raise the question in him about who he really was. I think possibly his mother's training had a lasting influence. Perhaps someone whispered the truth to him when he was a grown man. Or was it a touch of the Spirit that raised the possibility that he was not an Egyptian, but a Hebrew? Perhaps one or a combination of all three. We are not told. What we do know is that the future Pharaoh's deepest allegiance was crystalized in a very decisive way when he was forty years old. One day he went out to the Hebrew slave compound at Goshen and saw an Egyptian beating one of the slaves. Gripped with rage and indignation, he killed the Egyptian. He thought no one had observed his deed, but the amazing news traveled fast among the Hebrews and finally to the Pharaoh. The die was cast: there was nothing to do but flee for his life to the Midian desert.

That too was a part of God's plan. He got Moses out of the entanglements of the Pharaoh's court in order to prepare him to be deliverer of Israel. We are told that he was in the desert for forty years. During that time he came under the influence of Jethro, a Midianite priest, who was a worshiper of the Lord. (Midian was a son of Abraham by his second wife Keturah, Gen. 25:1-2.) Moses married Jethro's daugher Zipporah and had two sons, Gershom and Eliezer. As the shepherd of Jethro's flock, Moses learned about the ways of the desert, the travel routes, and the watering places. God was getting him ready for the strategic task ahead.

Most important of all, the Lord was hammering out a man who would be prepared to trust him completely. The elegant life of the Pharaoh's court was replaced by endless hours of silence in the lonely desert reaches. All the self-assurance had to be drained away. The dependence on human skill and cleverness ingrained by his Egyptian training for the responsibilities as the Pharaoh-designate had to be redirected in a new dependence on God. Moses was emptied of pride so he could begin to ask the right questions.

When we get inside the skin of Moses during that long period in the desert, we begin to feel the questions which must have tumbled about in his mind longing for an answer. Who was this God of his people? What he had acquired from his Hebrew mother gave him an intuitive sense of God's power. Perhaps contact with the Hebrews had furthered his awareness. Jethro must have introduced him to the name El Shaddai, the all-powerful God. But that must have raised other questions. If this God is all-powerful and if he has made a covenant with his people through Abraham, why doesn't he do something to help his people languishing in Egypt? Surely Moses pondered that for years as he tended Jethro's flocks. He knew about God, but he did not know God. And the answer to that need was the ultimate part of the lonely shepherd's preparation to be the deliverer of his people.

The other day I saw an old friend. "How are you?" I asked, not expecting the answer I got. "Not very well, thank you!" My face must have expressed alarm because he went on to explain some trying circumstances he was passing through which had loosened his grip on the assurance that God cares *and* would do something to help him. "What I've been through has forced me to face the fact that I don't know God very well. I really wonder if he is all-powerful when you need him." That was Moses' question in the Midian desert. What the man needed was what Moses needed—an authentic encounter with God.

That's what happened on that decisive day toward the end of Moses' sojourn of silence in the desert. While tending the flocks on the western side of Mount Horeb he was astonished by an acacia bush that was aflame but was not consumed by the fire. Moses watched with rapt attention. Surely he had seen the desert sun's spontaneous combustion of the dry bushes before, but this one burned at length and yet was not burned up. While he stood transfixed by the startling sight, a voice spoke out of the bush—commanding, demanding, undeniable. "Moses! Moses!" the Lord called. Moses was slow of speech, a stutterer at that time of his life. I am sure that his amazed response was stuttered, "He-e-re I-ii a-a-m." The Lord had his attention indeed!

What would it take to put us on our feet—or better still—on our knees, at full attention? Sometimes it takes a catastrophe, or an alarming blessing. *The burning bushes of God are all around us*—natural wonders in which God's signature is vividly written.

People in whom he is aflame with love and radiance. Excruciating problems in which he is our only hope. The desert time of waiting and wondering is always rewarded with a burning bush especially suited for our personal needs. What will it take for you? Right now as you read this the Lord is calling your name out of that bush. Do you hear it? Then answer with readiness, "Here I am!" Not later when you have heard what the Lord has to say, but *now*, indicating you trust him, need him, want him.

In response to Moses' attentive, awe-struck openness, the Lord revealed his essential nature. He had gotten to the core of Moses in the years of silence and now could expose his true nature to him. He was the God of Abraham, Isaac, and Jacob. He had heard the groaning of his people and was ready to deliver them. And Moses was to be the agent of deliverance. Confrontation with the Lord is now turned to consternation. "How, Lord, how?" Moses knew the military might of the Pharaoh and his dependence on the Hebrew slaves for continued expansion of the grandeur of Egypt. The most impossible thing Moses could imagine was that he could ever get the people of Israel out of Egypt.

Stay in Moses' skin. What would the most unimaginable possibility the Lord could suggest for you? Picture it! But note that the challenge to Moses was to do exactly what had been on his mind all through the years in the desert. Why didn't God do something about the plight of his people? Now the answer was given. Moses himself would be the one through whom his own prayer would be answered. *Authentic encounter with God always involves us in the answer.* What we want God to do for us, he waits to do through us.

And we respond with fear and trepidation, "Who am I? How could I ever do that?" We can't. But with the Lord with us, what more do we need? What else do we desire for assurance? Exactly what Moses needed. To know the true nature of the God who would be with him. When told that he should go to the people and say that the God of their fathers had sent him to them, he protested, "They will ask what is the name of this God who gave this impossible command. What shall I say to them?" It was then that the God of the burning bush gave Moses a gift which would sustain him all through the perilous years ahead. "I AM WHO I AM" God told him. The phrase uses the causitive Hebrew verb *to be* in the future tense. *The creator of all, who caused all things to come to be, will make things happen.*

Various translations of the I AM have been offered by scholarly expositors through the ages. As I have written elsewhere, my conviction is that the use of the essential Hebrew verb *to be* in the future tense means, "I will make happen," or "I will cause to happen what I cause to happen." See my book *The Bush Is Still Burning* (Waco, Tex.: Word, 1980). The Verb, the active Mover, of all creation will act out his unfolding strategy in history and in our personal lives. He is all-powerful, all-knowing, and all-loving and therefore he will be the all-things-possible God over what is considered impossible for us. Moses met the Lord of the impossible!

The new name given to Moses by God is Hayah, from the verb *to be*, rendered YHWH, or Yahweh—the Lord. In later years it became so sacred for the Hebrews that it was forbidden to be spoken. The word *Adonai*, the Lord, became its synonym for use in prayer and in referring to God. But for Moses, I AM was a clarion call to hope and action. God was not just the aloof El Shaddai, the powerful God of the mountains, but the God who would make happen what seemed impossible.

The Lord had not forgotten! He was waiting to get Moses to a place where he could accept the awesome truth that God could do anything he willed. While the people languished in Egypt thinking God had forgotten, the liberation had begun in the desert!

It is difficult for us to imagine that Moses would question God about how he would use him to lead his people out of Egypt. But before we become too critical, remember the many times we have argued with God's promises and guidance. The questions Moses raised are faithlessly proffered by most of us all the time I AM offers to do miracles. We want to scrutinize every aspect of how he will do them.

"What if they do not believe me?" Moses asked. The real problem was that Moses didn't believe yet. He put off on the people his own deepest fears. For this the Lord told Moses to throw his staff on the ground. It became a serpent. Then the Lord told him to take it by its tail. Moses had developed a healthy fear of snakes in the desert. Imagine his fear as he followed the command. Think of doing it yourself! When he did, the serpent became his staff again. Only now it was the rod of God.

The next sign was equally astonishing. "Put your hand in your bosom, Moses," the Lord commanded. When he did it became leprous, the most abhorred, fearful disease of the time. "Put your hand back in your bosom, Moses," the Lord rejoined. It was restored. What more than that did the would-be deliverer need? Wouldn't that be sign enough for you? Careful how you answer. What about the signs of God's power that we have rejected as inadequate?

Moses raised a further self-doubt. As we noted earlier he was a stutterer at this time in his life. How could he rally the people and confront the Pharaoh as a stammering leader? For this lack of faith, I believe the Lord provided second best. Surely the I AM who had told him that he would make things happen could free his tongue. In fact, evidence indicates that this did happen later. But for that moment, the Lord offered to use Aaron, Moses' brother, as the deliverer's mouthpiece. Clearly second best, but the best Moses was able to accept at that time. So often we miss God's best because we argue too long. His perfect will must be replaced by his permissive will because of our self-doubt rooted in lack of trust in God's first and finest promise. Has that ever happened to you?

But the innovative I AM who makes things happen in spite of us, always has a secondary strategy to get his work done. He takes us as we are. Eventually Moses spoke for Yahweh with clarity and power. The Lord never gives up!

Moses went back to Egypt with the words of the Lord ringing in his heart. The task ahead was humanly impossible. But he had had an authentic encounter with the Lord of the impossible.

We are back to where we began in this chapter. Let us not miss the awesome message. The Lord never forgets us. He hears, be sure of that. And when we least expect it, or deserve it, or have the courage to believe it, he comes to us to assure us that he will liberate us. What we think is the end, is only the beginning. We are not finished because God is not finished with us! He is preparing us for an exodus. It is to that we must press on with the heat of the burning bush at our heels and its radiant assurance living in our hearts. The sure sign we've had a burning bush experience is that the fire has leaped into us to set ablaze the dry kindling of our hopelessness. We can go into our Egypt as men and women with I AM-centered courage.

God never forsakes, He never is gone
So count on His presence in darkness and dawn.
Only believe, only believe;
*All things* are possible, only believe,
All things *are* possible, only believe!

Paul Rader

# CHAPTER FIVE

# The Lord of the Impossible

## —Moses, the Deliverer—

Moses went out of the Midian desert, back to the Israelites in Egypt, with clear orders. The idea of the Exodus was not a figment of self-aggrandizement or a need for the spectacular. Moses did not have the full strategy of the Exodus unveiled to him. What he had was a vision and a first step. All he was told to do was tell the people that I AM, Yahweh, had sent him. God had heard his people's plea and was going to lead them out of Egypt to a promised land. Moses was to go to Pharaoh with a command from the Lord, "Let My people go!"

That was enough for openers. The Lord seldom shows us more than we need for daily obedience. Doing today what he tells us to do opens the way for what he will show us tomorrow.

We should not expect a cheering section to applaud our daring attempt of the impossible. It's absolutely dangerous to take our signals from other people. Progress usually has to climb over the stiffened backs of the reserved and the recalcitrant. *Moses had to learn to trust God only.* His people did not greet his guidance from the Lord with enthusiasm, and Pharaoh hardened his heart to the idea of letting go of his slave force. But the Lord was at work; he arranged circumstances to force the people of Israel out of the questionable security of the familiar. The people begged God for deliverance and when it was offered, they resisted his appointed liberator. Amazing! Egypt had to be made absolutely intolerable before they would accept the possibility of what seemed an impossibility. They were in deeper bondage than the Egyptians imposed; the bondage to fear.

Moses' contest with Pharaoh was no less formidable. The ruler's disdain for Moses was a complex composition of virulent hatred and competition. My theory is that he was the Pharaoh who succeeded to the throne destined for Moses. Perhaps they had known each other in the days of their youth. Exodus 2:23 tells us that the Pharaoh who was the father of Moses' Egyptian mother died "many days after," a long time after Moses fled into the Midian desert. The Pharaoh with whom Moses contested would have known about Moses' defection and would have wanted to win in the battle of wits which ensued. What Pharaoh did not accept, until it was too late, was that he was not contesting with Moses, but with Yahweh. The plagues, especially the last one when the angel of death took the life of the Egyptians' sons, were too much for him.

We can learn much about the Lord of the impossible in the dramatic events of the Exodus from Egypt. God gave Moses and the people a sure sign of guidance in a pillar of cloud by day and a pillar of fire by night, and Moses led the people with obedience. When the cloud moved forward, he advanced the people; when it stopped, they camped and waited. The Scripture tells us that the triumphant procession of the Israelites out of Egypt contained six hundred thousand men on foot, beside the women and children. Figuring about five to a family the number in total could have been as great as two million. What is particularly crucial for our consideration is the route the Lord led them. He did not lead them directly to Canaan along the trade routes of the land of the Philistines, because there would be warfare with the Philistines, as the people of Israel sought to pass through. He told Moses, "Lest the people change their minds when they see war, and they return to Egypt." Added to that, the Lord wanted to prepare the people so he could display his power in a way they would never forget. Moses had the burning bush; now the people had to be galvanized around a similar experience.

The psalmist caught the urgency of that need when he reflected on the twofold assurance the Lord provided. "The Lord performs righteous deeds, / And judgments for all who are oppressed. / He made known His ways to Moses; His acts to the sons of Israel" (Ps.

103:6-7 NASB). The burning bush had revealed to Moses the powerful nature of the I AM, Yahweh, who would make things happen in spite of human circumstances. Moses learned what William Cowper later penned:

> God moves in a mysterious way
> His wonders to perform;
> He plants his footsteps in the sea,
> And rides upon the storm.

Now a mighty act was needed to prove beyond doubt that God was with the people and that Moses was his chosen leader.

Careful study of the way the Lord guided the people provides fascinating insight. Exodus 12:37 tells us that God led them from Rameses in the north of the Nile delta, south to Succoth. There they observed the Passover in celebration of their release from Egypt and in memory of the fact that the angel of death had passed over the Hebrew houses in the last plague. They had not come very far, for Succoth was in the heart of the land of Goshen where some of the people had been enslaved. Exodus 13:20 indicates that the Lord next moved the people from Succoth south again to Etham, which is on the north side of the Bitter Lakes; to the east of the lakes is the Wilderness of Shur. They were actually in the wilderness beyond Etham when God gave Moses an amazing instruction. "Tell the sons of Israel to turn back and camp before Pi-hahiroth, between Migdol and the sea; you shall camp in front of Baal-zephon, opposite it, by the sea" (Exod. 14:2 NASB). They were to go back north and west, back into Egypt. Moses was given the deeper reason for this strange reversal. "For Pharaoh will say of the sons of Israel, 'They are wandering aimlessly in the land; the wilderness has shut them in.' Thus I will harden Pharaoh's heart, and he will chase after them; and I will be honored through Pharaoh and all his army, and the Egyptians will know that I am the Lord" (Exod. 14:3-4 NASB). And so would the people of Israel! The Lord was about to perform a miracle which would become a metaphor of his might for all generations.

I've pored over the maps of ancient Egypt and the biblical text, particularly Exodus 14:2 and 9, trying to identify what happened. Visits to the area have helped picture it in my mind, even though the building of the Suez Canal has radically changed the topography. My postulate is this: the Israelites were instructed to

turn back, actually back into Egypt, around what at the time were
the Bitter Lakes and south to Pi-hahiroth, which means the
meadows west of the lakes, to Migdol, which was a tower and an
outpost of Egyptian troops. Baal-zephon was an Egyptian god
worshiped in a mountain range on the western shore of what is
now the Gulf of Suez.

The Israelites were now hemmed in by the mountains on one
side, the Migdol garrison on the other, and the northern
extremities of the Red Sea, in Hebrew *Yum Suf,* Sea of Reeds.
Then panic struck when they saw the cloud of dust from
Pharaoh's chariots moving across the meadows from the only
open area. They were trapped. *A cul-de-sac of impossibility. And the
Lord had led them there!*

Picture the situation: Moses could not move south because of
the mountains, or west because of the approach of Pharaoh, or
north because of the Migdol garrison, or east because of the Sea.
Exodus 14:9-10 makes the plight of the Israelites very vivid.
"Then the Egyptians chased after them with all the horses and
chariots of Pharaoh, his horsemen and his army, and they overtook
them camping by the sea, beside Pi-hahiroth, in front of
Baal-zephon. And as Pharaoh drew near, the sons of Israel
looked, and behold, the Egyptians were marching after them, and
they became very frightened; so the sons of Israel cried out to the
Lord" (NASB).

The Israelites' analysis of the situation was based on human
potential, not on God's power. They could not see what God was
up to. In five days they had forgotten the plagues, the liberation of
God's intervention, and the deliverance from Egypt.

I've found it helpful to divide this section of Exodus into the
various segments of dialogue: what the people said to Moses, what
Moses said to the people, what Moses said to the Lord, and what
the Lord said to Moses in preparation for the realization of the
mighty revelation of his power as the Lord of the impossible.

What the people said to Moses is typical of *the human analysis of
the impossible.* "Is it because there were no graves in Egypt that you
have taken us away to die in the wilderness? Why have you dealt
with us in this way, bringing us out of Egypt? Is this not the word
that we spoke to you in Egypt, saying, 'Leave us alone that we may
serve the Egyptians'? For it would have been better for us to serve
the Egyptians than to die in the wilderness" (Exod. 14:11-12

NASB). It's easy to be amazed at the lack of gratitude. Notice the transference of blame which fear causes—it's all Moses' fault. Why did he get us into this? The people were crying out for assurance that their decision to leave Egypt was right, truly guided by Yahweh, and that he would see them through.

Now we see the greatness of Moses begin to emerge. Because he is sure of the I AM of the burning bush, he is free of defensiveness. He does not come down to the level of the people to argue or defend his leadership. His experience of God has made him gracious rather than grim. People do what they do because of what they are. They cannot change what they do until God heals their fear. Moses was sustained by the realization that God had arranged the cul-de-sac of impossibility. There would be a way out!

What Moses said to the people and what God said to them all gives us *five basic things to do in confronting the impossible.* Notice the five verb forms of vital endurance and courageous living in Exodus 14:13-15. They show us first the natural, human response to the impossible, then what God wants us to do and to be when the impossible confronts us, and finally what he can do with the impossible if we trust him. Moses said to the panic-gripped people: "Do not fear! Stand by and see the salvation of the Lord which He will accomplish for you today; for the Egyptians whom you have seen today, you will never see them again forever. The Lord will fight for you while you keep silent." Then the Lord said to Moses, "Why are you crying out to Me? Tell the sons of Israel to go forward" (NASB).

Here is the prescription for perplexity: (1) fear not, (2) stand firm, (3) see the salvation of the Lord, (4) keep still, (5) go forward. Those verbs form an antidote for anxiety that works! I know from years of facing impossibilities. What I am writing here has been tested and lived.

The first instruction of Moses to the people is *fear not.* The only way to become free of fear is to know that God is with us. He is in charge of the impossibility. And not only that: God has allowed it, often arranged it for our growth and his glory. So often we blame people, wring our hands over evil, blast life for what it's doing to us. Growth in grace comes when we accept that nothing can happen without God's permission. With that tough fiber in our thinking, we can ask God for power and intervention in what he has either allowed or arranged.

The same channel of our emotions through which fear flows can be the riverbed for trust and loving obedience. Fear is only a hairbreadth away from faith. When we surrender our fear, telling God how we feel, we allow faith to force out fear. Tell God, "I'm afraid. I don't understand what you are doing with me! But I know there is something greater than this fear I feel. I know that you are in control and will allow nothing which will not bring me into deeper communion with you. What you give or take away is done that I might know you better." That's courageous praying in an impossibility.

It's foolish to say that we will never be fearful again. That simply means that we will pare down life's challenges so that we are never in a position to face anything we can't handle by ourselves. Fear is usually the first reaction to our impossibility. Don't be afraid of fear. It reminds us we are alive, human. Like pain, it's a megaphone shout for God—a prelude to faith. We would not need God if we weren't attempting something beyond us. Fear is a negative attitude toward reality which must be replaced by positive faith. Faith is a gift. Only God can give it. And he offers it to people who dare boldly enough to need the gift. But how is the gift given; what can we do to receive? That leads us to the second verb of vitality for the impossible.

*Stand firm!* The American Standard Version translates it "stand by." The Hebrew means, "take your stand." Fear makes us frantic, frenetic. The tendency is to run off in all directions to escape the fear dogging our steps. Instead, stand firm. A time of fear is not a time for crucial decisions or making moves. First, allow God to quiet you until you are sure of him again, of what he has told you he is going to do, and in the light of that, what he wants you to do. We need God's renewed perspective on the impossibility.

*See the salvation of the Lord.* That is expectation rooted in a promise. God told Moses that he would do a great miracle. Moses therefore was expectant, hopeful. There is both a retrospective and a perspective quality to the Hebrew words here. To see the salvation of the Lord is to look back at what God has done and forward to what he has said he will do. Moses is reminding the people of the spectacular things God had done already. That should be enough basis on which to trust him in the present problem. Each miracle God performs in our lives is preparation for greater trust in the future. But we forget so quickly! The people of Israel had surrendered inner peace for panic. They saw the seemingly impossible sea on one side and Pharaoh's armies approaching on the other. They looked north, south, east, and west, but they failed to look up—to God and his faithfulness!

God has done so much for you and me. We stand on this side of Calvary and the open tomb, and still we wonder if God can do anything about the impossibility he has ordained to bring us into more intimate union with him. The command to see the salvation of the Lord has profound implications. In the Old Testament, salvation meant safety, deliverance, extrication from suffering. In the New Testament through Jesus Christ, it means forgiveness, reconciliation, acceptance, wholeness, and abundant life now and eternal life forever. What is worth the energy squandered on panic in the light of that? The only things that can hurt Christians are those things they refuse to turn over to God. Stand firm and see what he will do because we belong to him through salvation. We are his beloved.

Next, *keep still.* That comes as a part of the awesome assurance that God will fight for us. Moses' instruction was to keep still *while* the Lord fought the battle. We are not to get in his way! So often in conflict we become defensive with elaborate self-justifying explanations. Or we insist on having the last word to be sure we come out on top. Or we barge into the battle the Lord is winning for us. Imagine what would have happened that day if instead of waiting on God, the Israelites had decided to fight the Pharaoh beside the sea! There would have been no Hebrew nation. To be sure, there is a right time for righteous confrontation, but only under God's guidance and timing. Later on, the Israelites cooperated with the Lord in winning many battles. But this time, the oncoming Egyptians were in a contest of strength with God, not with the people of Israel. They were God's problem so that he could display his triumphant adequacy for his people.

There's a time to keep still, to be silent, to listen, to observe God doing battle for us. So many of our lost battles in life were never ordained for us, or were those very special ones in which the Lord wanted to do the fighting for us. It's only in silent listening that we can know the difference.

There is a right time to move, but we can only learn it in
stillness. And that is final word from this Scripture. *Go forward.* It
tells us a great deal about Moses and about God.

Moses displayed courage and daring before the people. Inside,
he too was trembling with the crisis before him. His carefully
trained military eye calculated the steady movement of the
Pharaoh's armies toward them, estimating the size of the force.
He looked at his straggly, ill-prepared men, who were no warriors.
Then he looked to God. His prayer to God is not recorded for us.
From similar experiences in our own lives we can word it for him.
"Lord, what do you want me to do? The people are panicked.
Their fears are becoming my own. God help me!"

The Lord's response is startling. He is not impressed with
Moses' prayer. "Why are you crying out to me? Tell the people of
Israel to go forward." *Forward! Lord, which way? We are blocked on
all sides.* Was God testing Moses? Hardly. He was teaching him
that both guidance and power are given at just the right moment.
Never ahead of time; never late. The specific shape of the vision
will be revealed. The soul's only movement is forward.

Now it was time for the Lord to tell Moses how and which way
to go forward. The people were told what they were to do in trust;
Moses was told what he was to do in obedience; and God assured
him what he would do in response. Moses' staff, which had
become the rod of God, would be an instrument of magnificent
power. The Lord said, "Lift up your staff and stretch out your
hand over the sea and divide it, and the sons of Israel shall go
through the midst of the sea on the dry land. And as for Me,
behold, I will harden the hearts of the Egyptians so they will go in
after them; and I will be honored through Pharaoh and all his
army, through his chariots and his horsemen" (Exod. 14:16-17
NASB).

The cloud that had led the people to this place of impossibility
now moved around behind them, separating them from the
rapidly advancing Egyptians. The covering protection of the
Lord! It hid them from the Pharaoh all through a day and a night.
This would have been very distressing to the Pharaoh, a worshiper
of the sun god. The middle letters of his title, *Ra,* indicated that he
was a divine descendant of the god. But a greater than Ra was
calling the shots that day. Yahweh who had made the sun was
giving spiritual light to guide his people.

The Scripture suggests by implication that it was in the night that Moses was moved to follow the mysterious instructions of the Lord. "Then Moses stretched out his hand over the sea; and the Lord swept the sea back by a strong east wind all night, and turned the sea into dry land, so the waters were divided. And the sons of Israel went through the midst of the sea on the dry land, and the waters were like a wall to them on their right hand and on their left" (Exod. 14:21-22 NASB).

Maps of Egypt before the building of the Suez Canal show an upper portion of the Sea of Reeds which protruded southeast. An east wind of the force described in the Scripture would actually divide the waters of the sea so that the passageway was southeast. A peninsula of land near Baal-zephon extended into the sea like a finger. I suggest that this was the source of the passageway which reached southeast to the other shore. It was deep enough for the parted sea to be like walls and long enough for Pharaoh's armies to be trapped when it closed.

You know what happened. But don't allow familiarity to blunt the impact. When the cloud of protection which had hidden Moses and the Israelites was lifted, they were well through the sea to the other side. Pharaoh was gripped by compulsion and blind rage. He might well have waited and taken the longer route around the top of the sea. Instead, he ordered his chariots and troops into the passageway. He was arrogantly confident that Ra was greater then Yahweh. His confidence was contradicted when the bottom of the sea, which had been miraculously hardened for the Hebrews, softened again and oozed around the wheels of the chariots.

When the army was fully in the passageway, Moses was given fresh orders for the crisis. "Stretch out your hand over the sea so that the waters may come back over the Egyptians, over their chariots and their horsemen" (Exod. 14:26 NASB). It happened exactly as the Lord promised. The waters returned and the army was drowned. The people of Israel were saved by the Lord of the impossible. "And when Israel saw the great power which the Lord had used against the Egyptians, the people feared the Lord, and they believed in the Lord and in His servant Moses" (Exod. 14:31 NASB).

Yahweh, he who would be what he would be, the all-powerful creator of all, had done what he told Moses he would do—make things happen! Indeed! It took the burning bush to get Moses moving, and the parting of the Red Sea to free Israel to believe that what Moses said about God was true. Israel was brought into Egypt as a disorganized nomadic shepherd people. When they left Egypt they became a nation through the parting of the sea, which became the metaphor of what God can do with impossibilities. Nothing would be impossible now.

The same God, who did the impossible in opening the sea, is the Lord who came and lived among us. Jesus Christ boldly used the words I AM when he declared who he was—Yahweh with us! And Calvary was the place where he parted the waters of death so that we could pass through to eternal life. All the power of God dwelt in Jesus Christ and that same power is available to us through his abiding, ever-present, living presence! We have more than a burning bush, more than an opening of the sea, more than any memory. Time and memory fade. The Lord is the same yesterday, today, and tomorrow. The same extricating love that blessed Israel has liberated us from the bondage of sin, guilt, self-doubt, and condemnation, through a cross, an empty tomb, and the indwelling power of Pentecost.

Stack up the impossible against that! Heap up the things that have forced you into a wedge of improbability. And then give back to God the situation, circumstances, disability, or inadequacy which makes you cry out, "Impossible!" He is in it with you. It's dawn; the night is past; put your rod, the cross, in your impossible sea; the waters are going to part!

> Forward! But whither shall we go?
> The desert is on either side,
> Behind us the Egyptian foe.
> Before, the interposing tide!
> Yet while we Thy command obey
> Our road impossible pursue,
> The ocean yields an open way
> And lets Thy people through.
>                    Maclaren's *Expositions of Holy Scripture*

# CHAPTER SIX

# Fresh Grace

## ——*Moses, the Leader*——

I greeted a friend with the customary, "How's it going?" Her face clouded over with a worried look and her reply was filled with grim tension. "I'll be okay," she said, "if I can just make it through today!"

My response surprised her. "Dear friend," I said with empathy, "today is all you were meant to make it through. In fact, today is all you have!"

That made her laugh, and she loosened her white-knuckled grip on the problems of that day. Then I asked her a question that I need to answer for myself on days when pressures pile up. "Is the inflow matching the outgo?" She knew what I meant and confessed that she had walked into the battle of that day without taking time to talk with God about the day's demands or to get his guidance and direction. The best she had hoped for was to endure the trials of the day and get on to tomorrow. Then I dared to ask her something I wish my friends would ask me when I get grim. I encouraged her to share with me the pressures and offered to pray with her. She was amazingly ready and willing. We asked God what he wanted her to do that day and that she would receive an equal proportion of his power for what he guided her to do. You guessed it. Her day was transformed. Much more than just enduring the day, she had a triumphant, power-filled day.

The most difficult discovery I've been forced to learn about the abundant life is to live one day at a time and receive fresh grace from the Lord for each day. God has graciously measured out life in day-tight compartments so that we can be present in the present with the power of his presence. But that's not easy to hear, or to remember.

It is the most crucial truth God taught Moses and his people during the first few months in the wilderness after they had passed through the Red Sea. This is the period from the entrance into the wilderness to the arrival at Mount Sinai where they received the Ten Commandments and beheld God's glory. It was a time in which the Lord of the impossible taught Moses and the people of his unlimited grace to meet their daily needs. In all the crises the Lord molded Moses into a great leader and his people into a nation that would trust him.

The people were ill-prepared for the rigors of the desert. The sand and the limestone became like an oven under the blistering sun. They quickly ran out of water and food. Forty-five days into the wilderness and they were parched and famished. The water stored in their leather bags at the Oasis of Elim along the way had been consumed. The stock taken with them from Egypt had been slaughtered and eaten. The people's lips were blistered and hunger gnawed at their stomachs.

Once again they criticized Moses for taking them away from the flesh pots and bread of Egypt, and their murmuring mounted into threatened mutiny. Imagine two million people clacking their tongues on the roofs of their mouths in hateful disdain, coupled with discontented "Ohs! Errs! and Hisses!" No longer did they sing songs of praise with timbrels and cymbals which they had done a month and a half before when celebrating the Lord's victory over the Egyptians. Now there was petulance blended with panic. Lack of faith has a short memory. Fear of the future causes an easy forgetfulness of past blessings. The people became restless and rebellious. What could Moses do? The only thing he knew to do was cry out to God. "Yahweh, what do You want me to do?" What the Lord told him to do, and then provided for the people, gives us the secret of how he wants to care for us. His promise was astounding considering the circumstances of the desolate desert.

The Lord told Moses that he would send meat in the evening and bread in the morning. And it happened exactly as he told

Moses it would. Picture it in your mind's eye. At the end of one day, as the crimson sun set on the desert horizon, the people staggered to a resting place, weak with hunger. Hopelessly, they prepared for one more night battling their hunger pangs and parched throats which made sleep a stranger.

Only a few saw it at first. Then the whole multitude stood staring at the strange dark brown cloud that appeared on the horizon and moved toward them. Soon they heard an amazing sound. The chirping of quail! A gigantic flock of quail was flying directly toward them. Could it be? Yes! And then, as if the birds were making a desperate attempt to make the last lap of their appointed journey, they flew low and landed exhausted at the feet of the astonished Hebrews. They were limp and easily caught by the excited people and prepared for cooking over quickly set fires. As the game sizzled over the fire, the fat ignited the blaze and the hundreds of fires made holes in the darkness which had fallen across the desert. The people ate ravenously and once again began to sing praises to God. Now they could sleep.

Research into the migratory habits of quail in the Middle East makes the miracle of the Lord's provision all the more exciting. Each autumn, the birds fly from central Europe to Turkey. There they prepare for a crossing of the Mediterranean. The flight across the ocean is done in a single flight at a very high speed. Any bird that falters falls into the sea. When the birds approach the land they drop down in altitude but maintain their high speed. As soon as they are over the coastland they land exhausted and completely drained. They lie motionless for hours while they regain their strength. For years Bedouin who lived near the coast harvested the easy prey. Recently a law was passed and enforced which prohibited quail trapping.

The amazing thing about the biblical account of the provision of the quail is that the birds must have kept flying until they reached the wilderness of Sinai where they became the source of survival for the hungry Hebrews in the desert. How did the quail know to fly on farther after their already exhausting flight? Only the Lord who created them could have pressed them on to be his blessing for his people in desperate need.

When the people awoke in the morning, they were startled by still another evidence of the Lord's loving care. All over the ground was a frost-like substance, like coriander seed, with a yellowish tinge and a resinous appearance like bdellium. The people cried out, "Manhu!" meaning, "What is it?" The name "manna" comes from that. When they tasted it, it was like honey or fresh oil. They found that they could grind it in their mills, beat it with mortars, then boil it in pots, and make it into cakes.

Moses was quick to tell the people that the Lord had provided them bread from heaven. He also carefully instructed them in what the Lord had told him about it. The manna would be given them each morning. They were to collect only enough for each day and for two days on the day before the Sabbath. Whenever the people tried to hoard more than a daily provision, except to last over for the Sabbath, it became rancid and wormy. The message was clear: the Lord would provide for the people on a daily basis. They would have to accept his blessing fresh each day. There could be no stale manna.

The same is true for us. There is fresh grace for each new day. We cannot live on yesterday's inspiration. As the Lord gives each new day, he shows us the way. Old experiences of his grace will not be adequate to get us through today. Each day we must open ourselves to his new guidance and power. When we pray and study the Scriptures at the beginning of each day, the Lord gives us exactly what we will need in that day. Our task is to relinquish our fears and frustrations, problems and perplexities, and trust him completely. He will give us strength, insight, the right word to speak, and a blessed sense of companionship with him.

Moses and the people had to learn that all through the wilderness wanderings. And God was faithful. As they pressed on into the wilderness they were forced to trust him each step of the way. It wasn't long before they were attacked by the Amalekites, who were descendants of Esau, and closely related to the Israelites. Their fear of losing their grazing lands to the invading tribes made them fierce in their attacks. The Israelites were not prepared for war. The Lord had fought for them at the Red Sea; now they had to learn how to fight with his help. He gave Moses the formula. All he had to do was hold his holy rod in the air and Israel's armies would win over Amalek. The same rod that opened the Red Sea was the Lord's appointed symbol of his presence in battle. But the people were forced to cooperate with the Lord and with one another. He taught them that they must be mutually dependent and supportive for his blessing to flow.

As long as Moses held the rod up high, Israel won, but whenever he rested his arms at his sides, the soldiers of Amalek won. When the battle drew on for a long time, Moses was not strong enough to keep the rod uplifted. That's when he realized his dependence not only on God but also on Aaron and Hur. They would stand next to him, holding his arms up. Joshua would then be able to lead the armies to victory. Moses learned that greatness was being willing to receive strength from others as well as from the Lord.

We were never meant to make it alone. We need one another to win in life's battles. Our ministry to one another requires prayer *and* involvement. The Lord has ordained that his blessings will be released as we pray. He wants his children to identify our family likeness as brothers and sisters in his eternal family. That's why he often withholds his best until we pray for his interventions. I could not make it through any day without the knowledge that people through their prayers are holding up my arms in the battle. But prayer must be implemented by getting with people and their struggles. Aaron and Hur held up Moses' arms and Joshua fought as the general of the army. They were all indispensable for victory. And so are we. The key is seeking God's guidance for learning whom he has put on our agenda and what he wants us to do to express his love. The battle is the Lord's, but he chooses to win through our cooperation. Moses had to rediscover that repeatedly.

These two events during the period between the crossing of the sea and the arrival at Mount Sinai teach us a great deal about the Lord of the impossible and the way he works in our lives. His grace is given in daily portions and we need one another to appropriate his strength.

Each Sunday morning, the elders of my church gather in my study to pray with me. Just before prayer, one of them asks, "Lloyd, what do you need today?" The question focuses on the particular blessing I need that Sunday. I am amazed how my needs change. What was needed on a previous Sunday may not be the need of the following one. Sometimes I need physical strength after an exhausting week. Other times I need to confess problems which are troubling me. Still other times I need boldness to preach with freedom. And often I need the courage to be personal and vulnerable as I illustrate my exposition of the Scriptures from discoveries in my own life. When I have articulated the specific aspect of fresh grace needed, the elders begin to pray. They talk to God in an unstudied, forthright way. There is no general "Bless the service, Lord" but rather a straight arrow of intercession for the specific need. In this way, before and during the preaching, the elders hold up my arms.

Whenever I am complimented after a sermon or people express how the Lord spoke to their needs, I am quick to explain that the accolades go to the Order of Aaron and Hur, made up of the praying elders who are faithful in claiming God's best each Sunday. The question they ask me is one I need to be asked not only on Sunday, but every day of the week. In a very penetrating way, it is the question the Lord asks me each morning when I begin my prayers for the day.

As I've written this chapter on fresh grace and an interdependence in the family of God, I've been forced to get in touch again with a weakness in my life. I don't like to admit weakness! I'd like to be able to live the Christian life for the Lord, but not by his power. And I'd like to be able to be free of needing the constant prayers of people. My conditioning as a child put a high priority on self-reliance and independence. As a teen-ager, I was trained to lead, not to be led. For years after I became a clergyman, I felt my responsibility to be an example precluded admitting my own needs. When I look back on all the power the Lord offered which I resisted out of pride, and all the encouragement from people I refused out of needing to be adequate, I am alarmed by what I missed. I am thankful that the Lord allowed me to get to the end of my rope in this false independence.

One day in my first parish I ran out of steam. Totally exhausted physically, emotionally, and spiritually, I cried out to the Lord for strength to endure. His answer amazed me. "Tell the elders of your church how you are feeling and ask them to pray with you." The orders were not easy to follow. Expose my weakness? What would they think? Would they lose confidence in me? The need was so great that I set these questions aside and told the elders how much I needed them. The response was astonishing. They felt loved and trusted. No longer kept at arm's length, they established a weekly Bible study, sharing and prayer meeting in addition to the monthly business meetings. Admitting my need freed them to talk about theirs. Allowing them to love me released them to be receptive to my love and leadership for them. The strain of being perfect was gone. An authentic renewal swept through the Session and marked the beginning of a spiritual awakening in the entire church.

Out of that new freedom, I discovered the secret of dynamic exposition of the Scripture. In addition to careful scholarship, I dared to be personal about my own pilgrimage. The thrust of each message was illustrated not only by quotes from great thinkers and scholars, but also by what I had or needed to experience from what the Lord was saying in the Scripture. This revolutionized my preaching. Less a presentation, it became a dialogue with my people. I'll never forget the response of one man as I was explaining the power of this new freedom. "What's happened to you? I don't feel you're preaching at me anymore. You have let me into your heart. I feel that now we are partners in a great adventure." That was years ago, but the secret I discovered remains the source of joy in communicating with people. Surely, there are times I tighten up and fall back into privatism. But not for long. I now know it when it happens and realize that I blocked God's fresh grace and help from others. The misery of trying to be adequate forces me back to prayer and honest fellowship with others.

The Lord of the impossible wants us to discover what he taught the people of Israel. As was mentioned at the opening of this chapter, all we have is today. Our challenge is to live it as if it were our last and to live it to the fullest. He offers us the fresh grace to meet our specific needs and faithful friends to spur us on. Tell him what you need. Ask others to intercede for you. Don't depend on yesterday's inspiration, or last week's insight. New manna is available and Aaron and Hur are at your side.

# CHAPTER SEVEN

# The Ultimate Miracle

## —Moses and God's Presence—

Living in Southern California, I often hear people say, "I'm going up to the mountains to get away from it all!" Most, however, find that the one problem they can't leave in the valley is themselves. The reason some feel refreshed after a time of quiet and rest in the mountains is that they have given the Lord a chance to deal with their needs, priorities, and goals. They return to the valley of life with new purpose and power.

Recently, a member of my church put the "going to the mountains to get away from it all" idea very differently. He said, "I'm going to the mountains for a few days, not to escape life but to more fully appreciate the exciting things that have been happening in my life." The man is a great prayer warrior and recently he's received a succession of miracles through his prayers for God's intervention in impossibilities in people's lives. He's been entrusted with the gift of healing the hurts of people. The Lord's blessing on his ministry recently had left him breathless. Through his prayers relational, psychological, and physical healing has been given to him by the Lord. He shared a crucial insight. "The time I need to be quiet is not just after failure or fatigue, but after success. I'm tempted to ride the waves of power and forget where it comes from. I've learned that times of effectiveness in ministry with people are a prelude to a deeper experience of the Lord in my own life. I don't want to miss that. See you in a few days!"

That's essentially what the Lord wanted to do with Moses. The leader had been through taxing, exhausting challenges. He also had witnessed spectacular interventions of the Lord of the impossible. The release of the Israelites from Egypt, the awesome opening of the sea, the coming of quail and manna to feed his people, and the victorious power revealed in the battle with the Amalekites—all had left him reeling with wonder and amazement. The greatest impossibility lay ahead. It was proverbial among the people that no one had ever seen God and lived. Now after God had displayed what he could do, he wanted Moses to know who he was. To do that he led the emancipator to Mount Sinai for an emancipation of his own soul. The Lord knew that the most urgent need in Moses was not for one more miracle, but for the ultimate miracle—to know him personally.

In preparation for writing this book, I asked a group of people what they believed was the greatest miracle of the Lord of the impossible in their lives. One man spoke up with confidence in his voice and radiance on his face. "No question in my mind," he said. "The greatest miracle for me is that I can know him. Anything else he does in my impossibilities is an added bonus. Just to be able to talk with the Lord of the universe, experience his love, and be guided by him, is wonder enough for me. That seems impossible, but it happens every day!" So many people long for that joy. Why?

We cannot know God until he chooses to reveal himself. Left to ourselves, our minds are closed, our wills are in bondage, and our emotions are blocked. Only as he draws near to us do we want to go to him. The desire to know God is his gift. When I look back on my conversion it was his doing from start to finish. Now thirty-three years later, I can honestly say that he has always been the initiator. He initiates prayer by creating the desire to pray. The longing to know his will is because he has guidance ready to give me. The expectation of his interventions comes when he is ready to break through with insight, wisdom, or a resolution of some problem. And in it all, the Lord himself is the best gift he gives. To long to know God for God and not for what we want him to do for us is preparation for experiencing the relationship with him that we were born to have.

That's the gift the Lord called Moses and the people of Israel to

receive at Sinai. He summoned Moses to the heights of the
mountain to reveal himself. On each ascent, Moses learned more
about the mysterious Yahweh who had displayed his power so
spectacularly in his life. The Lord revealed his holiness in the
thick darkness of the cloud, fire, lightning, and thunder. Then he
disclosed his righteousness by giving the people the Ten
Commandments as the basis of a right relationship with him and
one another. His compassion for the infant nation, still unskilled
in the basics of health, cleanliness, and the management of life,
was given in specific regulations for daily living. In repeated
encounters with Moses, the Lord gave them feasts to express their
gratitude to him as the source of their prosperity in the land which
would be given to them. He told them how to worship him, how to
atone with sacrifices for their sin, and how to build a tabernacle
where he would be worshiped. Then he pledged his indefatigable
faithfulness in a covenant, a promise to be their God and to bless
them as his people. Still Moses longed to know God better, more
personally.

When the people sinned by forging and worshiping a golden
calf while he was on the mountain, Moses was led deeper in his
knowledge of God. He learned in experience the meaning of a
word the Lord had taught him on the mountain: *atonement*. The
Lord had used it when explaining the sacrificial offerings the
people were to make for their sin. In a moment of excruciating
anguish over what the people had done, Moses offered himself as
a sacrifice for his people's sin. The Lord was not impressed with
his self-oblation. He would deal with the people's sin. Moses' task
was to lead them, not be a substitutionary sacrifice. His love was
not enough. Only God could atone for their idolatry.

Those were turbulent months as Moses discovered a growing
understanding of his God. As the leader was ready, the Lord
showed him more of himself. "Thus the Lord used to speak to
Moses face to face, just as man speaks to his friend" (Exod. 33:11
NASB). When the Lord told Moses that it was time to depart from
Sinai and leave for the promised land in Canaan, Moses grew
uneasy. He desired to know more of God and feared leaving the
mountain. That led to a prayer to God which resulted in one of the
greatest revelations of the nature of the Lord of the impossible.
What happened has tremendous implications for us today. The

Lord wants to give us what he gave Moses: the assurance of his presence and the gift of his glory.

Like so many of our prayers, Moses talked to God until he knew what he wanted to say. He began with a complaint. "See, You say to me, 'Bring up this people.' But You have not let me know whom You will send with me. Yet You have said, 'I know you by name, and you have also found grace in My sight.' Now therefore, I pray, if I have found grace in Your sight, show me now Your way, that I may know You and that I may find grace in Your sight. And consider that this nation is Your people" (Exod. 33:12-13 NKJV).

The sublime moment had come. The Lord had given Moses the freedom to open his heart completely. Note how he progressed from complaints to the desire for communion. The Lord allowed him to go deeper with each request. Moses wanted to know his God. The same longing is in all of us. We want to tear down all the barriers we've erected and let God know us as we are. But we also long to know him as he truly is.

The Lord's response to Moses is one of the greatest promises in the Old Testament. People through the ages have staked their lives on it, martyrs have faced their death with it on their lips, and the troubled have grasped it tenaciously as their only assurance. The Lord said, "My presence shall go with you, and I will give you rest" (Exod. 33:14 NASB). My presence! The word for presence in Hebrew can also be translated "face." The face of the Lord with his watchful eye would not leave his people. *He would be with them.*

Moses responded in a very human way. "If Your Presence does not go with us, do not bring us up from here. For how then will it be known that Your people and I have found grace in Your sight, except You go with us? So we shall be separate, Your people and I, from all the people who are upon the face of the earth" (Exod. 33:15-16 NKJV). Moses' understanding of his God was being stretched. He was not just a localized deity of Sinai. Moses and the people could dare to move forward to claim the promises the Lord had given for their future. Nothing has meaning without God. No place is safe or satisfying without him. Now Moses not only knew of the power, holiness, righteousness, compassion, and forgiveness of Yahweh, but he was assured also of his omnipresence.

Moses' deepest desire had been hidden in his heart for a long time. He had wanted to tell God, but had not dared. When the

Lord assured Moses of his presence and that he knew his name
and he had found favor in his sight, Moses dared to express the
longing of his heart that had been growing ever since the burning
bush encounter with God. The months at Sinai had only made his
desire more poignantly acute. Finally, he burted out the desire of
his heart. "Please, show me Your glory."

The word for glory in Hebrew is *kabod*. When used for
describing a person it meant his wealth, worth, stature, standing,
and power. What did Moses want when he asked to see God's
glory? Did he want to see God's presence in a physical
manifestation? No, more than that. What he was asking was for an
encounter and experience with God's true nature. In a way, he was
saying, "Lord I want to know You better, love You for Yourself,
realize a heart-to-heart intimacy." Audacity? Blasphemy? Hardly.
The Lord had been the instigator and initiator of the desire. And
that tells us something we all need to be more sure of than
anything else. God not only wants to know us, He also wants us to
know, love, worship, and adore him as our God. That's why he
created us in the beginning. The ultimate prayer in the light of that
is, "Lord, show me Your glory!" Have you ever asked God for
that? It's the sure sign that he has been working in us to bring us to
the threshold of the holy of holies in his own heart. There is an
emptiness in the heart of God which only you and I can fill. He is
lonely for us to come home and desire him more than anything or
anyone else.

The answer the Lord gave Moses' awesome request tells us
what the Lord means by his glory. He said, "I will make all My
goodness pass before you, and I will proclaim the name of the
Lord before you. I will be gracious to whom I will be gracious, and
I will have compassion on whom I will have compassion" (Exod.
33:19 NKJV). There it is. The essential nature of God is
goodness, enabling power, and grace.

The Hebrew word translated "goodness" means constancy and
consistency. Goodness is the unchangeable, reliable, dependable
nature of God, the same yesterday, today, and tomorrow. In a
world of change, he can be counted on to be what he has said he is,
His mind does not fluctuate about us. That goodness is expressed
in the consistency of his character. His name is his character. And
that character is revealed in his power to create and recreate. His
name is Yahweh which, we learned earlier, means that he is the

ultimate power of the universe. But power for what? That leads us to another word the Lord used in defining his glory. "I will be gracious." Grace is the unlimited, unchanging, unmotivated love of God. It is not dependent on our performance or instigated by our adequacy. We do not deserve it and cannot earn it. God loves because he is love. His compassion is the lengths to which he will go to reach us, forgive us, and make us right with himself.

Our minds leap from Moses and Mount Sinai to Jesus and Mount Calvary. Christ is the glory of God for us to see, behold, experience, and receive. All that God explained to Moses about his glory is manifested in Christ. Paul articulated this with soaring rhetoric that never ceases to stir our souls. "For it is the God who commanded light to shine out of darkness who has shone in our hearts to give the light of the knowledge of the glory of God in the face of Jesus Christ" (II Cor. 4:6 NKJV). That doxological statement was made at the conclusion of the apostle's description of Moses' experience of the glory of God on Sinai. Moses beheld the glory of the Lord and put a veil over his face when he returned to the people. The reason for that was that the radiance of his face created by beholding the Lord was fading. Paul wanted the early Christians to realize that Christ is the unfading glory of God continually with them. He told the Colossians, "Christ in you, the hope of glory" (1:27 NKJV). Christ is not only beheld; he comes within us. The Lord's goodness, power and grace are implanted within us. We become like our Lord!

Now the prayer "show me Your glory" takes on profound implications. Not only does the Lord promise to go with us, but *he also desires to live in us.* Can that happen? Now you see why really knowing the Lord is life's greatest impossibility—except as he chooses us, calls us, conditions us with a hunger and thirst for him.

To make that possible he came himself as the mediator. Talk about impossibilities! That's what he faced in the hostile, rebellious, fallen world of human sin and misery. Only a cosmic atonement could accomplish the reconciliation of man to God. And the same power revealed in Christ's miracles, and explained in his message, was the power that defeated death and the power of evil on the cross. That power raised Jesus from the dead. Impossible? Yes, but the Lord of the impossible did it! And beyond that, the same power returned to fill the ready followers of Jesus in the Upper Room. The church was born and a new humanity was begun. As indwelling Lord, he regenerated them and made them new people, entrusted them with power to do what he had done as the incarnate Christ, and astounded the world with his glory that radiated on their faces and in their fellowship. And nothing less than what happened then can happen to you and me. When we pray Moses' prayer, "Show me Your glory!" it is answered in more than a vision of a distant Lord which will fade. For us it is an invitation for the Lord of glory to take up residence in us.

So much of our talk about life's impossibilities centers in the problems and perplexities we face with human inadequacy. Following Moses to Sinai has given us a new perspective. We don't need just an intervention in our problems, we need an infusion from the Lord of the impossible in our inner persons. Moses received the promise that the Lord would be with him; we have the promise that he will make his home in us. Not just beside, above, around, but within!

I have talked at length about this promise because it increases our understanding of the fact that the same Lord who intervened in the needs of the people of Israel is the One who dealt with the impossibilities of sin, death, and the re-creation of human nature when he lived among us as the Christ. Each event foreshadows that ultimate defeat of the impossible.

We wonder why we claim so little of the glory offered to us. We continue to struggle in our own strength. That's why we can identify with Israel's reluctance to trust that the Lord's presence would be with them. We know so much more of God's glory than they did. And yet we are afraid to claim the promise of power he offers. It's to the deeper causes of that fear that we turn our attention in the next chapter.

CHAPTER EIGHT

# Later!

## —Israel on the Border of Canaan—

A new abridged version of the old parting words, "I'll see you later," has now gained slang popularity. People just crisply say, "Later!"

A friend of mine ends every phone call abruptly "Okay, pal . . . later!" and hangs up.

The other day I was grappling with some soul-sized issues in my prayers that demanded the response of new commitment to the Lord. Suddenly the word popped into my mind. I wanted to end the prayer and get off the hot spot on which the Lord had me. My impulse was to put off the decisions and say to the Lord, "Later!"

Unless I miss my guess, each of us is struggling with some decision or response which makes us want to close our conversation with the Lord with a, "Later, Lord, much later!" What is it for you? What challenge have you put off? What promise have you tabled? What opportunity have you tucked away in the tomorrow file that should be done today?

"Later" was a persistent word Augustine of Hippo used during the time he was holding God at bay. "And when Thou didst on all sides shew me that what Thou saidst was true, I, convicted by the truth, had nothing at all to answer, but only those dull and drowsy words, 'Anon, anon,' 'presently,' 'leave me but a little.' " We can empathize with Augustine. We've done that with the basic decision to let God love us and guide our lives, and then in thousands of things we know he wants us to do. But most dangerous of all, we say "Later!" to the Lord when he finally opens up an opportunity for which we've been praying for a long time. Often the very things for which we have been petitioning are offered to us and we step back, afraid to grasp the gift we have been asking for.

Mark Twain gave some advice we accept too readily. "Never put off until tomorrow what you can put off until the day after tomorrow." That's dangerous advice. We know. Yet, we all live by it, almost as a creed, putting off until some distant tomorrow the urgent opportunities the Lord has offered us.

That kind of living is called procrastination. The word comes basically from two Latin words. *Pro* means "forward" and *cras* means "the morrow." Procrastination is putting forward to some tomorrow what the Lord wills for today—now! It is the burglar of time, a thief which robs today of freedom and fills tomorrow with frustration. Hesiod was right, "The procrastinating man is forever struggling with ruin." And Erasmus was even more pointed. "Procrastination brings loss, delay, danger." Most of all, procrastination precludes the realization of the promises of God. The strange mystery of our willful nature is that we resist the promises of the abundant life—peace, joy, and blessing—by putting off until some distant future the response of decision or action God has scheduled for today. And often we do it with beautifully formulated reasons and carefully worded equivocations. But one word summarizes our attitude: *Later!*

That's exactly the spiritual sickness which gripped the people of Israel with virulent proportions fourteen months into the Exodus. Three months out of Egypt brought them to the wilderness of Sinai. There, during nine months, the Lord gave them the Ten Commandments, the instructions for building the Tabernacle, and the sublime sacrificial system for atonement. Then the Lord said, "You have stayed long enough at this mountain" (Deut. 1:6). According to Numbers 10:11, it was on the twentieth day of the second month of the second year after leaving Egypt that the pillar of cloud by day and fire by night moved out, calling the people to press on to claim the promised land of Canaan. They were led north to the wilderness of Paran at Kadesh on the borders of the promised land. There the Lord instructed Moses to send twelve spies into the land. The command was not to determine whether it was possible to invade the land, but to assure the people that the promises which had sounded in their souls for fourteen months would soon be a reality. "Send out for yourself men so that they may spy out the land of Canaan, *which I am going to give to the sons of Israel"* (Num. 13:2 NASB, italics mine) was the Lord's propitious reaffirmation of his promise. The purpose of the reconnaissance was to give the people courage.

Moses didn't procrastinate. Immediately, he selected twelve strong and trustworthy men, one from each of the twelve tribes, and sent them into the Negev, the rocky, mountainous southern part of Palestine, and on to the hill country. They were gone on their mission for forty days. When they returned they gave two very different reports of their feasibility reconnaissance. The majority report of ten was negative and filled with panicked fear. The minority report, given by Caleb and Joshua, was courageous and daring. Caleb catches our attention and admiration when he says, "We should by all means go up and take posession of it, for we shall surely overcome it" (Num. 13:30 NASB). We admire his promptness, daring, and complete lack of procrastination. It earned him one of the finest accolades the Lord ever gave a person. "My servant Caleb, because he has a different spirit in him and has followed Me fully, I will bring into the land" (Num. 14:24 NKJV). Caleb's spirit was filled with the Lord's Spirit and he followed the Lord without question. Later, looking back on his career, Joshua sounded the same note of praise about Caleb, "because he followed the Lord God of Israel fully" (Josh. 14:14 NASB).

Sadly, it was not Caleb's minority report which won the day. The fearful majority report appealed to the people. They put off accepting the promise of God. The account in Numbers 13 gives four disturbing things about the cause and cure of the spiritual malady of procrastination. They increase our understanding of this strategic event in the people's experience of the Lord of the impossible. The account becomes pointedly personal when we focus our own promised land of anticipated blessing from our Lord only *if* we dare to go ahead and claim it.

First, *procrastination is questioning in the dark what God has promised in the light.* The Lord's promise had not changed as they camped there on the border of blessing. In the quiet of prayer, the Lord had repeatedly told Moses and the people that he would be faithful to give them the promised land. The majority report brought back by the ten spies left out the truth of that promise and the power offered to back it up. They left out the Lord as the primary factor in the equation of victory. Yes, the land was flowing with milk and honey, as the Lord and Moses had promised. But there were grave dangers. The people who lived there were strong, the cities were fortified. Most frightening of all, they had seen the sons of Anak, "the people of the neck," they were called, because of their long necks and giant proportions. These were the predecessors of Goliath, mercenary soldiers who were adopted as the warriors of the Amalekites and later, the Philistines. "It's too risky, too dangerous, the odds are against us," the ten furtive spies said with their teeth rattling. They went on with blood-curdling facts that confirmed Israel's procrastination. "The land through which we have gone, in spying it out, is a land that devours its inhabitants; and all the people whom we saw in it were men of giant size" (Num. 13:32 NASB).

Procrastination is usually the preferred alternative of the coward's heart. We all know that. When we leave the Lord's presence and power out of our analysis of a challenge, we will be gripped by panic and put off a crucial decision or action. What God has made clear in the light, we question in the darkness. Courage is fear that has said its prayers. Procrastination is fear that has forgotten what was promised in its prayers.

Questioning in the battle what God has quickened us to believe is his will for us is fatal. He is the same yesterday, today, and tomorrow. The Lord never goes back on his word. He does not shift his strategy or remove his strength to accomplish it. Our God wants to give us staying power when the going gets difficult. James Thurber's analysis of editor Harold Ross is all too personal. "He lived at the corner of work and worry." What an inadequate location for life! God, work, willingness, and courageous hope would be much better. What is our address? What are the ingredients of life for us? I'd like to live at the intersection of faith, hope, and love. What about you? Christ is not only truth and the life for us. He is the Way! He is leading on to our promised land of an abundant life now and eternal life forever. Now is the time to begin to follow the Way. Not tomorrow. William Temple once said of the Way, "It starts where each one stands. We do not need to find its starting place. It starts where we are!"

Procrastination locks us on dead-center. It immobilizes us as we try to make life stand still for a while. But life moves on, passing the procrastinator, leaving him or her with unrealized dreams and hopes. At base, procrastination is sin, as R. E. C. Brown put it, "the refusal to control what can be controlled, and the attempt to control what cannot be controlled."

The second thing this account tells us is that *things become what they seem.* The Israelites used the God-given capacity of imagination to picture the worst. The epitaph on the death of their courage was stated in the words of the majority report: "We became like grasshoppers in our own sight, and so we were in their sight." (Num. 13:33 NASB). Their image of the sons of Anak was distorted and their image of themselves was diminished. The Israelites became what they seemed in their own sight: inadequate, impotent grasshoppers! That's the way they acted and responded. Fear makes us grasshoppers first in our own sight and then in the sight of others. Nathaniel Hawthorne in *The House of the Seven Gables* said, "What other dungeon is so dark as one's own heart! What jailer so inexorable as one's self!"

God wants to give us a creative self-image which includes all the talents and abilities he's given, plus the power of his indwelling Spirit, plus a picture of ourselves accomplishing what he has given us to do. With that we can be more than conquerors. Paul discovered this. He did not say, "I can do all things for Christ," but, "I can do all things through Christ who strengthens me!" And so can we. Image the challenge you are tempted to put off. See yourself in the thick of the battle equipped with superhuman strength. Now hold that picture. We are giants!

> I fear no foe, with thee at hand to bless;
> Ills have no weight, and tears no bitterness. . . .
> I triumph still, if thou abide with me.
>
> Henry F. Lyte

Third, consider the *contagious infection of procrastination.* The fear in the ten appealed to the fear in the whole nation. It spread throughout Israel leaving the people prostrate. When you and I step back from meeting life head on, we spread the mood of delay to family, friends, and fellow-adventurers in Christ. We need Caleb to be our patron saint as we promote pertinacity in others. What the Lord guides, he provides.

What we decide and do today will radically affect the spiritual boldness or lack of it in others. They are watching, listening, all the time! I talked to a young man whose father had retreated from the difficult challenge of trusting God to help him make his marriage work. He evaded confrontation and healing. Rather than working through the problems, he accepted the easy way of having an affair with another woman. His son's urgings to resist spreading his relational ineptness to another woman were brashly rejected. The son said, "My father stood up to bat for his life. When he got one strike against him he left the mound. With some courage, he could have hit a home run with my mom. Instead, he struck out by default. Now I don't know what to believe; whom can I trust? I don't want to be simplistic. Not all divorce is striking out. But it was for him. He procrastinated so long that he lost his nerve."

In differing circumstances, it happens to all of us. A delay in a decision. To make no decision is disastrous. Of course, there are waiting times when we listen for God's marching orders. That's creative and necessary. It is not procrastination to wait until we have clear signals from the Lord before acting. Procrastination is reluctance to act on what he has made abundantly clear. Mark Twain again: "It's not so much what I don't understand in the Bible that bothers me; it's what I do understand and fail to do." We can start with love, forgiveness, and affirmation for openers. There's little doubt about the disciplines of discipleship for most of us. And for the gray areas of life's decisions, the Lord has told us he will give us all the guidance we need to act according to his timing. It is a spiritual law that we must act today on however much guidance we have if we want more tomorrow.

The fourth truth this account of Israel's procrastination affords us is that *we can miss God's best* by saying, "Later!" We can wait so long that we lose our power to say, "Now!" The people of Israel not only said, "No!" to God's promises, their guilt drove them to insurrection and an attempt to impeach Moses. Even after fourteen months and all the evidences of God's miracles and provision, they wanted to go back to Egypt! Hard to believe. Or is it? When procrastination is fed into our memory bank as the only data for life's demands, the computer in the tissues of our brain becomes incapable of any answer except "later."

As a result, most of the generation of Israel who followed the procrastinating majority report never saw the promised land. They were forced to wander for thirty-eight years more in the wilderness until Caleb and Joshua once again offered Israel a new chance to go in and possess the land. Many Christians live in a powerless, unadventuresome, bleak, impotent wilderness without the fullness of Christ's indwelling power because they constantly step back from challenges that only his presence could pull off. We settle for substitutes. We major in minors because we are afraid to take and pass the major course that will require all we've got plus all the Lord can give.

I want to conclude this chapter with some questions I need to answer. What would I do today if I knew that success according to God's standards was assured? What would I attempt if I were sure that the Lord would be there with me infusing wisdom, love, courage, and boldness? And you—what step of personal growth in faith have you been putting off? What forgiveness needs to be offered to or received from the people in your life? Who needs your love and assurance today in both words and actions? If this were your last day, what would you do? (As you answer these questions, write out your answers.)

Let us join the minority report. With Caleb, let's go in and possess our promised land saying with him, "We should by all means go up and take possession of it, for we shall surely overcome it" (Num. 13:30 NASB).

Later? No! Now!

# CHAPTER NINE

# Getting Our Feet Wet

## —Joshua, Crossing the Jordan—

Answering the questions with which we concluded the last chapter presses me to action. I don't know about you, but what I wrote out in response to each gave me marching orders. Did you sense, as I did, that your answers quickened the pace of our consideration of the Lord of the impossible? Suddenly, I realized that the Lord shows the way, offers his power, promises to intervene to help us, and then calls us to take a first step. It's almost as if he waits to be sure we really want to receive the answers to the prayers we pray. He loves us so much that he wants us to cooperate with him in the accomplishment of his will for us.

That's the thrust of this chapter. Our study of the unfolding drama of the Lord's revelation of his power to the people of Israel brings us to the edge of the River Jordan. The people had arrived at the edge of the promised land after wandering in the wilderness for thirty-eight years, procrastinating the challenge to go in and possess the land that the Lord had prepared for them. And to end the period of equivocation and to begin a forward movement, the Lord called a man called Joshua. When God gets ready to accomplish his purposes in us, he creates a desire in us to go forward, and then he reveals the specific steps we must take.

Joshua, the successor to Moses, dominates center stage in the book that is called by his name. He had been carefully trained by the Lord through Moses for the challenge of invading and occupying Canaan. He had been with Moses in his conflicts and concerns, his victories and his vicissitudes. Joshua had heard the great liberator in his prayers and in his messages to the people. He knew the valleys of failure and the mountain peaks of success. With Moses, he had been tested to the point of breaking because of the stiff-necked, rebellious, murmuring people. Joshua became a seasoned man of God, a brilliant general, and a believer in the accomplishment of the impossible through the Lord's might. He had shared Moses' bitter disappointment when the people would not trust Caleb and his report and admonition about entering and possessing the promised land. Now thirty-eight long, excruciating, wandering years later, Joshua was determined to discover and follow God's strategy for crossing the Jordan. I have selected this event in Joshua's leadership because it tells us so much about *how to make the future a friend.*

After Joshua had spent a prolonged time with God, he announced to the people, "Consecrate yourselves, for tomorrow the Lord will do wonders among you" (Josh. 3:5 NASB). We can imagine the lightning-bolt quality that call had for the discouraged, dejected people. Thirty-eight years of wandering had taken its toll on expectation. Like depleted people in every age, tomorrow had come to mean only more of the same.

How do you feel about your tomorrow, the future? Are you expectant? A sure sign that you are in communion with the living God is to believe in the future more than in the past.

Joshua promised a wonder-filled tomorrow for those burned-out Israelites. The word *wonderful* is too often a hackneyed word in our parlance. But its true meaning needs to be redefined and reclaimed. It means filled with wonder. Wonder is a combination of surprise, awe, and delight. It is our response to the serendipitous interventions of God. *A wonderful tomorrow is one in which God surprises us with the release of his power in the face of seemingly impossible challenges.*

There is a promised land for us to be reached in a wonder-filled tomorrow. For the Israelites it was the land of Canaan promised to them by the Lord—a land in which they would live under his providence, by his power, and in his provision. Canaan was a sure sign that they were the called, chosen, cherished people of Yahweh. Our promised land is that, and so much more. It is a combination of all the blessings of God, the abundant life in Christ, and the fullness of his indwelling Spirit. It is the joy of abiding in Christ in a new life, the resolution of long-endured impossibilities, and the realization of our full potential. In that light, a wonderful tomorrow is one in which we claim more of our promised land. But there is a River Jordan which flows between us and our fondest hopes—the river of life's perplexities. The third and fourth chapters of Joshua give us a strategy to crossing that river. They tell us what God promises; what we must do in response; what God tells us to do and how we are to do it; what God does with our cooperation; and how we are to remember with praise.

*The wonders of God for a different tomorrow require the consecration of the people.* Some translations of Joshua's command use the word *sanctify*. Both *consecrate* and *sanctify* are translations of the Hebrew root, *qdš*. Some Hebrew scholars hold that it comes from the root meaning "to cut," while others suggest "to be bright." Both root meanings are aspects of what is implied in being holy, belonging to God. The Latin basis of both *consecration* and *sanctification* have the meanings "holy" in them. The people of Israel were to cut themselves from the past and anything else that would hinder their absolute devotion and expectation. They were to be "bright" as they realized again that they belonged to God and he would get them to the promised land. For us, it means being cut loose from the past which binds our capacity to imagine what God can do. Today can be bright with anticipation of the realization of what God has imaged in our imagination for the future. So many of us expect little and are disappointed when we receive it!

Consecration of the people was necessary because what the Lord was about to do for them would require their cooperation, trust, and courage. The strategy the Lord had given Joshua was shared with the people. A priest from each tribe was to be selected to carry the Ark of the Covenant out ahead of the people. The promise was that when the soles of the feet of the priests were placed in the Jordan, the wonder of the rolling back of the waters of the river would begin. The riverbed would become dry and all of Israel would pass over. The waters of the Jordan were particularly high at harvesttime, when the regular riverbed, about fifty feet wide, overflowed filling the wider area along the banks, called the Zôr. To promise that all that water would be stopped up was quite a promise.

And a challenge, especially for the priests who carried the Ark. Imagine the courage required. The Lord of the impossible had decided to make his miracle dependent on the priests getting their feet wet.

Put yourself inside the skin of one of those priests as, early in the morning, you shoulder the Ark and move down toward that overflowing river. Now feel the strange mixture of panic and promise in your heart when the moment of decision comes. One step farther and your feet will get wet. I've always imagined that the courage needed to take that step came from the Ark itself. Two parts of it would have to be daring and nerve. Inside it were the tablets on which the Ten Commandments—given to Moses on Sinai—were carved. On top was the mercy seat, recalling the forgiving, atoning love of Yahweh. Surely those priests claimed both the covenant of commandments and the mercy of the Lord as they contemplated the awesome step of faith. There was no turning back. God and the people depended on them. And so all twelve of them with the Ark on their shoulders waded into the water. They had done their part.

Nothing happened! At least not instantly and not anything that they could see immediately. Joshua 3:16 is very careful to tell us that it was "a great distance away at Adam, the city that is beside Zarethan" (NASB), that the waters of Jordan "stood and rose up in one heap." My study of historical maps indicates that was nineteen miles away. The priests had to stand in the waters—waiting, hoping, praying as little by little the stoppage nineteen miles away caused the river to finally run dry. I think they had gone into the water up to their necks expecting an immediate miracle like the parting of the Red Sea when Moses' rod struck the waters. Not so. God is original in each of his interventions.

Surely Joshua was there in the fast-moving waters, encouraging the priests to stand firm and wait on the Lord. Capture in your mind's eye the expression on all their faces when the water around them began to recede little by little, until it was down to their

waists, then their knees, finally their ankles, and then the riverbed
was dry. The Lord had done it! He was faithful to his promise.
"You were right after all, Joshua!"

So many of the truly magnificent wonders God wants to do in
our tomorrows will *require that crisis time of waiting for the fulfillment
of his promise.* What if those priests had waded back out of the
water saying, "You see Joshua, it didn't work!" God must give us
both the courage to dare and the patience to wait for his timing.
We need jubilant feet to tap while we wait knowing God will be
faithful.

> Be jubilant, my feet!
> Our God is marching on.
>
> Julia Ward Howe

But that was not the end of the endurance test for those priests.
They had to remain in the middle of the riverbed until all the
thousands of the Israelites passed through. That would take a long
day of persistent trust. When would the river begin to flow again?
Only God knew, and he was worthy of their trust.

There are two later accounts in history when the Jordan was
similarly dammed up at that same place. One was on December 7,
1267, when the waters were dammed up for ten hours because the
marl banks along the Jordan collapsed and filled the river,
stopping its flow. A similar phenomenon occurred for twenty-one
and a half hours in 1927. The high, dry marl banks, unprotected
by turf, had been undercut by the swift flow of the river. At an
unexpected moment, again the banks collapsed and the waters
were trapped behind the natural dam. Some people have
suggested that this is what happened in Joshua's time, implying
that it was no miracle at all. But we must also ask why it happened
on that day and why in complete fulfillment of a promise? If an
earthquake had caused the collapse at Adam, who was behind the
earthquake? We cannot explain away the wonder of the timing and
the circumstances. We need to reclaim the word *coincidence.* For
me, it means two incidences that occur simultaneously producing
an effect beyond reason. Or as someone has cautioned, "Stop
praying and the coincidences stop happening!" It was God who
stopped up the Jordan, whatever natural circumstances he used to
do it.

Joshua would never have questioned that, even if he had been able to go up to Adam and observe what was happening there. He was too busy getting the people across to do that kind of proof-texting. When you're in the middle of a miracle, you don't stand around analyzing it. Joshua was totally involved in experiencing what God was doing, in giving him praise, and in listening to him tell him how to help Israel remember what he had done for them.

That brings us to the ending of a great day. We need to know how to conclude a wonderful tomorrow. The Lord told Joshua to select twelve more men, once again from the twelve tribes. While the priests remained standing firm with the Ark in the Jordan, these men were to take twelve stones from the riverbed and carry them on their shoulders to the Canaan shore of the river. These stones were to be carried with the people as a memorial of the impossible miracle God had accomplished for them. The twelve men, spurred on by Joshua's courage and the faithfulness of the priests still standing resolutely in the Jordan riverbed, followed instructions. The memory stones became cherished memorabilia of God's power and providence.

But that was not all. The endurance of the priests was further tested when Joshua built his own altar of twelve stones at the place where they were standing. He could not praise God enough for what he had done. *Thanksgiving and gratitude at the end of a day of wonders make it the first in a succession of wonderful tomorrows.* The Book of Joshua is filled with the general's Spirit-guided victories. The confrontation of the enemy, the battle of Jericho, and the successful invasion and possession of the land were the result of Joshua's capacity to give God the glory.

And how about you and me—our tomorrow, our promised land, and any Jordan standing in the way? The first step is the hardest. We must get our feet wet. Why are they so often dry, dirty with the dust of resistance? Step into your Jordan! I want to step into mine. Now, will we wait for the waters to recede? God is faithful, he decided to make his miracle dependent on those priests, and they certainly could not have done it without him. Who is depending on you and me to stand in the Jordan so they can pass over to God's promised land?

He has sounded forth the trumpet that shall never call retreat;
He is sifting out the hearts of men before his judgment seat;
O be swift, my soul, to answer him;
   be jubilant, my feet!
Our God is marching on.

Julia Ward Howe

# CHAPTER TEN

# Six Keys to Unlock the Impossible

## — Gideon —

During the past few years, I have had the privilege of giving the invocation for the annual banquet meeting of the Los Angeles Philanthropic Foundation, at which the Distinguished American Award is given to truly outstanding, great people. It has been a delight to meet and come to know people whom I have admired from a distance. Many of them have been people of profound faith which they lived out in a heroic way. Before one of the meetings one of them said something in a conversation that I will never forget.

"Please don't either idealize or sentimentalize me. If I have accomplished anything worthy of being called great, it is because of the greatness of God. He took an ordinary person and did extraordinary things."

An ordinary person who did extraordinary things! The same can be said of all heroes of the faith. It is both comforting and challenging to discover the ordinary people behind the extraordinary accomplishments. We are comforted to discover that they faced the same struggles and inadequacies we all face. But also, we are challenged to realize that the reason for their greatness is what God did in them and then through them. We are left with a lingering disquiet. Could not God do the same with us if we were willing?

We admire friends who seem to live the abundant life courageously. We long to be like them. Then the more we get to know
them, the more surprised we are by their humanity. We find that
they feel the same physical, emotional, and interpersonal
difficulties we all feel. As we penetrate into their personalities we
see the same traces of human frailty that are common to all men
and women. And yet, they do extraordinary things. Why?

Some years ago I lived through a parable which thundered this
truth in my soul. I was caught in a hurricane on a small island.
After the storm was over, I noticed that a two-by-four had been
ripped from an old building, and its splintered point had been
driven two feet into a concrete wall. When I pulled the board out, I
realized that it was a very ordinary, weather-beaten, old piece of
wood. And yet, under the velocity of the violent driving wind, it
had pierced the otherwise impenetrable concrete and stone wall.
Great people are like that. There is no explanation of their power
and prowess other than that they were impelled by the wind of the
Spirit of God. And our question is, What is the secret of receiving
and experiencing that power?

The honesty of the Bible about its heroes gives us an answer
with hope in it. We are told of the impotence and ineptness of
ordinary people who, by God's power, did extraordinary things.
We are tempted to think that they were people of superior
intellect, spectacular talents, and special creativity which were
employed for the glory of God. Not so! They were people grasped
by the Spirit of the Lord, enabled to grapple with the impossible,
who received the grace to be great.

Gideon is a classic biblical example of an ordinary person
through whom God did extraordinary things. A careful study of
his biography in Judges, chapters six through eight, reveals six
keys which unlock the impossible. Consideration of each of them
gives us both a progression to an analysis of his life and an insight
into basic ingredients of greatness which are common to most of
the spiritual giants of history. Most crucial of all—these keys are
available to all of us.

*The first is an undeniable call given to an unlikely person facing
untenable circumstances.* The Gideon we meet in Judges 6 dispells
any illusion that any of us are unqualified for greatness. No
biographical profile in Scripture starts with a more honest
exposure of human inadequacy and furtive frustration. We find

young Gideon secretly flailing out the wheat of a meager harvest on a hidden winepress in a small valley. We can imagine his eyes darting fearfully around in anxiety. That tells us volumes about the man and his times. He did not mill his wheat at a threshing floor out in the open because of the danger of the marauding Midianites. Israel had known little peace since they entered the promised land. As nomadic people, they were ill-trained for an agrarian life. They tried to learn the methods of being an agricultural people and would have done well if it had not been for a fatal mistake on their part and the persistent invasion of the Midianites and the Amalekites. To be sure of agricultural success, they adopted a blatant syncretism of religion, worshiping both the Baal god of fertility and Yahweh. They set up Baal shrines in their fields, along with the god's female counterpart, the Asherah, emulating the pagan religion of the land. The worship of Yahweh was blended with fertility rites and rituals. If prosperity was their purpose, it was short-lived. The ravaging forces of Midian and Amalek would sweep down at harvesttime and carry off the fruit of their hard labor, their cattle, and their possessions. Such raids continued relentlessly. Israel was never out of danger.

No wonder Gideon flailed the wheat on a winepress! If the Midianites found him, he would lose both his wheat and his life. Look into his angry, anguished face—it is dark with futility and sorrow, resentment and fear. There is no more discouraging disability than knowing that the harder you work the more in danger you will be. The worship of the Baal gods had not worked. But where was the wonder-working Yahweh who had guided his people to the promised land? That's what Gideon and all of Israel wanted to know. What they should have remembered is that the one thing Yahweh would never accept was second place—not even an equal place—with any other god.

And yet, the Lord did not give up on his people. At a time of national despondency, he was ready for another big move to help his people. And Gideon was to be primary in his strategy. Nothing in his natural makeup made him a candidate for heroism. That's what makes his story so significant: what happened to Gideon can happen to us.

The Lord interrupted Gideon there at Ophrah where he was angrily, hopelessly, threshing the grain. The announcement must have astonished youthful Gideon. "The Lord is with you, O valiant warrior." Nothing could have been further from Gideon's self-image. The Revised Standard Version renders it, "The Lord is with you, you mighty man of valor" (Judg. 6:12). Actually, it was not an affirmation of Gideon at all. The Septuagint Version is much closer to the original, "The Lord is with you, even the Lord in valor," or "The Lord is with *you*, the mighty Man of Valor." Yahweh, not Gideon, is mighty in valor. The divine visitation was to remind Gideon of the greatness of God.

That led to the obvious question: the impertinent "if" and "why" of impotence. "O my lord, if the Lord is with us, why then has all this happened to us? And where are all His miracles which our fathers told us about, saying, 'Did not the Lord bring us up from Egypt?' But now the Lord has abandoned us and given us into the hand of Midian" (Judg. 6:13 NASB). Notice the complaining consternation. It's all the Lord's fault. No confession of apostasy or seeking what he and Israel might have done to bring the calamity on themselves. So often our demanding "if" and "why," challenging the Lord to accountability to us, expresses how far from fellowship with him we have drifted.

"And the Lord *looked* at him." What was in that look? Anger for his apostasy? Wrath for his willfullness? Both would have been justified. Rather, I think God looked not at the frail man, but at the faithful man he would become. How very gracious of God not to pick up the challenge of our argument over his providence. Instead, he enlists us in changing the very things that trouble us and our time. Gideon is given an undeniable call in his untenable circumstance. "Go in this your strength and deliver Israel from the hand of Midian. Have I not sent you?" (Judg. 6:14 NASB). The unlikely man filled with unbelief and self-doubt responds as most of us would today with our kowledge of our inadequacies and the world's injustice. "O Lord, how shall I deliver Israel? Behold, my family is the least in Manasseh, and I am the youngest in my father's house" (Judg. 6:15 NASB). The Lord's answer should have been all Gideon needed to know. What more do we need? He said to him and says to us, "Surely I will be with you, and you shall defeat Midian as one man" (Judg. 6:16 NASB).

We sense Gideon's lack of natural courage when he responds to that awesome promise by asking for a sign. The Scripture is deliberate in exposing how little human daring the timorous young man had. He asks, "If now I have found favor in Thy sight, then show me a sign that it is Thou who speakest with me" (Judg. 6:17 NASB). Gideon set the qualifications of the sign. He prepared a meal of a young goat and unleavened bread and placed them on a rock. The Lord, always ready to meet his prospective heroes at the point of their need for assurance, touched the meat and bread, and fire sprang up from the rock and consumed them. Gideon knew for certain that it was the Lord who had spoken with him. He feared death because he had encountered a face-to-face visitation of the Lord. But the Lord had life and victory planned for Gideon. He said, "Peace to you, do not fear; you shall not die" (Judg. 6:23 NASB). In awe and wonder the leader-elect built an altar and named it "Jehovah Shalom." The Lord is peace.

Strange. The word for Gideon's new, transforming relationship with God was *peace*. One called to do battle knew both the peace of God and peace with God. The peace of the Lord prepares us for battle with anything in us, our relationships or surroundings which rob others of peace. Inner peace enables us to live in immense conflict without fear. For Gideon it signified God's favor, affirmation, and blessing. And it is exactly that for us—and yet, so much more profound through reconciliation through Christ. The warfare within us is over because of the forgiving love of the cross, and now we can become peacemakers. The cost of that is usually high. Often it means confrontation with the enemies of peace which disturb us and others. God gives us a taste of his peace so that we can go on with him in fearless battle for peace in all of life.

That leads us to the second key to unlocking the impossible. *Gideon was called to unswerving obedience.* He could not do anything about the syncretistic apostasy in Israel until he cleaned up his own backyard. Literally. There was a Baal shrine in his own family's fields! The first thing Gideon was commanded by the Lord to do before he could lead Israel, was to take ten men and two oxen and deliberately pull down and smash the idol. Next he was told to take the wood of the female Asherah which was part of the shrine and neatly build an altar to God on which he was to sacrifice the seven-year-old bull. Quite an order! Especially when Gideon knew that such an act of obedience to the Lord would surely bring threats on his life from his neighbors who had become passionately committed to Baal worship in addition to allegiance to Yahweh. The future of his nation hung in the balance. The

Lord could not bless Gideon with victory over the impossible until he knew that he would obey his will without question. Gideon's obedience was complete: he did exactly what the Lord told him; he tore down the idol and sacrificed the bull to the glory of God.

We pause in Gideon's story to check the unfolding of our own. What is there in our life that corresponds to the competitive idol? What person, position, possession, plan, or purpose stands in the way of complete obedience? We all develop secondary loyalties that distract or debilitate. We wonder why we have little spiritual power, vision, or daring. The reason, often, is that we have blended our commitment to God with a god of our own or our culture's making. Remember that the Baal shrine for the Israelites was a "both/and" equivocation. They feared total dependence on God. How often we believe in God, but draw our security from what we have or are, our accomplishments, our self-image, or the approbation of others. What do you draw your security from? Don't read on until you have done an incisive inventory.

One of the best ways to do that is to consider what we would have to do without if we lived only in dependence on God. What loss would shatter your security? On what or whom do you depend for life's meaning or happiness in addition to God? Doing such an inventory confronts me with my "God/and" security system. It leaves me painfully aware of how important success and people's affirmation are to me. All of us have a desperate need to accomplish our goals—even if, at times, we use people and things to reach them. The danger is that they become false gods. Our god is anything or anyone that dominates our thinking and demands our allegiance at the exclusion of absolute obedience to God. What's the Baal in your backyard?

That kind of incisiveness usually does not win a popularity contest. It raises the ire and indignation of syncretists around us. For Gideon it put his life in jeopardy. When the men of Gideon's city saw what he had done, they formed a lynch mob and went to his father, Joash, with the demand, "Bring out your son, that he may die, for he has torn down the altar of Baal, and indeed, he has cut down the Asherah which is beside it" (Judg. 6:30 NASB).

Now we witness the power of courageous influence. Gideon's obedience to the Lord fanned into flame the banked fires of Joash's commitment. His son's faithfulness faced him with his own equivocation. Joash should be listed among our heroes.

Gideon would not have survived to do the Lord's will in liberating Israel if his father had not stepped in to confront the mob. Listen to his new-found courage and loyalty. "Will you contend for Baal, or will you deliver him? Whoever will plead for him shall be put to death by morning. If he is a god, let him contend for himself, because someone has torn down his altar" (Judg. 6:31 NASB). Then he did a remarkable thing which expressed confidence and admiration for his son. He gave Gideon a new name: Jerubbaal, which means, "Let Baal contend against him." He saw the transformation in his son. The man in the boy brought forth the man in the father. It was as if he said, "My son Gideon is a new person. Something has happened to him. Baal is not our god. He has no power over my son. You have no quarrel with Gideon. If Baal has any strength, let *him* use it against Gideon." Nothing happened. Gideon, now Jerubbaal, had defeated the spiritual enemy of the people.

There's a great need for Joash's courage in families and among our friends. We long to find people who are willing to share the cost of obedient discipleship. Parents have a great opportunity to affirm the first stirrings of God's call in their children even when it challenges their own faith. Equally so, we need to take a stand with our friends who make an unreserved commitment to the Lord. We all need people in our lives who put themselves between us and negative, critical, threatened friends and associates who are alarmed when we dare to put God first in our lives. Who is the Joash in your life? For whom do you need to be a Joash?

Gideon exposed the enemy within Israel. Now he was confronted with the enemy without. The Midianites and the Amalekites were pitilessly oppressing and exploiting the impoverished Israelites. Something had to be done. Gideon was God's called and appointed man of the hour. But he lacked power. Here he discovered the third key to unlocking the impossible task of freeing his people from the alien oppressor, whose army was 135,000 strong in the valley of Jezreel. *Such an impossible task prepared him to receive unlimited power.* "So the Spirit of the Lord came upon Gideon; and he blew a trumpet" (Judg. 6:34 NASB). The more accurate translation of the Hebrew is, "The Spirit of the Lord clothed Himself with Gideon." A potent image. The Spirit filled the frightened, inadequate man. Gideon's personality and humanity became the clothing of God! Natural talents were maximized, extraordinary gifts were given. Faith replaced fear, courage displaced compromise, charisma flowed through his bland personality.

Up to this point Gideon's conversion was a human response to a divine call. Now he became the riverbed for the flow of the Spirit of the God who called him. Blowing the trumpet, he called Israel to arms. From this point on, we witness what God can do with a person possessed with his Spirit. The hollow-eyed, indecisive, worried man we met at the winepress flailing out the grain in secret is now an inspired, impelled man. His complaints about God's providence over his people's plight are replaced by verve and vitality. The God of valor was indeed making him a mighty man of valor.

The response of the tribes of Israel to Gideon's call seems astonishing. Was it the fact that their distress over the Midianite and Amalekite oppression had made them ready to follow anyone who showed any sign of leadership? Or was it Gideon's courageous act of exposing the impotence of Baal? There is something else. God raised up the Israelite armies. He created the desire to get out from under the heel of the pagan invaders. This is a lesson Christian leaders need to remember. The response we long for from people to our leadership is God-induced. The moving force behind the whole Gideon movement is the Lord. Why else would thousands of Israelites rally to a trumpet blast from the youngest son of the least of the tribes? Gideon's experience will not allow us the luxury of thinking that little or nothing will happen if we dare to lead others in a cause of truth and righteousness.

The fourth secret tells us as much about God as it does about Gideon. It also reveals a comforting thought about our own need for assurance. Gideon needed further confirmation that the Lord not only had guided him to this point, but also wanted him to engage the invaders in battle. Why should that be needed after his call, his conversion to the Lord, his consecration to his will, and his experiencing the controlling power of God's indwelling Spirit? Many expositors of this passage label Gideon's need for a further sign an affront to what God had already told him. Not so. The Scripture underlines the dependence of Gideon on the Lord each step of the way. Good thing. *The fourth key to unlocking the impossible is an unquestionable answer to prayer for guidance.* God not only gives us a clarion call, he provides us with clear confirmation along the way.

Gideon's fleece test shows us that God will stop at nothing to be sure we are sure. What would it take to convince you that the guidance you have received from the Lord is right? For Gideon it took a strange form. We find him, not at the hidden winepress, but now out in the open, courageously praying to the Lord on the threshing floor (Judg. 6:36)—significant evidence of the daring of the new Gideon. One evening, he told the Lord that he would put a fleece of wool on the threshing floor. If by morning dew was only on the fleece, and the ground around it was dry, then he would be sure that God would deliver Israel through him as he had promised. We can imagine that Gideon did not sleep very well that night as he wondered what he would find in the morning. When he arose he found God's answer: the fleece was so full of dew that when he wrung it out he filled a bowl with water. Then, just to be sure, he reversed the test: "Please let me make a test once more with the fleece, let it now be dry only on the fleece, and let there be dew on all the ground." God was faithful to the test: in the morning the fleece was completely dry and the ground was covered with dew. How gracious of God!

There are fleece-assurances in answer to prayer all around us. We look at the evidences of his love. But in special times of challenge and danger, he provides a special gift to convince us that he is with us. He uses Scripture, the words of trusted friends, the direction of events around us to convince us of the rightness or wrongness of a particular direction. And yet, there are never substitutes for profound times of listening in the secret place of conversational prayer. The Lord uses outside events and influences only as a confirmation of what he has been telling us in our prayers. Remember, Gideon didn't know God very well at this point. The secret for us is that he will guide us in ways that match our level of growth. The important thing is to tell him exactly how we feel about the challenge we think he has called us to do for his glory. Give him lead time. Present the need, wait on him and be sure that he will use our minds, feelings, and sensitivity to make us aware of what he wants. Gideon refused to blunder ahead in his own might. God honored his need for assurance. He will do nothing less for us.

On this side of calvary there is so much that is clear about what we are to do and be. Our Lord's message, mandate, and election of us to greatness is not ambiguous. If we spend our time energetically following the Master in the basics of discipleship—loving, communicating his grace, seeking first his kingdom and righteousness, forgiving, being peacemakers and agents of reconciliation—we will be open to guidance on special challenges which need specific guidance. The secret is the will. When we will to do his will, as he promised, we shall know (John 7:17). Spread out the uncertainty before him. Does it fulfill what he has said in Scripture? Will it bring his ultimate good for all concerned? Is it an expression of his love? Will we grow in deeper companionship with him if we do it? Will the kingdom of God be extended? If we can say yes to these questions, we can cast doubt aside. If there is still a lingering uncertainty, tell him. He created the world; raised Christ from the dead; can he not get through to our open minds and receptive hearts? Indeed he can.

The next and fifth key to unlocking the impossible is an *unlikely strategy*. This is the most difficult key to receive and use. God's ways are not our ways. We plan, strategize, and marshal human potential to accomplish God's work on our power. The Lord did not allow Gideon to fall into that trap. When the armies of the tribes of Israel were gathered on Mount Gilboa, Gideon counted his army—32,000 in all. Then he looked across the Spring of Harod at the foot of the mountain and across the Valley of the Jezreel to the Midianites and the Amalekites camped on the southern slope of Mount Moreh—135,000 in all. (Judg. 8:10 verifies this number.) A four to one ratio. A fighting chance with the Lord's help, Gideon thought.

Empathize with the leader's astonishment when the Lord told him to thin the ranks! He was to put the newly gathered army through two tests. The first was to say the words that had been prescribed in the laws for warfare given by the Lord to Moses, "Then the officers shall speak further to the people, and they shall say, 'Who is the man that is afraid and fainthearted? Let him depart and return to his house, so that he might not make his brothers' hearts melt like his heart'" (Deut. 20:8 NASB). Though Gideon could not imagine going against the enemy with one less man than his 32,000, he obeyed the Lord and said, "Whoever is afraid and trembling, let him return and depart" Twenty-two thousand retreated in panic to their homes!

Did Gideon's heart sink as he looked at the remaining 10,000 and once again at the enemy camp? Surely, but he skewered up his courage and began preparations. But the Lord was not finished! He told Gideon to make a further test. He was to march the armies across the river in the valley of Ein Harod that starts in a small cave on the north side of Mount Gilboa at sea level and flows southeast down the valley until it reaches the Jordan River, below sea level. The crucial point was that the river ran between Gideon's now depleted army and the immense forces of Midian, so the soldiers thought they were marching across the riverbed to war. That's significant for understanding the test the Lord instructed Gideon to make. As the soldiers moved through the water of the shallow stream, some stopped, took off their armor, set aside their weapons, knelt down, and put their mouths into the water to suck up more than enough to quench their thirst. Others, keeping their eyes on Gideon's leadership and the movements of the enemy, dipped a hand in the water and lapped a few drops from their cupped palm. The Lord told Gideon that only those who lapped, putting their hand to their mouths, would qualify to be a part of his army. Perhaps another reason that some of the soldiers knelt down was to keep a low profile by drinking directly from the stream. This adds to our admiration of those who walked or rode through the stream not stopping to satisfy their own needs. The number who failed the test was 9,700. Gideon was left with 300!

The Lord knew what he was doing. He wanted only those who could follow Gideon faithfully and obediently. Those who thought more of their own selfish satisfaction were drummed out of the corps. James Stewart calls this the "strange strategy of God." The Lord wanted a vigilant, totally committed band of daring men. But there was a deeper reason for thinning the ranks. With such a minority there would be no question but that the victory was won by God's power alone. Our God delights to amaze us at what he can do with a few people who trust him completely, setting aside personal pride and comfort.

If we want to live a life in which God's gifts of impossibilities are given, we must use his methods and live on his power. Our fearful dependence on human talents, skill, and power often stand in the way. God must break that before he can give us his best. Putting him first in our lives, seeking the goals of his kingdom, living on his resources, expecting his interventions, and receiving his Spirit's power, is the only way to live a truly victorious life.

The last key to unlock the impossible is *our unflinching courage.* For that, the Lord gave Gideon a vision of victory. Before the battle with the enemy, he showed Gideon that there was no question about his success. Gideon was allowed to taste the sweet savor of accomplishing the Lord's will, before any fighting took place. Here's how the Lord prepared him to claim the triumph and go forward with courageous praise for what the Lord would do. Gideon was told to take his servant, Purah, and sneak secretly into the camp of Midian late at night. We can picture the two men making their way down the rocky terrain of Mount Gilboa, across the valley, and over to Mount Moreh. They made it past the sentries and crouched beside one of the black tents where they heard two of the Midianites talking inside. One was telling about his frightening dream in which a barley loaf came tumbling into the camp and struck their tent, turning it upside down. The interpretation of the dream by the other soldier was a special gift of self-esteem to Gideon from the Lord. He was astonished and assured all at the same time. "This is nothing less than the sword of Gideon the son of Joash, a man of Israel," the interpreter said. "God has given Midian and all the camp into his hand" (Judg.7:14 NASB).

How gracious of God to inflame courage in Gideon by letting him know that Midian knew of him and feared his growing power in Israel, and that victory was secure. We are comforted by the persistent efforts of the Lord to build up Gideon's God-confidence. The result was that Gideon was able to thank God in advance for the liberation of Israel.

Thanking God in advance for what he has promised he will do allows us to picture in our imagination what it will be like to receive the promise to unlock the impossibility in our lives. That requires prayer, attentive listening, and awareness of the messages he sends us through unexpected circumstances and people. Once the image of the victory is firmly set in our minds, the resolution of problems, the reconciliation of broken relationships, or the success in the projects or programs he assigns us can be accomplished with courage.

When Gideon returned to his 300 men, he was ready with the battle cry, "Arise, for the Lord has given the camp of Midian into

your hands" (Judg. 7:15 NASB). Victory was an accomplished
fact, though at this point a still-to-be-fulfilled fact.

Gideon's plan of attack was inspired, brilliant. I am sure the
meager three hundred questioned his sanity when they first heard
it. But everything else in their preparation for battle had been
strangely mysterious; so they followed orders obediently. Gideon
gave each of them a trumpet to hold in one hand and a torch to
hold in the other. Each torch was placed inside a pitcher. "Look at
me," he said courageously, "and do likewise. And behold, when I
come to the outskirts of the camp, do as I do. When I and all who
are with me blow the trumpet, then you also blow the trumpets all
around the camp, and say, 'For the Lord and for Gideon' " (Judg.
7:17-18 NASB). With only that for a plan of attack to guide them,
the Israelites moved out toward Midian.

In the middle watch of the night the 300 men completely
surrounded the enemy camp. At the signal from Gideon, they
broke the pitchers in their left hands, exposing the torches, and
blew the trumpets held in their right hands. And with triumphant
voices, they shouted, "The sword for the Lord and for Gideon."
The only sword they had was the imputed courage of the Lord.

The Midianites and the Amalekites were awakened from sleep
by the frightening sound of blaring trumpets and blood-curdling
battle cries. They staggered out of their tents in confusion,
brandishing their swords, and because they were so confused in
the darkness, they began to attack and kill one another. But note
the Lord's part. "The Lord set the sword of one against another
even throughout the whole army." Of the 135,000 men, 120,000
were slain by one another, thinking they were battling Gideon and
his men. The other 15,000 fled when they realized what was
happening. It was the Lord's victory for Gideon and Israel from
start to finish. And all the praise was given to him. The Lord of the
impossible had done it again!

The true nature of Christian courage is displayed in this
account for us to see and emulate. It is the courage of the Lord, not
courage for the Lord. As the called and chosen people of God, we
gain our courage from the vision of his involvement in our
concerns and crises. Then we have the sure picture of what he will
do and move forward believing that what he has promised will be
accomplished in his timing and way. Our only sword is the Lord!
Prayer is the key. When we spread out before the Lord the

impossibility we face, surrendering it to him completely, we are given a confidence to press on. Our courage grows the more we depend on him. We do not need to be defensive, self-justifying, or timid. Again as we have learned in our study of the other heroes considered thus far, there is no limit to the blessings we can receive if we are willing to acknowledge and give God the glory.

The conclusion of the account of Gideon is a mixed story of greatness and fatal failure. Once more the Scriptures are honest with us, so we can identify with the people they describe.

Gideon is very gracious with the men who had failed the Lord's test before the battle and had excluded themselves from the conflict. He calls them to help in the mopping up action in the pursuit and defeat of the remaining 15,000 Midianites and Amalekites. The inspired leader knew human nature: those who missed the crucial battle would be jealous and eventually hostile to him. He allowed them to share the glory. Even the men of Ephraim, who had not reported for duty at the first call were given sensitive acceptance when they angrily contended, "What is this thing you have done to us, not calling us when you went to fight against Midian?" (Judg. 8:2 NASB). It is somewhat astonishing that they claimed they did not know. How could any of Israel not know? They had suffered under the marauding invaders as much as the rest. And surely they knew that Gideon had been called to lead all of Israel against them. They had stayed out of the battle and complained. There are people like that in every age. They wait until the battle is over and then complain that they were not sent an engraved conscription to join what they knew was their battle also. Ever meet people like that? Ever been among them?

It is tempting to denounce their evasion of confrontation and obedience. But Gideon did not. The Spirit of the Lord was still pulsating through him when he said to the Ephraimites, "What have I done now in comparison with you? Is not the gleaning of the grapes of Ephraim better than the vintage of Abiezer?" The assuring affirmation of their part in the completion of the pursuit of Midian was further extended with anger-diffusing solicitousness. "What was I able to do in comparison with you?" It was then that Ephraim's anger was subdued. When the Lord gives us victory in some seemingly impossible situation, he gives us a special measure of humility to tenderly care for others who may not share our triumph. That too is a part of giving God the glory.

When Israel wanted Gideon to become their king and rule over the people, he refused. "I will not rule over you, nor shall my son rule over you; the Lord shall rule over you" (Judg. 8:23 NASB). He was not willing to usurp the place of God. He knew that it was only because of the Lord's power ruling in his life that he had accomplished anything worthy of the people's adulation. He had put God first in his life and he wanted nothing less for Israel.

We wonder, then, how Gideon's spectacular life could have come to such a pitiful end. Near the end of the eighth chapter of Judges, he commits an idolatrous sin which threatens his courageous record on the pages of history. He would not be king and rule over the people in God's place. He did, however, request that the people give him an earring from the spoil of the battle with Midian. The Midianites were Ishmaelites and each wore an earring. These earrings had been taken from the dead bodies after the battle. Did Gideon want the single earring as a memorial, a trophy, a symbol? Perhaps. But the people gave him not one but all the earrings from all the dead Midianites and Amalekites. That's 135,000 earrings! The gift weighed 1,700 shekels of gold. And the crescent ornaments, pendants, and neckbands were thrown in for good measure.

That's when Gideon went amiss. He made it all into an ephod, the upper garment of the high priest. It must have been a magnificent vestment of gold and jewels. We are not told that Gideon wore it, which would have been elevating himself to the status of a priest. But he placed it in his home town of Ophrah. Judges 8:27 says, "And all Israel played the harlot with it there, so that it became a snare to Gideon and his household" (NASB). What is implied is that the ephod became a shrine of memorial worship of the great things Gideon had done in defeating Midian and Amalek. It focused their attention on what God had done in the past rather than what he would do in the future. Gideon lived in the glory of his past heroics. He took the glory for himself which previously he had been so careful to give to God. The people idealized and sentimentalized him and forgot the God who had accomplished the victory over the enemy. His impotence without God was soon overlooked as the stories of his greatness were told. Now the cry in Israel was, "For Gideon and for the Lord." It became a snare in his relationship to God. He was tripped up by self-aggrandizement. The Baal shrine he had vigilantly removed was back in another form.

It can, and does, happen to us. When the pressures that forced us to depend on God are relieved, we forget who got us through the tumult. Prayers of thanksgiving are replaced by endless tales of what we accomplished. The past becomes more exciting than the future, heritage more precious than hope.

And yet the honest record of Gideon stands. It encourages us to daring and warns us of what can happen if we take our eyes off the Lord. Most of all, Gideon's life, even to the end, shows that the past blessings of the Lord of the impossible are nothing in comparison with what he will do with impossibilities in the days to come. What the Lord has done gives us the keys to unlock the impossibilities of today and all our tomorrows.

# CHAPTER ELEVEN

# A Question of Loyalty

## —— *Ruth* ——

A delivery truck had a bold promise painted on its side. "You can *always* count on us!" Someone expressed his disbelief, or at least his doubt, with spray-can paint. "Oh, really?!" was spelled out in crudely shaped letters.

We raise the same question whenever people assert their reliability or dependability. Words are cheap. Our experience contradicts the promise. Whatever happened to loyalty?

A true friend is someone who knows all about us, who will not go away, who loves us as we are and not just for what we are able to do, and whose faithfulness is absolutely dependable regardless of the ups and downs of our successes or failures. How many friends do you have like that? How many people would claim you as that kind of friend?

The missing ingredient of greatness today is loyalty. Authentic love is expressed in loyalty. It is commitment, consistency, and constancy that lasts.

A personal officer of a prominent American firm told me that the most difficult quality to find in people today is loyalty. The lack of loyalty is one of the major causes of the diminishing number of long-term marriages. Much of the loneliness afflicting people in our nation in epidemic proportions has come because loyalty seems to have gone out of style. At a pastor's conference recently I asked three hundred parish leaders to write down the word they longed to find in church members and found most lacking. *Loyalty* was the word used by two hundred and sixty of them. Lasting loyalty for the church and fellow members seems to be a thing of the past. Patriotism expressed in loyalty is now viewed as sentimental or simplistic by an alarming number of Americans. At the same time the sacredness of persons is up for grabs. Character assassination through careless gossip is seldom brought to the trial of indignation. Reputations are held cheap and easily assailed by deprecating analysis. Loyalty seems to have been cast aside in the self-indulgence of the "me generation." Who cares anymore?

Last summer, I studied how the ancient giant obelisks were dislodged from the quarries along the Nile. Holes were bored into the granite along the designated line of the portion to be excavated. These were filled with wood and then soaked with water. When the wood expanded it forced the gigantic cleavage which loosened and eventually broke off the long, monolithic, slightly tapered, square shafts. These were then floated on wood barges down the Nile to Luxor, carved with hieroglyphics, and erected as part of the temples. It was the way the wood expanded and caused the cleavage that fascinated me and gave me another parable. The holes are like our careless attitudes and the wood our cutting words and lack of affirmation. The cleavage in our society between friends, husband and wives, parents and children, citizens and government, leaders and their constituencies, is the result of disloyalty swelling up to crack the foundation of our life today.

When we look around us at all the broken and strained relationships, we are forced to acknowledge that evil is winning some crucial battles. Nothing is a greater cause of brokenness than the absence of loyalty—to God and to one another. God is going to win the final battle, to be sure, but in the meantime insecurity, lack of trust, absence of mutual encouragement, and careless criticism are having a field day. From the beginning of time, God's maximum has been minimized by Satan's strategy of disloyalty. We miss the possibility of greatness offered by the Lord of the impossible when his loyal heart is not reproduced in the quality of loyalty in us.

Let's recap where we are at this point in our portrait of the Lord of the impossible. We have focused on his powerful interventions at crucial times in the early history of his people. The heroes we considered are distinguished for what the Lord did in and through them. In each case, the real hero of the drama is the Lord himself. Now, as the Bible continues to tell his story, it moves from accounts of his power to a deeper revelation of his nature. We meet a God who is not only all powerful, but all loving. Behind his interventions to save his people in times of crisis is an essential attribute of his nature. He is loyal to his called and chosen people.

The Book of Ruth centers our attention on this quality of loyalty. We wonder how this little book, with its eighty-five verses, ever found its way into the Old Testament canon. Some scholars suggest that though its setting is in the period of the Judges, somewhere between Joshua and Samuel, that it was written during David's reign to honor his lineage. The mention of David at the end of the book definitely dates it during or after the Davidic kingdom. Others argue that Ruth's story was written down during the post-exilic period as an antidote to the brash exclusivism and prejudice of that period. The author's intent may have been to contrast the loyalty of a foreigner to the disloyalty of Israel before and during the exile period. Most of all authorities agree, however, that the central message of the book is the loyalty of God which he longs to duplicate in his people. At every period of history God's people have been tempted to be disloyal to the covenant and the commission to share his loving-kindness with all the people. Naomi shows us the power of loyalty in our witness. Ruth exemplifies what can happen to a person who expresses God's loyalty in a faithful person. Exclusivism is contradicted and inclusive love is commemorated.

Ruth has been immortalized as one of the great women of the Bible because of one perfectly phrased, beautifully balanced, poignantly poetic statement of loyalty expressed to her mother-in-law, Naomi. It is a well-known, oft-quoted affirmation of undying faithfulness which has endured the test of time in the literature of the world because it articulates a commitment of loyalty we all long to receive from, and be able to offer to, our loved ones and friends.

Ruth and Naomi shared a common grief. Both lost their husbands. Naomi offered Ruth freedom from the responsibility of remaining with her and caring for her. Ruth's response is found in verses 16 and 17 of chapter 1 of the little book of the Old

Testament which bears her name. Do you need to hear an expression of loyalty like this? Savor it in the loyalty-starved places of your own heart. Ruth said to Naomi, "Do not urge me to leave you or turn back from following you; for where you go, I will go, and where you lodge, I will lodge. Your people shall be my people, and your God, my God. Where you die, I will die, and there I will be buried. Thus may the Lord do to me, and worse, if anything but death parts you from me" (Ruth 1:16-17 NASB).

Some background is helpful to understand the full impact and implications of this speech. Years before, Naomi and her husband Elimelech set out from Bethlehem of Judah because of a famine. Along with their sons, Mahlon and Chilion, they traveled to the pagan land of Moab in search of food. It was not easy for these Hebrews to dwell in a land where the god Chemosh was worshiped and human sacrifices were made. But they remained faithful to Yahweh in the foreign culture. Grief pierced Naomi's heart when Elimelech died. Her emptiness was filled by concern for her sons and their Moabite wives. Mahlon married Ruth and Chilion married Orpah. They all lived together under the careful, loyal eye of Naomi. She loved her Moabite daughters-in-law as her own with unflagging zeal. Then tragedy struck again. Both Mahlon and Chilion died, and all three women were widows. This additional grief sent Naomi's heart on wings of memory back to Bethlehem. Prosperity had returned to her native land and she longed to go back. Her warm and gracious care for her daughters-in-law made them both determined to go with her. The three widows set off for Bethlehem together.

In a fork in the road, as they neared Judah, Naomi stopped and offered a magnanimous, selfless gift of freedom to Ruth and Orpah. She wanted them to be free to return to Moab, liberated from the care of an old woman. It would be difficult for foreign women to find husbands in Judah. There might be prejudice, and the encumbrance of worry for her would debilitate their chances of beginning a new life. She begged them to turn back. Orpah complied but she cried as she departed. Ruth, however, would not be dissuaded from her loyal determination to return the loyalty she had felt from Naomi. The two women journeyed on and settled in Bethlehem. There Ruth's response of loyalty was rewarded with the respect of the townspeople, and a tender love affair and marriage to Boaz, a wealthy farmer and close kin of her late husband. The fruit of her love with Boaz was a handsome son whom they named Obed. Our sense of history and the awesome providence of God is stirred when we realize that Obed was Jesse's father and Jesse was David's father. The genealogy of grace was begun which eventually led to the birth of Jesus Christ in the line of David! Loyal Ruth is mentioned in the hall of fame of the ancestors of the Savior (Matt. 1). A Moabite woman, converted to faith in Yahweh, became a woman of the covenant and an ancestor of the Son of God. The Lord of the impossible accepted her quality of loyalty as a part of his preparation for the incarnation.

There are three crucial things Ruth teaches us about loyalty. Each one is desperately needed in our lives and our society.

The first is that *there can be no loyalty without liberty*. And conversely freedom is denied its power without loyalty. Naomi gave Ruth the gift of liberty so that she could make the choice of loyalty.

For us, liberty and loyalty are Siamese twins born out of the womb of grace. They are mutually dependent. One cannot thrive without the other. The undeniable paradox of life is that we cannot choose to be loyal until we are free, but without loyalty, our freedom becomes careless and directionless. Loyalty maximizes our realization of interdependence.

We are living in an age which places great value on individual freedom. Freedom from restraints, freedom from rules and regulations, freedom from the restrictions of dicta and mores. Whatever "feels good" is okay. "Do what gives you the greatest pleasure and happiness!" is the liberation cry of our time. A half-truth is being paraded as the ultimate truth. What we have missed is that loyalty is the other half and is required for the realization of the first half.

We don't hear much about loyalty today. And yet, loyalty is the golden thread which knits the fabric of authentic freedom. Without it, the wardrobe of our character becomes flabby and shapeless, lacking style. Loyalty invests freedom with lasting commitments, liberating consistency, and loving constancy.

The Lord gives us immense liberty so that we can be loyal to him. He has called, chosen, and cherished us with covenant love. And yet, he knows there can be no reciprocal love without freedom. This truth pervaded Jesus' message. He presented both sides of the paradox. He came to set humankind free from sin, self-centeredness, and selfishness. But he called those who accepted their liberation to the loyalty of discipleship. Only those whose loyalty was expressed in putting him and his cross first, following in absolute obedience, could grow in the realization of his gift of freedom. His cross won us our liberty; the loyalty of taking up our cross will win us the liberated life.

The apostle Paul discovered this. The price tag on continuing freedom for him was the cost of discipleship. He never tired of talking and writing about the freedom of the Christian because of Calvary. But he seldom mentioned it without monitoring his own and others' growth in loyalty. His trumpet blast of Christian liberty in I Corinthians 3:21-23 sounded both notes. "For all things belong to you . . . the world or life or death or things present or things to come; all things belong to you, and you belong to Christ; and Christ belongs to God" (NASB). All things belong to us—that's liberty; we belong to Christ—that's loyalty. It's not the number of things which belong to us that is crucial, but to whom we belong. Really belonging to Christ gives us the belongings of all the Christian faith offers.

The message to the Galatians proclaims the same truth. "It was for freedom that Christ set us free; therefore keep standing firm and do not be subject again to a yoke of slavery" (Gal. 5:1 NASB). The Galatians were tempted to misuse their liberty by falling back into slavery to old legalisms rather than loyalty to Christ. The one who called himself a "bondservant of Christ" cautioned them about misspent freedom. Because he was a slave of Christ, he was free in Christ.

The same is true for us. It is our loyalty that preserves our liberty. We are to belong to Christ and then all that he offers belongs to us. When we are loyal to him and the people he gives us to love and care for, we become truly free people.

This is because of the second thing the Book of Ruth teaches. *Loyalty is what God offers and wants in return.* The word in Hebrew translated as loyalty is *chesed.* It is rendered "lovingkindness" in some translations. The word is used most often in the Old Testament by two in Ruth's family tree, David and Solomon. In Psalm 101:1 David says, "I will sing of loyalty and of justice; to thee, O Lord, I will sing." It was the limitless, relentless, consistent love of the covenant God which made David want to sing. He reproduces the Lord's loyalty in his loyalty to Saul in spite of the king's jealousy and fear of him. This is expressed in what he said to the men of Jabesh-gilead who were faithful to Saul to the end. "May you be blessed by the Lord, because you showed this loyalty to Saul your lord, and buried him! Now may the Lord show steadfast love and faithfulness to you!" (II Sam. 2:5-6a). David is remembered for his loyalties—to Saul, his sons who often rebelled, his troops who fought gallantly with him, and his friends who disappointed him. Even in the great failure of his life, David was brought back to the Lord in repentance and contrition because he remembered the loyalty of the Lord.

The wisdom of Solomon, David's son, was anchored in the loyalty of God to him and his longing to be loyal to God. Proverbs is punctuated by the repeated use of loyalty and faithfulness. "Let not loyalty and faithfulness forsake you; bind them about your neck, / write them on the tablets of your heart. / So you will find favor and good repute" (Prov. 3:3-4a). "What is desired in a man is loyalty" (Prov. 19:22).

Throughout the Scriptures, loyalty to God means placing him first, forsaking any other false god, and being to others the faithfulness he has been to us.

This leads to the third crucial message of Ruth. *Loyalty is the fabric that binds together the family of God.* The Lord of the impossible withholds his blessings until we respond with his loyalty in our relationships. The cross is our example of the lengths to which loyalty must go. It is through the lens of calvary that we can see one another and say what God says to us, "I will not let you go! You belong to me; I will not forsake you or leave you." The words of the poem "I Will Not Let Thee Go" that Robert Bridges wrote to his beloved capture the quality of loyalty God gives to us and wants us to give to one another.

> I will not let thee go,
> The stars that crowd the summer skies
> Have watched us so below
> With all their million eyes
> I dare not let thee go.
> I will not let thee go,
> I hold thee by too many bands,
> You say farewell, and lo!
> I have thee by the hands,
> And will not let thee go.

An accountability check again: Who needs to know that? From whom do you need to hear and feel it?

The rewards of loyalty are inherent in loyalty. Loyalty is its own reward because a God-imputed need in us is satisfied. He made us for himself and for profound relationship with one another. We fulfill our destiny when we are loyal. We become like our God. The events that happened to Ruth, the blessings she received, and the joy she experienced way beyond happiness, were because she complied with the basic spiritual law of loyalty.

Perhaps you are saying, "Wait a minute, Lloyd, what do you do when people disappoint you or do those things which are unworthy of your loyalty?" That presses us deeper into the ingredients of true loyalty. Faithfulness must be lived out with honesty, directness, exhortation, and encouragement. When people do things which stretch our loyalty, we need to care enough to share with them our perception of what's wrong. Loyalty is not blind. Rather, it sees through the eye of love to the person—what he or she is and can be. Directness is an absolutely necessary part of healthy loyalty. Disloyalty is giving an analysis about a person to others rather than giving it to him or her directly. Some years ago I made a commitment to God that I would try never to say anything about a person which I had not said to that person, or was able to say within a twenty-four-hour period. Now, I've broken that promise often, and it has forced me to seek forgiveness and make restitution. But seeking to keep that commitment has cemented lifelong relationships of mutual trust. We all need people whom we can count on to advise or criticize us. Anyone who gossips to us will surely gossip about us. We are to talk to God about things that trouble us about people, and then talk to the person directly in the perspective of those prayers.

What if people won't listen? What if they do things that hurt and destroy themselves and others, even after we have confronted them or expressed our alarm? We remain loyal! Loyalty is not approval. It is a giving, forgiving, "in spite of" love in action. Loyalty does not deny what's right or condone irresponsibility. In fact, out of loyalty to people we cannot stand by and wink at behavior which will destroy them. Being committed to loyalty spells consistent involvement in their struggles to help them discover and do God's will. That's not easy and demands untiring effort. We've all failed repeatedly to help people express their potential.

That's why exhortation and encouragement are such essential elements in loyalty. Exhortation is discovering people's true goals and spurring them on to accomplish them. Encouragement is pulling alongside and cheering them on. To have friends who share our dreams and want God's best for us is a taste of heaven. But having friends like that requires being that kind of friend. William James once said, "The deepest principle in human nature is the craving to be appreciated." Only God can fulfill that ultimately, but he uses us to help. There is no deeper sense of appreciation of a person than to understand her or him. That means knowing the hopes as well as the hurts in them, and becoming a loyal cheerleader as they race on to their goals.

Boaz gave Ruth the accolade of excellence because of her loyalty. Excellence is being all that God meant us to be. And the place to begin is with our acceptance of his loyalty to us expressed by an undying loyalty to him which will flower in unending loyalty to the people of our lives. Confession of the disloyalties of the past and commitment to loyalty in the future will move us to pray:

> Father, forgive the cold love of the years
>    As here in the silence we bow
> Perish our cowardice, perish our fear,
>    Kindle us, kindle us now.
>
> Lord we accept, we believe, we adore
>    Less than the least though we be;
> Fire of love, burn in us, burn evermore
>    Till we burn out for Thee.

Author unknown

# CHAPTER TWELVE

# An Ebenezer Long Before Scrooge

## —Samuel—

Some time ago, a group of seminary students visited me to talk about preaching. One of them asked a very personal question. "What goes through your mind as you look out over your congregation when you stand up to preach? What's the feeling you have as you look into the faces of your people?" As I answered, I realized that what I think about and feel is the same as when I begin a chapter of a book: identification, empathy, love.

All my readers become one person in my mind's eye. By the gift of discernment I see beneath the surface. What people have written in letters, shared in personal conversation, or expressed in discussions at conferences blend into a unified voice to thunder the real needs of people in my mind and soul. I suddenly hurt where they hurt, ache where they ache, hope where they hope, and want to dare where they are challenged to dare. At the same time, I must be honest about a deep longing: that what I write will make a difference.

That is especially true as I begin to write this chapter. My desire is that it can be a significant separation, a blessed break, of the past from the future. Listening to the pulsebeat of people's hopes and hurts I am aware that so many need the healing of memories. We need to let go of the past in order to be free to move into the future as liberated persons. The purpose of this chapter is to help you and me to begin a new past. And that begins right now. How we deal with the memories that haunt or hinder us will determine what kind of past episode we will live today.

Three presuppositions undergird what I want to say: (1) if we do not experience healing of the past we are destined to repeat it; (2) without the healing of memories, the only thing that we learn from the past is that we do not learn from the past; and (3) the only way to change the past is to own, then disown, it.

There are many inadequate ways we are tempted to use in dealing with the past. Remorse is one way. Many of us feel it. We look back on what we've said and done, or didn't say or do, and the hidden ache of remorse pulsates within us. "Why did I do it that way?" we ask. "Why did I ever let those words escape my mouth? How could I ever have reacted in that way?" There have been times that my morning prayers have included the request for the Lord to give me temporary lockjaw at repeated times throughout the day. I long to respond to the movement of his Spirit before I set my mouth in motion. Ever feel that way? Of course you do. And what about the residue of remorse from the carefully hoarded composite of unresolved memories? Failures, goofs, mistakes, misused opportunities. And we say to ourselves, "What right do I have to be happy with memories like that?"

Others of us feel regret about the past. Not as deep as remorse, regret still has the unsettling disturbance of present happiness. "If I could only do that all over again!" we plead. The faces of people we've hurt or neglected or mistreated march before our mind's eye.

Still others feel acute recrimination. That is to take the past into their own hands and assume the responsibility of punishment. We blame others for what they did or neglected to do that caused us a bad memory. Or, what's worse, we refuse to forgive what someone has done to us. The memory festers like a splinter in our souls. We take over the management of our part of the universe and demand God's abdication as the only one who can absolve us or others of what we've done or been.

Renunciation is used by others of us. We make firm promises that we are going to do things differently. We renounce the past without cleansing it. We try to close the door on what has been, but all we do is suppress the dragons of memory. Every so often they rap persistently and want to come out into our consciousness for a dress rehearsal in preparation for a rerun in a new situation or circumstance. Renunciation of our memories sounds so very pious. The only thing wrong with it is that it doesn't work.

In fact none of these ways of dealing with the past work. There is only one way to experience the healing of memories. That is to *rejoice over the past!* You read it correctly. *Rejoice.* Whatever it takes to bring us to a place where we can rejoice over what has happened to or around us, even in the most painful of memories, is the only way to find release. That means going back over, in fellowship with the Master, what was said and done by or to us. When we hear him forgive us and others, we are empowered to forgive ourselves and them. Then we can rejoice over what we've learned, allow the pus of the hurt to be expunged and the scar tissue to form over the raw flesh of the now cleansed memory. Then we know that the Lord wastes nothing and uses everything to bring us close to him and one another.

That's what Samuel did for Israel. The greatest prophet since Moses was also the last of the Judges of Israel. We do the memory of this giant of a man a great disservice when we remember him only as the one who reluctantly accepted Israel's demand for a king and anointed both Saul and David. His finest hour as God's person occurred long before that. He towers as the healer of memories at the end of the period of the Judges by helping Israel repent and rejoice over the failures of the past. Samuel enabled Israel to prepare for a new age by letting go of memories of defeat. Through him we have a word which is now the watchword for God's memory-healing power: *Ebenezer!*

The word reminds us of the central character of Dickens' *Christmas Carol.* But a careful study of the word in First Samuel introduces us to an Ebenezer long before Scrooge. The word means in Hebrew, "the stone of help." Samuel used it at a time of triumphant victory over the Philistines. He set a great stone between Mizpah and Shen and named it Ebenezer, saying, "Thus far the Lord has helped us." In so doing he took a bitter memory of defeat years before at a place called Ebenezer and replaced it with a memory-stone of gratitude. Through the ages the word *Ebenezer* has become so closely associated with his words, "Thus far the Lord has helped us," that the meaning is almost synonymous. Like Dickens' Ebenezer, Israel was transformed by the cleansing of painful memories with new memories of praise. Samuel is distinguished as one of the great personalities of the Old Testament because he exemplified in his own character and taught Israel the liberating truth of the inseparable relationship between gratitude and greatness.

A couple of paragraphs of background sketch the implications of Samuel's leadership for our lives today. The great prophet and judge of Israel gave leadership in the turbulent period toward the end of the settling of the land of Canaan and the beginning of the Hebrew monarchy. He was born at the lowest ebb of this period when Israel was brought to its knees, not in worship of Yahweh, but in defeat and humiliation from the Philistines. First Samuel, chapter one, makes it very clear that Samuel was a gift of God in response to the urgent prayers of his mother, Hannah. When she dedicated her son to the Lord before Eli the priest, she said, "For this boy I prayed, and the Lord has given me my petition which I asked of Him. So I have dedicated him to the Lord; as long as he lives he is dedicated to the Lord" (I Sam. 3:27-28 NASB). In the prayer of praise which follows in the first ten verses of chapter two we can see why gratitude became the source of Hannah's son's greatness in later years. The boy had learned his lesson well at the knee of a thankful mother. The attitude of gratitude made Samuel the man God could use in one of Israel's most ungrateful periods of apostasy.

Hannah left her son with Eli to assist him in ministering before the Lord. It was there Samuel received his call from the Lord. In a time when word from the Lord was rare and visions were infrequent (I Sam. 3:1), the Lord called Samuel by name. The young man first thought it was Eli calling him. He did not know the Lord. After repeated calls and counsel from Eli that if he heard the call again it must be from the Lord, the decisive encounter occurred. "Samuel! Samuel!" the Lord called again. Samuel responded with words taught him by Eli. They were to become the essence of the future leader's power. "Speak, Lord, for Thy servant is listening" (I Sam. 3:9 NASB). The Lord told young Samuel that he was about to do a great thing in Israel. It would begin with judgment upon Eli's family for the sin his sons had committed in taking sacrificial meat from the people and using it for common purposes of food for their own satisfaction. The next day Samuel was encouraged by Eli to share what the Lord had told him. It was a powerful moment of truth for the old priest who had indulged his sons' sacrilege. Eli confirmed that Samuel was a prophet of the Lord. From that time on all of Israel grew in respect for Samuel. His power as prophet and judge over the people was strengthened by further revelations from the Lord.

Then follow three chapters in First Samuel where Samuel is not mentioned at all. But what happened in Israel during those years set the stage for the prophet's finest hour. The armies of Israel were defeated miserably at a site called Ebenezer. Soon afterward the Ark of the Covenant, which had become symbolic of the presence of the Lord, was captured by the Philistines. Eli died and his daughter-in-law expressed the mood of all Israel in naming a newborn son Ichabod, which means, "The glory has departed from Israel." Her words expressed the pitiful plight of God's people: "The glory has departed from Israel, because the ark of God was taken" (I Sam. 4:21 NASB).

But the Lord was faithful to his covenant. Even though his people persisted in the syncretism of Baal and Ashtaroth worship along with a vague commitment to him, he did not give up on his beloved, chosen people. The capture of the Ark brought the Philistines nothing but trouble, sickness, and plagues. A strange twist of history: the Israelites adopted the foreign gods of the Philistines and failed; the Philistines tried to gain Yahweh's power by keeping the Ark and failed! Inside that Ark was the reason for both: the tablets of the Commandments which began, "Thou shalt have no other gods before Me." Neither Israel nor the enemy nations could trifle with Yahweh! Finally the Philistines cried out, "Get rid of that Ark!" It was returned to Israel. That brought an unexpected response from God's people. Instead of rejoicing and reveling, there was a national repentance.

The people went to Samuel to ask him to offer a sacrifice expressing their lamentation and longing for God's power. He told them flatly that the Lord would not bless them until all the Baal and Ashtaroth idols were removed from Israel. Reminiscent of Gideon's incisiveness about pagan worship, Samuel knew that the first step to a renaissance in Israel was purging the land of idols and false gods. *A healing of our memories always begins with a decisive return to the Healer!*

The prophet brought the people to Mizpah where he led them in worship of Yahweh. Word of the gathering of the people of Israel spread to the Philistines. Knowing that they would be vulnerable, they decided to attack. As they saw the Philistines approaching, Israel was thrown into panic and appealed to Samuel to call out to the Lord for help. All that Samuel had been through up to this point prepared him to grasp the hour of need as the opportunity for the display of Yahweh's power. A whole generation had lived and struggled without witnessing an incisive intervention of the Lord of the impossible. A realization of their sin of syncretism, coupled with the impossibility of facing the encroaching Philistines' military might, made them open to receive what God had been ready and willing to give through the long period of spiritual destitution. Samuel made a sacrifice of a lamb. In response, the Lord thundered in a violent storm. The thunder threw the Philistines into confusion. Israel seized the opportunity and attacked the Philistines, driving them out of the land as far as Beth-car. The people knew it was the Lord who had won the battle. Their contrition had been confirmed by his victory.

After the Israelites had won the victory over the Philistines, Samuel built an altar in gratitude to God. He named it Ebenezer, a stone of remembrance. Before all the people he said, "Thus far the Lord has helped us." Hannah would have been pleased. Her gratitude had become the power of her son's greatness. *Thanksgiving prepares us for a triumphant future.*

We all need resting places of gratitude from which we look backward and forward. The word "hitherto" implies both reflection and reconsecration. Two things thunder from this pivotal event in Samuel's life for our pilgrimage today.

The first is that *our God-given capacity of memory must be filled with his grace and our gratitude to offset the grimness of our failures.* How very sensitive of Samuel to call his altar of praise Ebenezer! The Israelites ached over the defeat at the site of Ebenezer years before. They could not forget that until they forged a new image of themselves as a blessed and victorious people.

That has tremendous implications for us. All the disturbing memories of the past must be brought under the transforming power of the Holy Spirit. We become the defeats of the past until he invades us with new memories to displace the debilitating ones. Our Ebenezer is a resting place of gratitude in the midst of the fast-moving currents of our experience. We are forced to praise and say, "The Lord has brought us thus far." We can own the failures in his forgiveness and then disown them, rejoicing over what we've learned.

We all experience the power of bad memories in unguarded moments. A familiar face, or a set of circumstances, brings back the realization of our lack of courage or the results of some compromise. We relive the whole mess of our inadequacy. Then the Lord begins to teach us through what we've been through. Jesus reminds us that only those who have been forgiven greatly can love graciously (Luke 7:47). And then we can say, "Ebenezer! The Lord has brought me to this place!"

Alexander Maclaren (*Expositions of Holy Scripture*, Baker Book House, 1974) once said:

> The best use of memory is to mark more plainly than it could be seen at the moment the divine help which has filled our lives. Like some track on a mountain side, it is less discernible to us when treading it, than when we look back at it from the other side of the glen. Many parts of our lives, that seemed unmarked by any consciousness of God's help while they were present, flash up into clearness when seen through the revealing light of memory, and glean purple in it, while they looked but bare rocks as long as we were stumbling among them. It is blessed to remember and see everywhere God's help. We do not remember aright unless we do.

The second thing we learn from Samuel's Ebenezer is that *the Lord is the great memory-healer*. He knows that we cannot grasp the present, or give ourselves to the future, until the past is expunged of its crippling memories. Samuel helped the people of Israel deal with the past and get on with the challenge of the future.

The word *hitherto* implies that future. It does not suggest that the people of Israel had arrived, but that God's best was offered to those who knew that the One who brought them thus far had an exciting future ahead.

What memories of the past still haunt and hinder you? There are memories of hurts we received and those we inflicted. People out of our past loom up in our mind's eye. The demons of suppressed guilt stalk about in our closet of memory. But also, there are memories of triumphs that we are tempted to claim as our own accomplishment. Pride invades and keeps us from praise. We need an Ebenezer to remind us that it is the Lord who has brought us thus far, not our cleverness or ability.

Paul knew the essence of oft-repeated Ebenezers. "Forgetting those things which are behind and reaching forward to those things which are ahead, I press toward the goal for the prize of the upward call of God in Christ Jesus" (Phil. 3:13-14 NKJV). We are never finished! This life cannot contain all that our Lord has prepared. That will require eternity. Spurgeon caught the dynamic of that. Speaking of our Ebenezers, he said:

> The word . . . points forward. For when a man gets up to a certain mark and writes "hitherto," he is not yet at the end; there is still a long distance to be traversed. More trials, more fights, more victories; and then sickness, old age, disease, death. It is over now? No! There is more yet—awakening in Jesus' likeness, thrones, harps, songs, psalms, white raiment, the face of Jesus, the society of saints, the glory of God, the fullness of eternity, the infinity of bliss. O be of good courage, believer, and with grateful confidence raise your "Ebenezer." (C. H. Spurgeon, from a sermon delivered March 15, 1868, at the Metropolitan Tabernacle, Hewington, England, quoted in Metropolitan Tabernacle Pulpit, Pilgrim Publications, Pasadena, Texas.)

Our confidence is that the Lord who has helped us hitherto will see us all our journey through! John Newton knew this. Christ redeemed his life, set him free of pride and petulance, and gave him such an experience of his love that he could write the hymn, "Amazing Grace." A slave trader became a liberated, winsome witness of Christ's freedom.

The slave trader became a priest of the Church of England and gave the world many hymns of praise. The epitaph placed on his grave epitomizes what God can do when we begin a new past.

JOHN NEWTON, clerk
*once an infidel and libertine,*
*A Servant of slaves in Africa:*
*Was by the rich mercy of our Lord and Savior, Jesus Christ,*
*Preserved, restored, pardoned,*
*And appointed to preach the Faith*
*He had labored long to destroy.*

Christ alone can deal with our memories. He persists with us until we can rejoice. For each mistake or failure we've done, or each destructive or debilitating thing which has been done to us, forgiveness is the only way to freedom for the future. If we try to judge or atone for ourselves or others, we stumble and the past is locked up like a fire in our bones. Samuel Johnson used to say, "A wise man will make haste to forgive because he knows the true value of time." We can achieve inner health and peace only through forgiveness—the forgiveness not only of others but also of ourselves. We can't do it ourselves. Forgiveness is one thing we cannot give until we have received it. To forgive others is the sublime result of forgiving ourselves as forgiven through the cross.

I remember walking in a cemetery some time ago and noticing a gravestone. "Forgiven" was carved boldly into the center of the marble and at the bottom was the name of a former Christian leader in that town. Not a bad tombstone to put on our memories. "Forgiven" is the secret of a new past. That reminds me of what Thomas Hooker, one of our settling and founding fathers, said on his deathbed in Hartford, Connecticut, in 1647. His loyal followers, whom he had led to the new world, gathered around his bed and said, "Mr. Hooker, you are going to your reward." His reply is a good motto for all our tomorrows, as well as our deathbed assurance. "No," he said, "I go to receive mercy." Robert Frost would have cheered that. He said, "You've had bad luck and good luck, and all you want in the end is mercy." So say I!

There's a stone in the New Testament which is the Ebenezer stone of all time. It is the stone over the grave of Christ in Joseph of Arimathea's garden. It was rolled in a groove-track over the tomb in which the sacred, nail-pierced body of the Savior was laid. But God had the final word. He rolled the stone away and raised Jesus from the dead. All our memories were suffered for on the cross. They were buried with Christ. Now the stone which stands between us and the future is rolled away and a new life can begin. As Paul put it, "Therefore we were buried with Him through baptism into death, that just as Christ was raised from the dead by the glory of the Father, even so we also should walk in newness of life" (Rom. 6:4 NKJV). This is our ultimate stone of memory. Ebenezer! Hitherto has the Lord led us—thus far the Lord has helped us.

Michelangelo's sculpture of David and Goliath, now in a garden in Florence, Italy, was sculpted by the great artist from a piece of marble that had been rejected and discarded by another artist. That's what God does with our past. He makes a thing of lasting beauty out of what we have rejected. He gives us the power to rejoice over the new person he has sculpted out of the misshapen experiences of our yesterdays. Our attention can now be focused on what shall be rather than what has been. God says, "I will remember their sin no more" (Jer. 31:34). And we say with the psalmist, "Remember not the sins of my youth." Because the people of Israel repented and trusted God for victory in their battles, an old Ebenezer of humiliating defeat became a new Ebenezer of humble delight.

God's "hitherto" implies the promise of henceforward. Samuel experienced that. The rest of his life was a struggle with Israel's second-best choice of demand in a king rather than maintaining trust in God alone. He saw his people accept the provisional will of God because they refused his perfect will. He lived through the bungling of Saul and found David to be a king "after God's heart." The turbulent days of the last years of Samuel's life had many an Ebenezer before he died. But what he said in his first response to the Lord remained the creed of his life. "Speak Lord, Thy servant hears." The prophet listened intently and spoke incisively. "Samuel judged Israel all the days of his life" (I Sam. 7:15).

Robert Robinson has immortalized Samuel's Ebenezer and helps us claim our own.

> Here I raise mine Ebenezer;
> Hither by thy help I'm come;
> And I hope, by thy good pleasure,
> Safely to arrive at home.

A further verse gives us a vivid description of what that means:

> Hitherto, Thy love has blessed me;
> Thou hast brought me to this place;
> And I know Thy hand will bring me
> Safely home by Thy good grace.

Anyone of us who has raised an Ebenezer of memory-healing, future-anticipating joy knows that he or she has come home already. Life's problems or death's power cannot assail us. Welcome home, now, and forever. Ebenezer.

# CHAPTER THIRTEEN

# Impeding the Impossible

## —Saul, A Willful King—

Thus far in our consideration of the Lord of the impossible, we have seen the magnificent examples of what he was able to do in the lives of people who were willing to cooperate with him. Now we must be as honest as the Bible is about our awesome capacity to limit his power in our lives. There are times when our attitudes and actions clearly indicate that we don't want him. The frightening thing is that sometimes he gives us what we want.

God is almighty and has all power. And yet, the mystery of his providential management of our lives is that he has given us the capacity to receive or resist his interventions in our impossibilities. We have been entrusted with both a will and the freedom to choose. That's our potential. We have the endowed ability to discern and do his will. When we do, exciting things happen. But we can also refuse his overtures of love and end up with less than the maximum he intends for us. And that's our problem.

I talked to an old friend on the phone the other day. He had checkmated the Lord at every turn. Consistently, he said no to his guidance. Now he was in a mess that was the natural result of a series of choices contrary to what he knew was right. When his marriage drifted into dullness, instead of getting help, he allowed an attraction for another woman grow into infatuation and eventually into an affair which destroyed his marriage as well as hers. Not really wanting his marriage, he acted out his inner frustration by those actions and forced his wife to seek a divorce. When life fell apart for him professionally, he asked me why God allowed this. I felt led to ask, "Isn't this what you wanted?" His true desires had become a reality.

Somewhat the same thing happened in a very different context to a woman who constantly resisted her husband's affection. He came to see me about what he could do. I suggested that it might be well to temporarily stop his words and actions of endearment. Some weeks later the wife came to see me. "What's happened to my husband?" she asked angrily. When she described his coolness, I asked, "Isn't that what you have been telling him in thousands of ways that you wanted?" Getting what she indicated she wanted frightened her so much that she faced the deeper problem of manipulation through the affection she gave or withheld.

An officer of a church in the Southeast unloaded the sad tale of what was happening in his church. There was no vitality, growth, excitement. He blamed the pastor. A few penetrating questions about the real dynamics of the situation revealed a power struggle between him and the pastor. Further conversation exposed the fact that the man had persistently scuttled every effort the pastor had made to renew the parish. Now the church was split into factions and the pastor had been asked to resign. "Why doesn't God step in and revive our church?" he asked. "Is that what you really want?" I responded. "It sounds like you've wanted just the opposite and you've gotten your desires."

After a meeting recently a woman stopped me to visit. She was concerned about the fact that God had not answered her prayers. The longer we talked the more I became aware of specific incidents in which she had refused God's answers because of her self-justifying, do-it-herself religion. She found it difficult to surrender her needs to him, fearing loss of her own control over her life. "Do you really want God to answer your prayers?" I asked. Her response of yes had the tone of a no. She had given God her agenda. Actually, he was trying to get her to live on his agenda. When she resisted, for a time he allowed her deeper desire beneath her words of prayer. He gave her freedom to run her own life. It's alarming to contemplate: there are times when

God allows us what we really want! Even when we miss his best for us, he waits to bless us until we seek with all our hearts what he wants for us. This woman had to go through heartbreaking difficulties before she finally surrendered her will to the Lord.

These examples are alarming. More alarming still are the host of good church people who are caught in the syndrome of needing and resisting God's interventions. We camouflage our willfulness under a surface religion. Sometimes we are busy working for him and don't really want him. In a multitude of ways we block his interventions in our problems. We persist in controlling people and situations, resist guidance when it requires behavior modification, and continue in patterns that intensify the very difficulties about which we pray.

It's possible to drift into Christianity without ever giving our wills to the Lord. Our life can be limited to what we can do on our own strength without him. Prayer can become shallow. It's possible for our churches to become a series of services and activities which never lead us to a decisive encounter with the living God. The life we really want is what we get!

Too severe? Perhaps. And yet, when I've shared this possibility with people, it has led to some of the most honest conversations I've ever had. Many have been forced to see that their deepest problems are caused by a lack of an intimate relationship with God. I'm happy to say that the shock of realizing that their words and actions betrayed a willful resistance to him eventually led to an authentic experience of his love and power.

This contemporary analysis of one of the most urgent needs in many Christians sets the stage for our consideration of Saul, the first king of Israel. The purpose of this chapter is more than a character study of him. It is that, but it has repeated application to our life today. Saul shows us a side many of us need to face and ask for power to change. He is a case study of the frightening possibility of saying no to God so long we lose the desire to say yes. We can see what happens when we continually stiff-arm the approaches of the Lord. His life alarms us with a vivid example of the disturbing truth that we may be granted what we want. And in the final analysis, Saul didn't really want God!

We first meet Saul in I Samuel 9. From the outset we are confronted with his mixture of promise and problems, advantages and disadvantages, strengths and struggles. Saul had an excellent family background. He was the son of Kish, the heir of a tradition of valor of the small tribe of Benjamin. We are told that he was a "choice and handsome young man. There was not a more handsome person than he among the children of Israel. From his shoulders upward he was taller than any of the people" (I Sam. 9:2 NKJV). This explanation of his physical stature stands out in contrast to what is implied in the story that follows.

Saul and a servant were sent out by Kish to find some stray donkeys. They searched for a long time and as far as the land of Zuph where Samuel was dwelling. Saul decided the search was futile. The servant, not Saul, made a telling suggestion. "Look now, there is in this city a man of God, and he is an honorable man; all that he says surely comes to pass. So let us go there; perhaps he can show us the way that we should go" (I Sam. 9:6 NKJV). The implication is that Saul did not know about Samuel or the great issues that gripped Israel. How could it be that any young man with Saul's potential for leadership in confronting the nation's enemies did not know God's prophet of the hour?

The meeting with Samuel disclosed more than how he could find the donkeys. In it the prophet announced to Saul what the Lord had told him. The son of Kish was to reign over his people and command the armies in the continuing battle with the Philistines. Samuel anointed Saul and gave him mysterious instructions. He was to go toward his home and on the way he would meet two men who would tell him that the donkeys had been retrieved. Further, he would meet three men on their way to make sacrifices at Bethel. They would offer him loaves of bread which he was to receive from them. After that Saul would meet a band of prophets. "Then the Spirit of the Lord will come upon you, and you will prophesy with them and be turned into another man" (I Sam. 10:6 NKJV). This must have seemed strange and mystifying to Saul. All he had wanted to do was find his donkeys. Now he was told that he was being conscripted by the Lord to be king and general of Israel's armies. The passage indicates no response. The final instruction from Samuel was more baffling than the others. In the future, Saul was to go to Gilgal where the prophet would offer burnt offerings and make sacrifices of peace offerings to God. The orders were that Saul was to wait there seven days and Samuel would tell him what to do. The chain of command was clearly established: the Lord, his prophet, and the king-designate. There was no question in Samuel's mind that this king would report to him. If Israel was to have a king in response to their demands, he would be a king who followed the prophet's orders.

When Saul turned to leave Samuel, he experienced a dynamic movement of the Spirit of the Lord within him. It was an affirmation of all that the prophet had revealed to him. We are told that God gave him a new heart. That means that he was endowed with a new disposition, an openness to the Lord, a desire to serve him, and an assurance of his call. Previously Saul's desires and disposition were totally occupied with himself and his domestic responsibilities. There's no indication that he had had any previous experience or interest in the Lord, his blessings, or his people's plight.

On the way home, all that Samuel had said occurred. Most important of all, he did meet the band of prophets and had another encounter with the Lord. He had been given a new heart and now it was filled with the Lord's Spirit. Saul joined the prophets in prophesying, which probably meant a combination of prophetic utterance, ecstatic praise, and exuberant singing. What is most significant, however, is the amazement of his countrymen. They were astonished and said to one another, "What is this that has come upon the son of Kish? Is Saul also among the prophets?" (I Sam. 10:11 NKJV). That further underlines the previous lack of any observable piety in Saul's life.

What did all this mean to Saul? We are told that when he met his uncle and was asked about his search for the donkeys, he told about his meeting with Samuel. The uncle, undoubtedly aware of Saul's experience with the band of prophets, was very interested in what happened to his nephew when he was with Samuel. "Tell me, please, what Samuel said to you." Saul's response was strangely guarded and reserved. He said nothing of his calling, his anointing to be king, or that the Lord had given him a new heart and quickened him with his Spirit. Some may interpret this as admirable humility. However, I wonder how deeply Saul really felt about his experience or the urgency of his new calling to lead the armies against the enemy.

Further evidence of this is revealed when Samuel gathered the people of Israel together at Mizpah. Once again the people demanded a king to reign over them. Reluctantly, Samuel, responding to the Lord's guidance to give them a king, announced that the king would be chosen from the tribe of Benjamin. And then to everyone's surprise, he declared that Saul the son of Kish, was chosen to be king. But he was nowhere to be found. Actually, tall Saul was hiding among the baggage and equipment! The Lord himself told them where to find their new king. They ran and brought him to Samuel. As he stood head and shoulders above all the people, Samuel's approbation seemed to contradict Saul's obvious reluctance. "Do you see him whom the Lord has chosen, that there is no one like him among all the people?" And the people, elated at finally having a king, shouted, "Long live the king!" But others said, "How can this man save us?"

This account of Saul's call to be king exposes the essential problems that persisted through his life. He was big in stature and little in character. He towered above the people and yet cowered at the challenge to lead them. He was empowered by the Lord for a cause which had not gripped his concern. People like that can be dangerous. They do what's required for the wrong reasons. There's no fiber to the fabric of their commitment. The Lord's plan and purposes get distorted in their own need for recognition and aggrandizement. In Saul the shift from doing God's work by God's power to doing God's work for Saul's glory is clearly discernible.

In his early military career, Saul was spectacularly successful. The Spirit of the Lord not only blessed him in his battles, but also gave him a magnanimous attitude toward those who had ridiculed his coronation. Both were reaffirmed in the people's adulation of their new king.

Two years later Saul made the first of several fateful errors that were the beginning of his demise. Before a battle, instead of waiting for Samuel to make the sacrifice, he took matters in his own hands. Saul's orders from the prophet were to wait seven days. When he did not come, Saul proceeded with the sacrifice himself. The issue was one of obedience to what the Lord had commanded through the prophet. When Samuel arrived in the camp, he demanded, "What have you done?" Saul made excuses, blamed the people, and expressed his impatience in waiting for Samuel. Saul had usurped Samuel's authority and denied the balance of authority between prophet and king in the fulfillment of the commands of God. Samuel's response was devastating to

Saul. "You have done foolishly. You have not kept the commandment of the Lord your God, which He commanded you. For now the Lord would have established your kingdom over Israel forever. But now your kingdom shall not continue. The Lord has sought for himself a man after His own heart, and the Lord has commanded him to be commander over His people, because you have not kept what the Lord commanded you" (I Sam. 13:13-14 NKJV).

We can imagine the panic that struck in Saul's heart. He had been reluctant to be king. Then when the approbation of the people and the savory taste of power began to fill his emptiness, he became imperious and impetuous. Because the Lord and his commandments were not the passion of his life, he persisted in disobedience. The fear that his new glory might be taken from him only intensified his compulsive self-determination.

But let's not be too hard on Saul. Let the full record stand. He often recognized that the Lord's power had won the battles he fought. He did erect altars to honor Yahweh. But the fatal shift had taken place. He had been called by God because of his weakness as well as his strength so that the people would be amazed at what God, not Saul, could do. What happened in Saul was that *he wanted God's strength for his own will and purposes.* Saul never seemed to have a trusting relationship with the Lord so he could yield each step to the Lord's strategy. Though he had been made king under very clear conditions, he constantly resisted God's authority and Samuel's unique position as God's spokesman. Because he had no center of companionship with the Lord he reacted to the enemy rather than acting on a clearly defined battle plan leading toward the Lord's goals.

The same thing can happen to us when we want God to follow our plans rather than us to follow his plan. It is possible to want God's miraculous power to pull things off for us, and at the same time not allow him to pull us together as an integrated person rooted in the firm foundation of his love and acceptance. God wants us but not just for what we can do for him. When he has us through the daily, hourly, consistent surrender of our challenges, then the impossible happens to us and around us.

But too often, like Saul, we become reactors instead of actors. We go from one problem to another crying out, "Lord, get me out of this!" rather than, "Lord, help me through this and on to your goals for me." The power of the Lord is for his plan and purposes, not just a temporary crutch to survive one problem to get ready for the next.

So many of Saul's problems were self-induced. We see a growing self-negation bordering on self-destruction. That kind of emotional turmoil usually produces a intractableness that gets people into trouble. Because we do not believe that God loves us, we begin to think that others are against us too. An example of this in Saul's life was his relationship with his son Jonathan. One day Saul commanded that none of his soldiers should eat any food until evening. Jonathan had not been present when the order was given. He was off winning battles against the Philistines. After he conquered a segment of the enemy, he rejoined the main forces of Israel. In a wooded area he found honey dripping from a honeycomb. Because Jonathan had not heard his father's order, he dipped his rod into the honey to be refreshed after his battle. Reports of his seemingly disobedient act quickly reached the king. Saul was enraged and called for a casting of lots between him and his son. When the lot fell to Jonathan, indicating he was guilty, Saul condemned him to death. The strange twist to the account was that Saul had asked for a roll call prior to his order forbidding his soldiers to eat any food until evening. He had learned that Jonathan was not present and therefore could not know about his order. Some interpreters suggest that Saul even created the situation by giving the order when he knew Jonathan was absent, thus creating a no-win situation in which his son might get into trouble. Jonathan was a very attractive, mighty warrior. His victories in battle brought him great acclaim. Was Saul jealous? Only the people's resistance to his order to kill the young man saved him.

*When the Lord ceases to be our security, we are tempted to set ourselves up for hurt and broken relationships.* Because we are out of a consistent flow of grace for our failures, we inadvertently create situations in which we are punished by what people do to us. We even turn on the people closest to us. The more significant the person who hurts us, the more painful and masochistically satisfying is the anguish that results. When we get out of a relationship with the Lord where he is our only judge and subsequently our only source of forgiveness, we engineer life and people to reinforce our bad feelings about ourselves. When we feel badly about ourselves, we can very easily create situations in which people will agree with our negative self-appraisal.

This is further illustrated in the way Saul compulsively did things which he knew would get him into difficulty with Samuel. The king was insecure in his own authority and, therefore, had to test Samuel's authority repeatedly. Really, he was forcing the hand of God. It happened when Saul went out to battle with the Amalekites. Through Samuel, the Lord gave him clear orders that he should take no spoil and no prisoners alive. The order seems cruel to us, but it must be understood in the context of that stage of history. The issue of the account for us in this present study of Saul is that he did not follow orders. He took Agag, the king of Amalekites, took a booty of the best sheep, oxen, lambs and "all that was good, . . . *unwilling* to utterly destroy them. But everything despised and worthless, . . . utterly destroyed" (I Sam. 15:9 NKJV, italics mine). If compassion had been Saul's motive it would have been a different matter. Rather, he could not follow orders so he had to create a situation that would further strain his relationship with God. When we don't really want God's authority over us, we will repeatedly do those things that strain his patience. Just as we set up people to become our enemies, so too we act out our resistance to God. If we have not known him as a friend, we often project him as an enemy in our minds. We end up thinking God is against us rather than for us.

Saul's spiritual neurosis was acted out in blatant arrogance when, following his victory over Agag, he went to Mount Carmel and set up a monument, not to Yahweh, but to himself! When Samuel heard that, his grief over what Saul had done in disobedience in the battles with the Amalekites turned into holy indignation. The encounter with the prophet and the king subsequently was filled with drama and pathos. When Saul greeted the prophet his words betrayed how out of touch with reality he had become. "Blessed are you of the Lord! I have performed the commandment of the Lord" (I Sam. 15:13 NKJV). But Samuel hearing the sheep of the forbidden booty said, "What then is this bleating of the sheep in my ears, and the lowing of the oxen which I hear?" (I Sam. 15:14 NKJV). Saul's answer is outrageous. Hiding the fact that he had built an altar to himself, he protested that he had taken the best of the sheep and the oxen to make a sacrifice to the Lord. Samuel's response is incisive. It exposes Saul's real problem of insecurity which he had never allowed the Lord to heal. "When you were little in your own eyes," the prophet said, "were you not head of the tribes of Israel? And did not the Lord anoint you king over Israel?" (I Sam. 15:17 NKJV). The point was carefully made. *Saul's problem was that though he was the tallest in Isreal, he was little in his own eyes.* Becoming king never healed that gaping hole in the fabric of his character. Samuel's judgment cut to the core of his problem. In response to Saul's pious protestation that he had taken spoil to sacrifice to the Lord even through disobedience, Samuel said, "Has the Lord as great delight / in burnt offerings and sacrifices, / As in obeying the voice of the Lord? / Behold, to obey is better than sacrifice, / And to heed than the fat of rams. / For rebellion is as the sin of witchcraft, / And stubborness is / as iniquity and idolatry. / Because you have rejected / the word of the Lord, / He also has rejected you / from being king" (I Sam. 15:22-23 NKJV).

This brought Saul to his knees at last. He begged for forgiveness, another chance, and for Samuel's approbation of him before the elders of Israel. The prophet did not offer cheap grace. Saul had rejected the Lord and the Lord gave him what his actions had indicated he really wanted. Samuel told Saul that because he had rejected the Lord, the Lord had rejected him as king over Israel. The kingdom would be given to another. When Samuel turned to leave, Saul clutched at his robe begging him to stay and forgive him. The significant thing is that the prophet helped Saul worship the Lord again indicating forgiveness for him as a person, but he had lost his chance to be king. That calling would be given to another. Saul had resisted the Lord too long. The Lord could no longer use him.

Shocking! Yes. God forgives, but our sin may have cost us our cherished position, relationships, or status. We dare not universalize from the way the Lord dealt with Saul. It cannot be applied to every person who has consistently refused God's will and gotten into trouble. God is infinitely original in the way he deals with us. The point is that persistently not wanting his authority over us can make us unusable. Our rebellion can weaken character to such an extent that we are incapable of great responsibilities. God loved Saul so much that he did not want him to continue in the position of king which had fed the worst of

Saul's neurosis. Saul hadn't really wanted to be king and refused to be the kind of king the Lord needed. He could have been a great king, had he realized that his self-conscious inadequacies were not liabilities but an opportunity to allow the Lord to do through him what he could not do by himself. That's the key. When we confess our needs to the Lord, he will glorify himself by doing in us what would be impossible without him. He delights to do that. If, however, our insecurities make us obstinate and obdurate, we deny the Lord the glory of using our humanity as a riverbed for the flow of his power in life's responsibilities. Saul's reluctance to trust the Lord, manifested in rebellion, finally resulted in actions which were intractable. *Saul didn't really accept himself as king. Eventually, the Lord agreed with him!*

Saul continued in the office of king without the blessing of God. That does not mean that the Lord had not forgiven him or that he had stopped loving him as a person. The Lord was moving on in the preparation of a new king. A shepherd boy who loved the Lord with all his heart was his choice. David, the son of Jesse, was singled out in the Lord's providence. It is interesting to note that this time the Lord chose a man who knew, loved, and trusted God before he called him to be king.

I can't help adding an aside as a biblical historian. Could it have been that the Lord's maximum will had been for Saul to serve with greatness rooted in his grace through a long reign and then at this death be succeeded by David? I think so. The kind of king Saul became was not what God intended. God's best was rejected. But his best for Israel could not be deterred or sacrificed at the altar of Saul's twisted ego. The Lord's providential plan can be delayed by us, but it cannot be deterred.

As for Saul, the rest of his life was spent in defensive manipulation. God's forgiveness that day at Gilgal with Samuel had not changed him. He resisted the Lord's love at every turn. The last chapters of his life were filled with intrigue, infighting, suspicion, and jealousy.

David became Saul's armor-bearer and remained faithful to the king throughout his life. A further evidence of Saul's self-centered self-possession is shown us when David slew Goliath. We remember the story well, but reflection on the incident gives us deeper insight into Saul. The Philistine and Israelite forces were drawn for battle. The pride of the Philistines was a six-cubit tall champion of battle. He was from the people of Anak, which means the people of the neck. He towered over the other Philistines and in full armor was a frightening sight to the Israelites. He taunted the Israelites with a formidable challenge. He would do battle with one of the Israelites. "Choose a man for yourselves, and let him come down to me. If he is able to fight with me and kill me, then we will be your servants. But if I prevail against him and kill him, then you shall be our servants and serve us" (I Sam. 17:8-9 NKJV).

Panic rippled through the Israelite forces. David took the challenge and with only a sling and a stone killed the giant Philistine. The question remains as to why the largest man in Israel, tall Saul, did not take the challenge on behalf of the Lord and his people. He allowed a young man to enter the danger. And after David's victory, suspicious Saul asked, "Whose son are you, young man?" Did he suspect that Samuel's prophecy meant that one of his countrymen had been chosen by the Lord to be king?

Saul's suspicions were deepened as David became a mighty warrior. Soon he began winning battles and Saul's suspicions turned to jealousy. The people didn't help. Amazed by David's prowess in battle, they made him their hero. After a great battle, the women chanted antiphonally, "Saul has slain his thousands, / And David his ten thousands" (I Sam. 18:7 NKJV). It was the beginning of the last chapter of Saul's demise. He made David an enemy and a wanted criminal with a high price on his head. Saul had a deep-seated problem with himself which he focused on David! His growing rage and jealousy finally scrapped the last ties with reality he had. He blasphemed by consulting a medium, acted irrationally, and at last committed suicide by falling on his own sword at Mount Gilboa. He had been doing that inch by inch for years as his self-hatred grew to monumental proportions. His last imperious self-determining act was to take his own life.

Saul had impeded the impossible happening in his own life, and for a time, in Israel. His story may seem beyond application to us today. But is it really? Writing this chapter has moved me deeply to think about our awesome power to say no to God's maximum. And yet, it has also brought me to the cross again, the regeneration of the resurrection, and the power of Pentecost. Christ died for that part of you and me that resists him in self-will. He set us free from the syndrome of self-justification which leads to self-hate. His resurrection offers the power to us for regeneration. We can become new creatures who will to do God's will. And when his Spirit invades us, the emptiness is filled with his power and we are enabled to say, "Not my will, but yours be done."

Suddenly we know that we do want what the Lord wants for us. Then we can say, "Lord I do want you, need you, and long to be your obedient person. Forgive my shallow wishes for self-control and look only on my deepest desire to know and love you!"

And then, in the quiet we know that the desire to pray that prayer was his gift. Perhaps we don't have as much power to limit the impossible as we thought. Could it be that the transformation of our desires to will to do his will is one of the greatest impossibilities he performs in us every day, right now? I believe it. And I for one, want that above all else!

# CHAPTER FOURTEEN

# A Person After God's Heart

## —David—

The secret of receiving the power of the Lord of the impossible is an open and receptive heart. David exemplifies this secret. He has been called the greatest saint and the greatest sinner of the Old Testament. Perhaps that's why we love him so much. We admire his strengths and empathize with his weaknesses. Our hearts soar with his in his psalms of praise and identify our own brand of fallibility in his confession and contrition.

The life of David becomes an essential ingredient of our understanding of the Lord of the impossible, because in David's life we see again what God can do with people who yield themselves to be channels of his power and seek his forgiveness in their failures.

I have included David in our consideration of the heroes of the Old Testament because he contradicts the myth that human strength or perfection are qualifications for experiencing the impossibility-defying power of the Lord.

David was a man after God's heart. "I have found David the son of Jesse," the Lord said, "a man after My heart, who will do My will." That amazing accolade focuses on the crucial issue in receiving the power of the Lord of the impossible. It tells us that God has a heart, we have a heart, and the secret of our abundant life is receiving his heart into our hearts.

The key words are *heart* and *after*. Hebrew psychology identified the heart as the seat of the mind and the will, together with the whole range of physical emotions. It was the inner dimension of human personality. Our contemporary division of intellect and emotion would be foreign to the Hebrew vision of the wholeness of personality.

What do we mean when we speak of God's heart? His heart is his essential nature. The ultimate divine intelligence, plus his indefatigable loving-kindness, plus his sovereign will equals his heart. The wonder of our created nature is that we can think his thoughts after him, receive and express his love, and will to do his will. The capacities of our hearts correspond sublimely to God's heart.

The word *after* brings God's heart and our heart together. It means in succession to, responding to, in search of, molded in a likeness of, and in complete harmony with. As a sculptor takes clay and sculpts a bust "after" our likeness, or a painter paints a portrait "after" our likeness, so a heart after God's heart is one in which God's heart is reproduced—intellectually, emotionally, and volitionally. David is distinguished as one of the greatest men of the Old Testament because he longed for the heart of God. From Israel's second king we discover the basic purpose of life: to be persons after God's heart. Most of all, we learn to echo his deepest desire to be moldable clay for the Potter's hand to shape into his likeness—to have his thoughts formed in the tissues of our brains, have his Spirit infuse our emotions, and have his will guide our wills so that we can follow his guidance.

We first see David as the young shepherd son of Jesse. What was it that God saw in this lad tending his father's sheep that identified him as Israel's potenial king? The twenty-third Psalm reflects David's humble trust in God as the great Shepherd of his life. When David penned that beloved psalm, he expressed the faith that gave him courage as a boy. God was all-sufficient for David. He was his protector, provider, and purpose. What David sought to be to his flock, God had been to him. The Lord was his companion and friend. The quality of unreserved trust God wanted most of all in his people, and found so lacking in Saul's rebellious nature, he found in a shepherd boy in the hills of Judah. The way David faced danger completely dependent on God, convinced the Lord that here was a lad soon to become a man, who could confront the dangers besetting Israel. David's mind was receptive, his emotions were open and free, his will was ready to obey. If he could confront and defeat the lions and wolves that attacked his flock by trusting in the Lord, his Shepherd, he would be able to be God's man to defeat Israel's enemies. *David was a God-captivated man who wanted to please and serve his Lord above all else.*

The dramatic episode of David's call and anointing by Samuel puts an exclamation point to the quality of heart God wanted in a new king for Israel. Jesse's older sons, all formidable specimens of manhood, were passed by Samuel's careful eye. As he evaluated each one as a potential king, the Lord cautioned him, "Do not look at his appearance or at the height of his stature, because I have refused him. For the Lord does not see as man sees; for man looks at the outward appearance, but the Lord looks at the heart" (I Sam. 16:7 NKJV). After looking over seven of Jesse's sons, the prophet said flatly, "The Lord has not chosen these." Then he asked, "Are these all the children?" Jesse had not even thought of his youngest as a candidate. "There remains yet the youngest, and behold, he is tending the sheep." Samuel asked that David be brought to him.

The description of the young shepherd brought before Samuel underlines the outward manifestation of his heart. "Now he was ruddy, with beautiful eyes and a handsome appearance." As Samuel studied David's face, the Lord spoke the undeniable command of his choice. "Arise, anoint him; for this is he." And so, the elderly prophet took his horn of oil and anointed David while his astonished brothers and father looked on in amazement. The Spirit of the Lord came mightily upon David from that day forward. God entrusted his heart to the receptive and ready heart of David.

God is seeking to find that quality of heart in you and me. In every period of history, circumstance, or time of personal or interpersonal crisis, he searches for a person whose heart wants his heart. The significant thing about David's call is that he did not think of himself as a future leader of Israel who would need God's help to accomplish his self-image of greatness. He longed for God's heart and God did the rest. When we put God first in our lives, he can use us. We do not seek God to accomplish our ends. We love God for God, not for what he can do for us. Our analysis of what he could do through us usually hits wide of the mark. An authentic call always has in it a surprise and a mystery. We are responsible only for what is in our hearts. Our minds, emotions, and will. Begin there and leave the results to him!

The anointing given to David signifying the invasion of God's heart into his is crucial. As I see what happened as a result in David's life, I wonder if that same infusion is available today. I believe it is. The Lord of the impossible is ready to anoint us today with his Holy Spirit. When we want God with all our hearts, he gives us special gifts which are way beyond the human level of talent. Anyone who has accepted God's love and forgiveness in Jesus Christ and opened his or her heart unreservedly with an unconditional surrender is a candidate both for an assignment that is humanly impossible and for the infilling of supernatural power—wisdom for the intellect, healing and release of the emotions, passionate willingness to know and do God's will. Right now, in this moment of time, God is saying of you and me, "Arise, anoint him, for this is he."

*The power of David's anointing is seen in his courage* as Saul's armor-bearer. As we noted in the previous chapter, David was fearless in his confrontation of Goliath. There is something awesome about the young man standing unafraid before the giant son of Anak. His unsophisticated sling and five smooth stones seem insignificant compared to the size of Goliath and his oversized sword and armor. And yet, the Lord's power, plus David's fearless heart, won the day. The author of First Samuel is very careful to paint a word picture of the impossibility of the situation. David's precision in sending the stone into the giant's forehead was the result of years of practice, but only the Lord's anointing could have added the ballistic force and accuracy to send that stone to the exact and fatal target. The victory over the Philistines that day assured David that the Lord was, indeed, with him. It also convinced Israel. The young man was propelled into immediate popularity and power.

That's the way God works. After he has found a heart after his heart, he gives special endowments, and then a vivid example of what he can do with that heart and that person's impossibilities. He wants all of us to be sure we can be sure of him!

David's years in Saul's court brought the maturing of his anointed heart. The convictions of his mind controlled the expression of his emotions. Like his ancestress Ruth, David's God-filled heart is loyal and faithful. There is a winsome freedom in David as he seeks to serve the king. At no time do we see him battling for power or position. Even while the deranged Saul was possessed with insane paranoia, David remained consistently committed to him as king in Israel. David is surprised that Saul is jealous and competitive. A guilelessness pervades his attitudes. When he is banished by Saul as an outlaw, he seeks an even deeper relationship with God's heart to be able to understand and endure the rejection and hostility. His psalms expressing the thoughts and feelings of his heart during this period reveal his total dependence on God. He experienced God in victory; he came to know him profoundly in vicissitudes. So often God follows the first blush of success resulting from his anointing with difficulties that drive us deeper into heart-to-heart communion with him.

During this period of anguish David exhibited other characteristics that we can admire and imitate. He exuded *a personal warmth* in his relationships with others. His friendship with Jonathan, Saul's son, made them closer than brothers. God's heart in our heart produces an inclusive, robust vitality in our relationships. A heart indwelt with God's heart makes us attractive, caring, concerned people who can enter into lasting friendships. "The soul of Jonathan was knit to the soul of David, and Jonathan loved him as his own soul" (I Sam. 18:1 NKJV). Because David had God's heart, there was room for a friend.

That same quality of warmth and faithfulness to his friends won David a band of men who pledged themselves to him during his years of exile from Saul's court. David was the kind of person who magnetically drew people to himself. He was dependable, gracious, thoughtful. His companions were willing to live and die for him. The reason was that God's Spirit reached out through David and gave them a sense of affirmation and self-esteem in his presence. When we enjoy the person we are because of God's Spirit in us, others will enjoy us and enjoy being themselves with us.

We see further into the depths of David's heart when we observe his *allegiance* to Saul as king even after repeated attempts by the jealous monarch to kill him. When David has opportunities to kill the king, he refuses. And after Saul dies by his own sword,

David grieves and commends the soldiers who risked their lives to bury the king.

After David is made king in Israel we see another aspect of his character. The new king's first act after unifying the kingdom by defeating internal and external enemies, is to bring the Ark of the Covenant to Jerusalem. We see him out in front of the procession leading the Ark, dancing with abandon and praise. David was a man of *immense emotion*. His intellectual beliefs about God released his emotional expression. "And David was dancing before the Lord with all his might" (II Sam. 6:14 NKJV). A heart filled with God's heart is free both to glorify and to enjoy God. There was no grimness in David's relationship with God. He could weep out his loneliness and fear to the Lord, but he could also dance with unrestrained fervor. When we love God with all our heart we can openly express our emotions to him, and then to others. He wants us to be real with him. When we are in the valley of despair or the mountain peaks of sublime joy, we can express it.

David's abandoned freedom to express his praise is contrasted with his wife Michal's reserve and contempt. She abhorred the king's lack of religious decorum before the Ark of God. Her embarrassment was caused by her own lack of freedom. Michal was like her father Saul. Her emotional energy was not guided by firm beliefs about God's sovereignty and grace. There was little in her mind about God's loving-kindness, and therefore, little capacity of emotional delight in him. What she could not express herself, she ridiculed in David.

There are Michals in all our lives, people whose minds are starved for liberating truth about God and whose emotions are stunted by malnutrition of lively belief. The conviction of God's grace results in the expression of joy. We cannot contain our joy. The tragedy of religion is that it produces more Michals than Davids. I am always gratified when my congregation shakes the rafters of the Hollywood church singing one of the great, historic hymns of the faith, or is free to express foot-tapping delight while singing a contemporary hymn of joy. I praise God for a people who can laugh and clap, weep when deeply moved, and talk with emotional zest about what God has done in their lives. A heart that has never felt God's presence in sorrow or pain, will seldom express his delight in adoration and praise.

The fires of God's Spirit burning in our hearts will make us glow with radiance and warmth. We are left to wonder: Are we most like David dancing before the Ark, or like Michal, restricted with a reserve and cankerous with criticism?

A friend of mind tells of attending an evangelical church that had lost its joy in fanatical legalism. He heard people talking about being "born again" and actually thought they were confessing that they were "bored again." That may say more about his transference onto the people of his own attitudes or about his hearing capacity, but it does underline the lack of sparkle, gusto, and attractiveness of many Christians who look and act as if they were "bored again."

There was nothing bored or boring about David. His lively heart was filled with exuberant adoration in times of both exhilaration and disappointment. No consideration of the quality of David's heart can overlook how he dealt with the Lord's rejection of his grand plan to build a house for the Lord. "See now, I dwell in a house of cedar, but the ark of God dwells inside tent curtains" (II Sam. 7:2 NKJV). David sent Nathan the prophet to inquire of the Lord's guidance. That is crucial. David, unlike Saul, honored the position and power of God's appointed prophet in the land. The king's heart was ruled by the Lord, and therefore, he ruled in Israel in cooperation with the Lord's prophet. The answer the Lord gave through Nathan was not what David expected. He would not be the one to build a house for the Lord. Now feel the heart of David respond in this prayer of faithfulness and obedience. We are given an intimate look into the depths of his loyal heart.

> "Now therefore, O Lord God, the word that Thou hast spoken concerning Thy servant and his house, confirm it forever, and do as Thou hast spoken, that Thy name may be magnified forever, by saying, 'The Lord of hosts is God over Israel'; and may the house of Thy servant David be established before Thee. For Thou, O Lord of hosts, the God of Israel, hast made a revelation to Thy servant, saying, 'I will build you a house'; therefore Thy servant has found courage to pray this prayer to Thee. And now, O Lord God, Thou art God, and Thy words are truth, and Thou hast promised this good thing to Thy servant. Now therefore, may it please Thee to bless the house of Thy servant, that it may continue forever before Thee. For Thou, O Lord God, hast spoken; and with Thy blessing may the house of Thy servant be blessed forever." (II Sam. 7:25-29 NASB)

Now we can understand why God called David a man after his own heart, who would do all of his will. There are times when our hearts must be realigned with God's heart. Often when we get an idea of what we want to do for God, it is not his plan for us. For David, building a temple for worship of God seemed so logical, natural, and magnanimous. Think of the elaborate plans we have wanted to execute for God. They seemed so right, but they were not God's best. He has a unique and special plan for each of us. When He says yes to some strategy and no to another, we are challenged to obey him. The task of building the temple was to be done by Solomon, not David. And the prayer David prayed guides the intellectual understanding, the emotional response, and the volitional obedience of our hearts when God closes one door and opens another.

How then, we ask, could the same David who prayed that prayer and others like it that are recorded in the Psalms, ever be the David who committed adultery with Bathsheba, the wife of Uriah, one of David's faithful warriors? The way David dealt with his sin shows that he had a heart after God's heart. It is not necessary to rehearse the pitiful details of the sin of adultery or of the subsequent deception that ended in Uriah's death. What is important is how God dealt with David. He sent Nathan, the prophet, to expose the king to himself. With the masterful use of parable, Nathan leveled the sword of truth at David's heart before he knew what was happening. With his "You are the man!" Nathan thrust the spear into David's conscience. David's heart was broken by what he now realized had broken the heart of God. His prayer of repentance in Psalm 51 reveals a new depth to David's character. Our brand of sin and failure may be different from David's. But confronted with its reality, we too can be horrified by the defection of our own hearts. I believe it was Nathan's assurance of God's forgiveness that enabled David to pray this prayer of longing for rightness with God.

> Be gracious to me, O God, according to Thy lovingkindness;
> According to the greatness of Thy compassion blot out
>     my transgressions.
> Wash me thoroughly from my iniquity,
> And cleanse me from my sin.
> For I know my transgressions,
> And my sin is ever before me.

> Against Thee, Thee only, I have sinned,
> And done what is evil in Thy sight,
> So that Thou art justified when Thou dost speak,
> And blameless when Thou dost judge. . . .
> Create in me a clean heart, O God,
> And renew a steadfast spirit within me.
> Do not cast me away from Thy presence,
> And do not take Thy Holy Spirit from me.
> Restore to me the joy of Thy salvation,
> And sustain me with a willing spirit.
> Then I will teach transgressors Thy ways,
> And sinners will be converted to Thee.
>
> (Ps. 51:1-4, 10-13 NASB)

People with great hearts have experienced the anguish of confronting their sin by praying that prayer. The point is that God looks at the deeper desire in our hearts, deeper than the misguided desires that got us into trouble. His purpose is to introduce us to the real person inside us who longs to be reconciled with him. He allows us to see the distorted loyalties, selfishness, or passion that got us into sin. Then he helps us both to own the wrong and to disown it in the blessed atmosphere of his forgiveness.

Don't miss the terror in David's heart when he begs God not to take his Holy Spirit from him. He knew that God's anointing was the only secret of his leadership and ability. He had witnessed what had happened to Saul when the Spirit departed from him. More than anything else, David needed and ached for God's forgiving presence. He did not try to explain away his sin or offer sacrifices. All that David had left to offer God was *a broken and a contrite heart.*

So often when we consider a heart after God's heart we think of sinless perfection and human impeccability. Not so. It is in both success and failure that we break open our hearts. And God's heart is perfectly responsive to our need. Whenever we have done the thing we've said we would never do, his heart is open and ready to receive us. I am always moved by the fact that David never forgot God's graciousness to him. In fact, he named one of his children Nathan (I Chron. 3:5), in memory of God's goodness in exposing his sin and forgiving what he had done. David's heart had a healed memory.

We wish there could be a "they all lived happily forever after" ending to the account of David. The honesty of the Scriptures about our heroes is shown again. The later days of David's life were filled with war, internal strife, incest in his own family, sibling rivalry, and heartbreaking anguish over his rebellious son, Absalom. The king knew little but grief over the people he loved most. Just as David had broken God's heart, so too, his own heart was shattered by what happened in his family.

Absalom had his father's charisma without his father's heart. He was handsome and talented like David, but did not seek or follow the Lord's guidance. David loved Absalom and grieved that his son did not have a heart like his own. When Amnon violated his half sister Tamar, Absalom took matters into his own hands. With dishonest intrigue, he mysteriously arranged for the death of Amnon and fled. David wept bitterly, mourning for Absalom daily. He was forced to perceive the deeper recesses of God's heart as he tried to balance justice and mercy. Finally, at the prompting of his general Joab, through a wise woman of Tekoa, he was convinced that mercy for Absalom was greater than his justified banishment.

Absalom expressed little thanks. He was engulfed in a lust for power and finally led an insurrection against David. He found dissidents and mounted a formidable army. David was forced to flee Jerusalem. Absalom's struggle for power caused division and unrest throughout Israel. David finally had to do the most painful thing in his life. He organized his army and sent them into battle against his own son. Joab was wise in cautioning David not to go with them. Good thing. David could not have done what Joab had to do. When Absalom was caught by his long hair in the branches of a great oak, Joab killed him. When word reached David, the king's heart was crushed with grief. He cried out, "O my son Absalom, my son, my son Absalom! Would I had died instead of you, O Absalom, my son, my son!" (II Sam. 18:33 NASB).

David did not blame God for what had happened. He knew that he had failed to impart his heart to him. His grief was a turbulent mixture of grief over his loss and his own failure as a father.

Life has its blows that hammer our hearts. The disappointments with people we love in our families or among our friends are the most poignantly painful ones. Perhaps some loved one is giving you the same cause for lament as Absalom did David. Or perhaps some friend you've trusted has turned on you. And what do you do when all of your efforts to help someone you love are rebuffed and rejected? That's when you and all of us need a heart after God's heart most of all. Our grief drives us to his heart. There's nowhere else to go! And he's waiting there to help us. In heart-to-heart prayer we can tell him our anguish and receive his patience and love. One of the greatest miracles of the Lord of the impossible is the healing of hearts broken over people.

I've experienced that miracle often. When my heart is bursting with the pain of disappointment and frustration, I've found that only a fresh experience of the Lord's heart can give me the courage to endure. He listens while I pour out my feelings. Then, in response, he helps me feel toward the person with his heart. He presses me to deeper empathy for the real cause of the problem. Then I ask him to show me what my attitude and actions should be. In my imagination he gives me a picture of the kind of person I would be with his heart expressed toward the person. Most important of all, he gives me the gift of faith to trust him with the person's future. I am given a picture of that person filled with his love. That breaks the worry-bind. Soon I feel his heart flowing through my heart resulting in a renewed desire not to give up. When I think of the Lord's patience with me, I am given new willingness to pray, "Lord, help me to be to this person the love You've been to me." The result is a new heart in me.

Seeking a heart after God's heart isn't easy. It means giving up our judgments, the need to be right, and the feelings of hurt. Often, it requires a daily, sometimes hourly, renewal of our hearts with God's heart. And then when we've done all that we can do, we are forced to wait, leaving the results to God. And in the meantime, he gives us a recall to our basic purpose. He puts us back to work serving him. When we feel we've failed miserably in some effort to care, he puts us back on our feet with a new challenge.

That's what God did for David. He gave him the strength and courage once again to be the leader his people needed. The kingdom needed unification and healing. Only a strong king could do that. David had to realize again that his ultimate purpose was to know and do the will of God. He was more than his failures. He was God's man with a future. And the confidence of the Lord in him in spite of everything became the antidote to his grief. David spent the rest of his life battling against Israel's enemies, seeking to weld the people into a unified nation, and giving dynamic leadership to the kingdom being prepared for his son Solomon. To the very end, David's heart was being shaped into the likeness of God's heart.

Israel never forgot the shepherd-king. David became the personification of Israel, and the prophets, long after his death, looked forward to the Messiah who would be born in his lineage and likeness. And when Jesus came in the fullness of time, many called him the Son of David. Through him we discover the real meaning of being a person after God's heart. Jesus Christ came as the heart of God incarnate. John understood the wonder and mystery of this. "No one has seen God at any time. The only begotten Son, who is in the bosom of the Father, He has declared Him" (John 1:18 NKJV). Our quest to know the heart of God is now fulfilled. We can behold his glory and crown him as our Lord.

Now what it means to be a person after God's heart is shown to us with undeniable clarity. The more we know of Christ the more of God's heart we experience. The deeper our relationship is with him the more his character is transplanted in us. The heart of God, full of grace and truth, who dwelt among us revealed what he is like and what we were meant to be. He taught us what it means to open our hearts unreservedly. His message guides us in how to put God first in our hearts. Throughout his teaching he revealed that our hearts are the real treasure. The Greek word for treasure used to translate Jesus' Aramaic word, is *thēsauros*, meaning container. He used *treasure* and *heart* almost synonymously. Matthew 6:19 is a play on the word *thēsauros*, "Mē thēsaurizete hūmin thēsauros epi tēs gēs" really means "Do not treasure up treasures on the earth." Or in my interpretation, "Don't fill the treasure container of your heart with earthly treasures." The reason is in another verse. "For where your treasure is there is your heart also." The total impact of Jesus' teaching on the heart is that it is the divinely created repository of the treasure of the Spirit. He went to the cross to break open our hearts and to prepare us to be able to receive his resurrected presence in them! That's what happened at Pentecost. His followers' hearts were filled with his Spirit.

So for us today, a person after God's heart is one whose mind, emotions, and will are filled with the living Christ. When he is our purpose, passion, and power, we are anointed with his Spirit and grow in his likeness from one degree of glory to another. We experience in ever-increasing measure what the Lord of the impossible has in store for us. This life is but a small part in the endless eternity in which our hearts and his heart become one.

I have never outgrown the simple beauty of the prayer hymn I learned when I first became a Christian. I sing it daily in my prayers. When my heart is troubled or joyful, broken or jubilant, in failure or success, in grief or triumph, I sing,

> Into my heart, into my heart,
> Come into my heart, Lord Jesus;
> Come in today, come in to stay,
> Come into my heart, Lord Jesus.[1]

Harry D. Clarke

And he has—and does!

---

# CHAPTER FIFTEEN

# Fire out of the Ashes

## —Elijah—

My friend was very discouraged. At the urging of his wife and pastor, he had come to a businessmen's retreat at a mountain resort where the topic I was speaking on was burnout. After one of the evening meetings, he and I sat alone in a cabin before a blazing fireplace, talking late into the night.

The man was a Christian, but he had a series of disappointments that had sent him spiraling into the pit of discouragement. He shared with me an inner pervading ache that would not go away. The high-pressure environment in which he worked was getting to him. He was physically and emotionally exhausted from working too long and too hard at a very demanding job. A combination of perfectionism, overcommitment to work, and conscientiousness had produced high expectation and disappointment with his own performance and with that of others.

"Nobody cares as much as I do . . . nobody works as hard as I do . . . nobody is as responsible as I am," he said grimly. This forced him to work all the harder with less results. His defenses were down and his temper was revved up. This made him ill-prepared for the crises that hit him. He was shocked when he sensed that his superiors didn't appreciate his heroic efforts that bordered on what he perceived as martyrdom.

Things weren't going any better at home. Since most of his energy was spent at work, he had little time or patience for the needs of his wife and two children. The least they could do for him, he said, was acknowledge what he was doing for them by keeping life trouble-free at home. They didn't schedule their crises according to his availability and ability to cope. Exercise, recreation, and relaxation had been sacrificed at the altar of pressure at work. At the same time, he realized that he could not say no to added responsibilities which only multiplied his syndrome of discouragement. Lately his marriage had been strained and his family life distressed by the same overcritical attitudes that dominated his attitudes at work. Restless and sleepless nights were wearing him down. The whole world was on his shoulders, he thought. In it all, he was taking himself too seriously, and not taking God seriously enough.

As we talked, the fire in the fireplace burned down into embers and then seemed to go out, leaving the grate full of ashes. "That pile of ashes is just like my life," he said discouragedly, "all burned out!" Then he said something that indicated the depth of the ache in him. "If God cares, how could he allow this to happen to me?" Now even God was an enemy and under the same scrutiny of the man's judgment which he had leveled on his fellow workers and family.

I assured him that God was not against him and that he could help him reorder his priorities and get his life back in order. We talked about his faith. Though he had been active as a member and officer in his church, he had never made a commitment of his life to God. He believed in God but had not experienced the release of entrusting himself and all areas of his life to God's lordship. This accounted for the immense lack of freedom and healthy self-acceptance that drove him on to the questionable goals that he had never surrendered to God. We talked about the great difference between working to achieve our goals for God and allowing God to work in us to accomplish his plans for us.

Next, it was time to talk about what he could do to rediscover new romance and delight in his marriage. The Lord was there guiding both of us as the man thought about the time and tenderness that would be required. And what about the children? They needed him badly. He would have to give up his "drop-out" status as a father and allow God to free him from transferring to his children his own drive for perfectionism. They needed encouragement and affirmation in order to be all that they could be.

We concluded this in-depth analysis of his life and then I asked him to form in his imagination a picture of himself free of the discouragement and living a life in the flow of grace and acceptance. What kind of rest, relaxation, release of judgmentalism would it take? What would happen if he loved himself as much as God loved him? What different attitudes would guide his relationships? How would he prioritize his life as God's man, committed to be a receiver and transmitter of hope and vision?

It was time to pray. I suggested that we ask the Lord to heal the ache of discouragement inside him. God would show him the way and give him the courage to act on the specific steps he had been guided to take as a part of his commitment to a new quality of living.

While we prayed, some unburned pieces of wood in the ashes of the fireplace flickered into flame. Hearing them crackling, we looked up. "You see," I said, "God can bring fire out of the ashes!"

To drive home the implications of the parable we felt the Lord had given us, I took some dry pine logs and asked my new friend to designate each one for the steps he knew that his new commitment demanded. As he prayerfully placed each one on the flickering flame leaping out of the ashes, the fire began to blaze even more brightly than when we first began to talk earlier in the evening. "God not only can bring fire out of the ashes," I said, "He can use the kindling of our surrender and willingness to set us ablaze again with new joy and courage." The man smiled with relief and then retired for the first full night of sleep and rest he'd had in a long time.

I kept in close contact with my new friend in the months which followed that decisive event in his life. He drafted a personal description of the kind of person he wanted to be, incorporating the specific steps he had to take. Each day he rereads that as part of his morning prayer and study time. Along with his wife, he wrote out the essential elements of a new style of life. Each week the two of them honestly check out his progress. He has become part of a small group of businessmen who meet weekly to discuss how to manage stress and pray for one another. He is accountable to them for the maintenance of his new priorities. The Lord of the impossible is transforming his life. My friend has discovered the secret of allowing the Lord to fuel the fire out of the ashes.

Discouragement. We all experience it at times. Some are seldom free of the spiritual malaise. This chapter is for three kinds of people. There are those who are suffering from the spiritual sickness of discouragement right now as they read this. Others have known this debilitating virus of the soul in the past and know they are ill-prepared for the next attack. Still others are very concerned about loved ones or friends who are immobilized by discouragement and long to help them. I know from experience that whenever I speak all three groups are present in an audience. Hearing from people who read my books indicates all three are among my readers. It is with profound love and concern for all of these that I want to grapple with the causes and cures of the crippling ache of discouragement.

Once again, I am amazed at the practical way the Bible helps us find answers. Elijah, the ninth-century B.C. prophet, is a classic case study of discouragement. What happened to him and what God did to cure him gives us specific guidance for burnout. It is the story of what the Lord can do to bring fire out of the ashes.

Elijah was a Tishbite of Gilead, an area in the north of Palestine east of the Jordan. God called him to be a prophet at a time of crisis in Israel during the reign of King Ahab. This weak and vacillating king had married a foreigner, Jezebel of Tyre. She brought with her the priests and worship of Baal and Asherah. Her passion in life became the obliteration of the worship of Yahweh and the establishment of Baal worship as the national religion. The problem of syncretism we considered in previous chapters became more serious than ever before. But now there was a frightening difference. The queen did not foster a blending of religions, but the exclusive worship of Baal as god in Israel.

At the darkest hour of apostasy, the Lord sent Elijah to confront the king. The prophet's name spelled out his mission: Yah is El, Yahweh is God. Elijah established his prophetic credentials and shocked Ahab to attention with a grim judgment. "As the Lord, the God of Israel lives, before whom I stand, surely there shall be neither dew nor rain these years, except by my words" (I Kings 17:1 NASB). With that he left the king to ponder who, indeed, was God in Israel. And a long drought began as Elijah had predicted.

Then the prophet disappeared as quickly as he had entered the court, but it was not the last that Ahab would hear from Elijah.

During the months that followed, the Lord prepared Elijah for a decisive battle with the spiritual sickness which gripped his people. He sent him east of the Jordan where he discovered that the Lord could meet all his needs. He was fed by the ravens which brought him bread and meat. Then he was led north to Zarephath, a city of Sidon, where he was cared for by a widow. The meager resources of the woman were miraculously multiplied by the Lord so that she could feed the prophet. Then, as affirmation of the hand of the Lord upon him, Elijah was given power to heal her son and bring him back to life. The Lord wanted his prophet to be sure of his power. Since nothing can happen through us which has not been demonstrated in us, the Lord was preparing Elijah to trust completely in the power of the Lord of the impossible. When he was ready, the Lord gave him his impossible task. He was to return to Ahab and engage the prophets of Baal and Asherah in a battle to the finish.

Elijah returned to Ahab with a challenge which would decide who was God in Israel. "Send and gather to me all Israel at Mount Carmel, together with 450 prophets of Baal and 400 prophets of the Asherah, who eat at Jezebel's table," Elijah demanded. Ahab accepted the challenge and called all of Israel to come to Mount Carmel.

When the people and the foreign priests and prophets were gathered on the mountain, Elijah thundered his decisive message. "How long will you hesitate between two opinions? If the Lord is God, follow Him; but if Baal, follow him" (I Kings 18:21 NASB). To help them decide, he set up a test of Yahweh's superior power. Two altars were built, one for Yahweh and the other for Baal. Two oxen were selected for sacrifice, one on each of the altars. Elijah carefully explained the conditions of the contest. "Now let them give us two oxen; and let them choose one ox for themselves and cut it up, and place it on the wood, but put no fire under it; and I will prepare the other ox, and lay it on the wood, and I will not put a fire under it. Then you call on the name of your god, and I will call on the name of the Lord, and the God who answers by fire, He is God" (I Kings 18:23-24 NASB). All the people agreed saying, "That is a good idea."

The battle was on. The prophets of Baal wailed all day long, "O

Baal, answer us," but no fire came on their altar. After relentlessly taunting them with their impotence and Baal's silence, Elijah prepared his altar in a way that only the Lord of the impossible could bring fire. He had the people pour twelve barrels of water on Yahweh's altar. The water flowed around the altar and filled the trench around it. Then when it was evening, Elijah prayed, "O Lord, the God of Abraham, Isaac and Israel, today let it be known that Thou art God in Israel, and that I am Thy servant, and that I have done all these things at Thy word. Answer me, O Lord, answer me, that this people may know that Thou, O Lord, art God and that Thou hast turned their heart back again" (I Kings 18:36-37 NASB). And fire fell on the altar consuming the ox and the wood and licking up all the water in the trench. Elijah and God had won. The people were convinced. "The Lord, He is God; the Lord, He is God," they cried, falling on their faces.

That would have been more than enough to exhaust the spiritual resources of Elijah. But he was now revving at high speed. Fire on the altar was not adequate for him. With frenzied compulsion he marshalled the people and killed all the prophets of Baal and Asherah at the brook of Kishon.

Then it was time to pray for rain. Expending superhuman energy, Elijah put his face between his knees and poured all that he had within him in prayer for rain to end the drought. At long last a cloud appeared on the horizon over the sea. Soon the sky grew black with clouds and a heavy rain descended on the land. The Lord had answered again.

When Ahab saw the rain descend, he knew it was time to return to Jezreel to tell Jezebel the amazing thing which he had witnessed. He harnessed his chariot and drove through the rain at high speed. We can only imagine his astonishment when he saw Elijah running beside and then ahead of his chariot with unbelievable energy. The prophet of the Lord outran Ahab's chariot to Jezreel!

At the end of that eventful, spectacular day, Elijah was exhausted and depleted. All his spiritual and physical resources had been completely spent working for the Lord. There was nothing left. Fire had descended on the altar, but Elijah was burned out. He was ill-prepared psychologically for the most excruciating test of his endurance which was still ahead of him.

Jezebel was enraged when Ahab told her about what had

happened on Carmel and about the slaying of her prophets. She sent a bitter, threatening message to Elijah. "So may the gods do to me and even more, if I do not make your life as the life of one of them by tomorrow about this time" (I Kings 19:2 NASB).

At any other time Elijah would have taken that message in courageous stride. But, after all he had been through, expending all he had within him in his battle for the Lord, the message crushed him with unbearable discouragement. He had thought that Mount Carmel was the final battle with evil. Jezebel saw it as a skirmish. And Elijah knew an emotion he had never experienced before. He was afraid. The mighty prophet ran for his life. With ashes of bitterness in his soul, he ran south to Beersheba and then on into the wilderness. When he could run no farther because of sheer exhaustion, he fell down under a juniper tree and begged God to let him die. The spiraling descent from self-doubt to disappointment to discouragement hit bottom in despair. "It is enough," he said, "now, O Lord, take my life, for I am not better than my fathers."

Burnout. The components of what I call "the Elijah complex" are worth analyzing because they can happen to all of us. There are five things which contributed to Elijah's depressing discouragement.

First of all, he was *totally exhausted* from working for God. There is no depletion as dangerous as that which comes from overextending ourselves for righteous causes. Elijah had expended his energies for Yahweh instead of being a channel for his power. God had answered with fire on the altar and rain from the skies, but Elijah had felt the display was dependent on his preaching and persistence. He had not realized how much it had cost him to reestablish God as Lord in Israel.

Second, Elijah was naïve. Simplistically he believed that the defeat of nine hundred and fifty prophets would settle the threat of evil in Israel. He had, however, only touched the tip of the iceberg. His "once and for all" battle was only a beginning. But he was too exhausted to realize that. Jezebel's threat was all it took to snap the thin thread that tied his weary mind to reality. Like many of us, one little disturbance can defeat us when we are down. We too get caught in the web of thinking that accomplishing some task for the Lord will finish the battle. In contrast to generals like Napoleon and Washington who were never more dangerous than after defeat, Elijah, and many of us, are never more vulnerable than after a victory which has drained all our human resources.

Almost every day I talk to or receive letters from Christians who have burned out working for God: pastors, church officers, members of churches, and people active in good causes. Our strenuous activity for God can be the most dangerous threat to our relationship with God if we work in our own strength rather than in the flow of his Spirit. The shift from dependence on him to self-generated, self-justifying effort is subtle. Our work for God can become a source of pride and an extension of our own egos.

I see this happening in three ways. There are those who come up with good ideas which, however admirable, are not guided by the Lord for us. We expect his accolades and strength to be provided for what we determined was his will. The second way is much more frustrating. We seek God's will, feel guided to take a particular direction, and then run ahead of his timing and strategy. We lose contact with God when the task becomes more important than he is! That's when we redouble our efforts to assure success, become critical of others who do not share our commitment and vision, and eventually turn the impatience in on ourselves. The third is most difficult to break. It happens when we confuse our worth with our performance. Whenever we are tempted to assume that we are loved by God for what we do rather than who we are, we overload our lives with more than we can handle. The Spirit is quenched and burnout is on the way.

The next aspect of the Elijah complex is closely related to that: *perfectionism*. The prophet expressed that intoxicating narcotic when he said, "For I am not better than my fathers." Whoever said he had to be? The Lord had called him to be committed to the task given to him, not to compare himself with anyone else. The biblical meaning of *perfect* is to accomplish the end or purpose for which we were born. Perfectionism is very different. It is our effort to have everything maximum on our own strength. We are never satisfied, always restless with our own and other people's accomplishments. Elijah had the proud desire to outdistance his forefathers and everyone else around him. He lost touch with his humanness and blocked out the precious gift of vulnerability to receive God's grace.

Many of us know what he went through. We, too, want to set standards and meet them impeccably. The mistake is that we take our readings of how we are doing from the performance of others rather than from God. But when is enough, enough? Seldom. And we burn out trying to pressure ourselves toward some image that never gets fulfilled.

Perfectionism leads to *isolation.* That's the next thing we see in discouraged Elijah. On Mount Carmel he had arrogantly said, "I alone am left a prophet of the Lord." He had forgotten that a hundred prophets of the Lord had been hidden by Obadiah (I Kings 18:4) and surely there were others. Not all the people had been duped by Jezebel. There were knees that had not knelt to Baal. But Elijah was too possessed with his own passionate efforts for the cause to notice. When his strength burned out and Jezebel threatened him, all he could say was, "I alone am left; and they seek my life, to take it away." In wounded pride he abandoned even his faithful servant. There was no one left to share his grief, to talk over his discouragement. The loner was left alone to make his solo flight into the bottomless pit of self-condemnation.

A major cause of burnout is our separateness, our willful independence. We all need people who can help us realize that what we are feeling they have felt. Discouragement deepens in the false idea that no one else feels the way we do. There is powerful healing in the words of a friend, "I know how you feel; I've been there!" And in an even more sublime way, the incarnation expresses the ultimate power of empathy. There is nothing we can go through that the Lord did not face as our Immanuel. God knows, understands, cares!

Finally, Elijah's discouragement reached its peak when he felt the *futility of the future.* He was so tied up in himself that he heard Jezebel's vitriolic message as the call to close the curtains of history. Why try? What could he hope for? He lost his vision of the sovereignty of God. Most of all, he had given up the meaning of his name Elijah—"Yahweh is God." *Elijah* was really god of Elijah!

What can God do with discouragement like that? What he did for Elijah is exactly what he is ready to do for us. It is exciting to note that as there were five elements to the prophet's complex, there were five ways God dealt with him. The cure of discouragement is in all of them for us.

The first remedy was to put the exhausted warrior for the Lord to *sleep.* He was too physically depleted to be open to reason or new hope. There are times when we get so down that rebuilding our

physical strength is absolutely essential. The first step out of
discouragement is to love ourselves enough to reorder our lives so
we can get adequate sleep, recreation, exercise, and times away
from demanding schedules. The problem, however, is that when
we are down we keep thinking that redoubling our efforts will pull
us out of the tailspin. That's why we need friends to discern the
telltale signs that we are about to break and help us leave the
universe to God while we regather our energies. When Elijah
awoke, he was at least rational enough to know that he was hungry.
The battle on Mount Carmel had worn him down. He needed
*food.* The Lord met his need. "Arise and eat" was the simple
command. The prophet ate and drank the cakes and water that
had been provided and fell asleep again. God who knows us better
than we know ourselves provides exactly what we need to get us
going.

When Elijah was rested, the Lord told him to go on in the
wilderness to Mount Horeb. The place where Moses had met
God and received the Ten Commandments was to be the place of
healing. When Elijah arrived the Lord asked a very strange
question: "What are you doing here, Elijah?" Why, when the Lord
had told him to go to Horeb, would he ask Elijah what he was
doing there? For a good reason: to help the prophet *get in touch both
with what was happening to him and with his real feelings.* Elijah's
response did just that. He rehearsed the whole discouraging
situation. "I have been very zealous for the Lord, the God of hosts,
for the sons of Israel have forsaken Thy covenant, torn down
Thine altars and killed Thy prophets with the sword. And I alone
am left; and they seek my life, to take it away." With his feelings
and perceptions focused, the Lord could begin to deal with the
deepest need that was causing his discouragement.

The Lord does that with you and me. What are you doing here?
In this condition? What caused this? How did it happen? The
question to Elijah was an expression of profound love. The Lord
did not rebuke him for his discouragement; he simply asked for an
account of the circumstances and of his feelings. A crucial
dimension of the healing of our discouragement is to spread out
before the Lord exactly how we feel and the things that caused our
condition. The Lord seeks to use us with others to ask these same
questions tenderly and incisively. When we are challenged to

answer how we got to where we are in our discouragement, we are at the beginning of the way back to health.

God did not debate with Elijah over the blame he transferred to other people. What he said in response was the next step to healing. He told Elijah to stand on the mountain before him. The prophet's greatest need was *a rebirth of his relationship with the Lord.* He needed a demonstration of the Lord's power, a reassurance that in spite of all that happened, the Lord was still in control. That's exactly what happened. First there was a mighty wind which split the mountains, breaking the rocks around the prophet. Then an earthquake made the earth beneath Elijah's feet tremble. Finally, a fire leaped up out of the mountainside. The prophet was shaken and shocked at the physical manifestations of Yahweh's presence. But greater than the wind, earthquake, and fire was the internal experience of grace in Elijah's soul. The Spirit of God spoke to him in a still small voice—a quiet whisper—which brought calm and assurance. The outward displays of power were matched by an inner manifestation of love and encouragement. The wind of God blew out the tension of self-justification. The earthquake in Elijah's heart helped him move from the old ground of perfectionism to the new foundation of being loved and accepted as he was. The fire of God burned out the chaff of despair and rekindled the flame of willing service in Elijah's heart. The most dynamic gift of God to the dismayed is to set a new fire of hope for the future. Enthusiasm is returned; excitement for the Lord and his cause is rekindled. The Lord's fire is for burned-out people!

The final cure for Elijah's discouragement was to *put him back to work.* The Lord gave him specific instructions that would solidify the prophet's assurance that God was not finished with Israel or the unfolding drama of history. He was told to anoint his successor. Elijah's work would go on! Then he was to anoint Hazael king over Syria and Jehu king over Israel. The Lord had plans for his chosen people. Elijah didn't have to carry the universe on his own shoulders alone. To make that undeniably clear to the prophet, the Lord told him about seven thousand people who had remained faithful and had not worshiped Baal. Elijah's isolation was cured by the humbling and then uplifting knowledge that he was not the only faithful man of God in Israel.

What God did for Elijah, he can do for you and me. If the ashes of discouragement smolder in your heart, be sure of this: God can and will cause a flame to be ignited. He is not finished with us. Therefore, we are not finished. Listen for the wind. Sense the quake of his power. Feel the warmth of new fire. Most of all, listen. And the Lord will speak. Do you hear? "I love you. I will never give up on you. We have work to do together. You don't have to work *for* me any longer. Let me do my work *through* you! I am still the Lord of the impossible."

# CHAPTER SIXTEEN

# The Power Struggle

## —*Jonah*—

We hear a lot about power struggles these days. The endless battle for dominance and authority goes on at every level of life. Who's in charge here? Who is calling the shots? Who is in control? The wrangle for power pervades our existence.

The media never allows us to forget the struggle for world leadership between Russia and the United States. There is a constant maneuvering for power in our local and national governments. Companies jockey with competitors for first place. Within their ranks, people wrestle for positions and recognition, climbing over one another as rungs on the ladder to the top. Everyone wants to be head of something—from the shipping department to the executive suite. Unfortunately, the church is seldom any different. Denominations vie for statistical superiority. Church leaders contend for popularity. Within congregations saints often act very unsaintly in seeking to gain, keep, and assure their footing on some turf of the kingdom business. Families are not exempt. Husbands and wives strive to control one another in subtle and brash ways. Dominance is often determined by what is given as well as what is withheld. Children get caught in the no-win situations of sibling rivalry and learn in early years how to manipulate their parents. Friendships often are limited by the superiority-subservience syndrome. Life is a power struggle.

But the greatest struggle of all is between us and God. The most awesome risk of history was taken when God entrusted humankind with free will. He wanted us free to decide to receive or to reject the power of his love. With the power of our volitional gift we are capable of saying yes or no to God. We never escape the question, Who is running my life? The question faces us when we are challenged to begin the Christian life; we must answer it daily as we meet each opportunity or perplexity. To will to make God Lord of our lives and follow his guidance is not easy. Often we resist. Frequently we think we know what's best and question his direction. We miss his blessing in a battle of wills. The crucial power struggle is in our own souls.

E. Stanley Jones once said, "Life is either awfully simple or simply awful." The difference is that we receive or resist what God wants us to do. We desperately need his power, but so often we clog the channel of its flow by engaging him in a power struggle.

A television viewer once asked me a question that focuses the problem. "What I want to know," he wrote, "is how to cooperate with God's best for my life. I'm tired of fighting against him. I want to know God's will and work with him, not against him." This chapter is my response.

We've considered the power of the Lord of the impossible. Now we turn our attention to the power struggle that takes place when we decide something he's guided us to do is impossible for us, not because it is unfeasible, but because our prejudices and judgmentalism make it so. To forgive those who we've decided are unforgivable, to accept the unacceptable, to love our enemies—these challenges meet with stubborn resistance in our hearts. We say no and the power struggle is on!

The prophet Jonah is a classic example of a person in a power struggle with God. The name of this Old Testament prophet means "dove." "Hawk" would have more explicitly captured his combative character. Jonah came from Gath-hepher in the Zebulun territory, now known as Galilee. He prophesied during the reign of Jeroboam II. The historical reference to Jonah in II Kings 14:25 exposes his nationalistic fervor. Jeroboam "restored the border of Israel from the entrance of Hamath as far as the Sea of Arabah, according to the word of the Lord, the God of Israel, which He spoke through His servant Jonah the son of Amittai, the prophet, who was of Gath-hepher" (NASB). It was some time after this cooperation with God that Jonah began his struggle with God over the prophet's hatred of Israel's arch-enemy, Assyria. The Lord clearly instructed Jonah to go to Nineveh, the capital city of the Assyrians, and preach judgment. The prophet's power struggle over that command forms the content of the little four-chapter book which bears his name. The struggle was later recorded as the basis of a disturbing message leveled against exclusivism.

The account of Jonah is more than a whale of a story! Rather, it confronts us with the battle of wills which many of us experience today. Jonah personifies the ways we question God's guidance and resist what, in our deepest hearts, we know he has been urging us to do or to be. We are a "Jonah" whenever we find it difficult to say yes to God's best.

I am going to retell the familiar, fast-moving story of Jonah with some not-so-familiar exposition applicable to our own power struggles with God. To prepare ourselves for what the Lord may want to say to us, I'd like us to focus in our mind's eye on the people we find it most difficult to love. On the screen of your consciousness flash the faces of the persons, the types and groups of people of whom you are most critical and judgmental. Think of the personalities you write off, hoping never to have contact with or responsibility for them, the person or group that prompts you to say, "If I never see them again it will be too soon," or "Whatever happens to them it is less than what they deserve!" These are the people who have become enemies in your mind because of what they do, say, or believe. God may have some marching orders for us that will challenge us to a power struggle over his will for us.

That's what happened to Jonah. "The word of the Lord came to Jonah the son of Amittai saying, 'Arise, go to Nineveh the great city, and cry against it, for their wickedness has come up before Me' " (Jon. 1:1-2 NASB).

"Nineveh, Lord? You must be joking! The capital city of the Assyrians? The center of power of Israel's worst enemy?" The power struggle had begun. Jonah could agree about the wickedness and sin of Nineveh. But what concern was that of his? Yahweh was the exclusive God of the Hebrews. Palestine was his realm. What if the Ninevites responded and repented? That was the inner core of Jonah's resistance. The last thing Jonah wanted to do was become responsible for the salvation of his enemies. He would not go! The rest of the Book of Jonah records the sprints of the reluctant missionary. I like to call him the most rebellious runner of the Old Testament. We see him run from God, run to God for his life, run with God in a brief time of prophetic success, and then run ahead of God in anger and judgmentalism. Each lap focuses the basis of the progression of the biographical sketch of Jonah.

When the shocking revelation of God's will came to Jonah's exclusive, nationalistic heart, he resigned. *He started running—away.* He had worked for the Lord, but he was unwilling to work with him. Nineveh was situated overland to the northeast, on the east bank of the Tigris River, north of the confluence of the river with the Upper Zab. Excavations of its walls, eight miles in circumference, indicate a city of great size. The ancient Hebrews actually thought of Nineveh as a combination of cities that included Calah, eighteen miles south, Resen, between Calah and Nineveh, and Rehoboth-ir which means, "broad places of the city." For Jonah, Nineveh meant simply the center of Assyrian power—the place from which bloodthirsty emperors planned Israel's destruction. He would not go! Instead, he ran off to Joppa, paid his fare, boarded a ship, and sailed off to Tarshish, a sleepy fishing village on the coast of Spain. Told to go northeast, Jonah went west. Nineveh and Tarshish. Two cities in opposite directions, each of which meant something very different to Jonah. Nineveh was the epitome of everything he had been taught to hate. This dreaded enemy of Israel was the synonym for destruction and bloodshed. It was an expansive, idolatrous, pagan, sin-ridden city for Jonah, and nothing could have been more repulsive or repugnant than going there to preach repentance.

Jonah's attitude reflected Israel's narcissism. Inverted self-love and pride precluded the possibility that God's chosen people were to be agents of reconciliation for the salvation of the whole world. Like Narcissus of Greek mythology, Jonah was smitten with the sickness of contemplating his own image. He was committed to exclusivity and separatism. There was no room in his prejudiced heart for concern about his enemies. In reality there was no room for God either. When Jonah ran away he thought he could get away from Yahweh. He had a funnel concept of Providence—that

God's power and control were limited to Palestine and his covenant people.

Tarshish was the farthest place Jonah could think of to get away from the presence of God. The quiet little village symbolized escape and freedom from the call *and* the presence of God. Only a few weeks' journey would bring him anonymity. He was in flight from the reality of Yahweh in avoidance of any responsibility. Most of all, Jonah thought it would end the power struggle.

Most of us have our own Nineveh and Tarshish. One is the city of obedience and confrontation; the other is a place of escape and equivocation. Our Ninevehs are those undeniable revelations of the will of God for us focused in people, opportunities, problems, or perplexities. Whatever or whomever our judgments have rendered an enemy can be our Nineveh. Some are uncomplicated. Nineveh can be simply the Lord's urging which we turn off, some obedient action that demands more than we are ready to give. Whatever else, Nineveh is the call of God sounding in our hearts to serve him, to be his person, to give him first place in our lives.

Running off to our Tarshish can happen in our souls long before we physically head for a Joppa or board a ship to Spain. Some of us are running away from God without ever leaving our geographical location. We can run away by so filling our lives with good things that time for God is precluded, whether with a specific work or with people he has placed on our agenda. Some of us are running off in many directions, but not under God's direction.

At a conference some time ago, I asked a group of Christians to identify their Nineveh. For most, it did not mean going to some place but being God's faithful people where they were and expressing love, forgiveness, and reconciliation to others. One man confessed, "I've spent most of my life running away from God! He's been tracking me for years. I believe in him and attend church regularly. In fact, I'm very active as a leader and contributor. People think of me as a 'good' Christian. But inside, deep in my heart, I've been trying to escape really doing his will. I live a frantically active life, but I'm running in the wrong direction." Years ago the Lord put a finger on a raw place in his attitudes and change was mandated. He's still evading the impact of that. Tarshish can be inside our own souls!

Don't miss the startling implication of the call that sent Jonah running away from God. When we become Christians, God begins a character transformation of our narcissistic self-concern. He seeks to deploy us in the central business of the kingdom, to get us moving with him in loving people and expressing to them what he's done in us. There are no solo flights. We can't clutch God as our private possession to help us accomplish our unsurrendered goals. He has us targeted for some unexpected surprises with some unlikely people and unanticipated challenges.

Jonah bet his life on the false idea that he could flee the presence of God. He lost. At Joppa he boarded the ship for Tarshish and immediately anesthetized his rebellious heart with sleep. What he had momentarily forgotten was that Yahweh was Lord of land and sea. The broad reaches of the Mediterranean were as much under God's providence as his beloved Gath-hepher. The winds began to blow and the sea became tumultuous with white-capped, turbulent waves. The captain of the ship and its crew were panic-stricken. The gods were angry, they thought—angry at someone on board. Lots were cast to find which one on the ship was the culprit. The lot fell to Jonah. "Who are you? What is your occupation? Where did you come from?" they asked urgently. Jonah told them that he was a Hebrew and belonged to the God of Israel. Then he confessed that he was fleeing the presence of his God. The sailors begged Jonah to pray to his God, and all joined in a fervent plea for safety. To no avail. Finally, Jonah asked to be thrown overboard. Strange twist. The sailors tried everything before complying with Jonah's self-destructive request. Masochism is a hairbreadth from narcissism. When we can't build our world around ourselves, often we expect and sometimes assume the responsibility of inflicting pain on ourselves.

You know what happened. Jonah was finally thrown overboard into the sea and the storm subsided. God was the author of the storm and he wanted to get on with the next chapter of his struggle for Jonah's will. The intervention of the "great fish" or whale reminds us that God has "plans for welfare, and not for evil, to give you a future and a hope" (Jer. 29:11). The account in the second chapter of the Book of Jonah tells us that inside the belly of the fish *Jonah ran in spirit to God.* The magnificent prayer he prayed, filled with moving quotations from the Psalms and faithful sayings of Israel, express Jonah's rediscovery of Yahweh's omnipresence and his willingness to deliver those who turn to him in their distress.

We've all known those desperate "God help me, please!" times when we've fallen flat on our faces while running away from him. We've made a mess of things. Life has tumbled in on us. The Lord from whom we've been trying to escape becomes our only hope. We don't deserve his intervention or a second chance, but there's nothing left to do but cry out for his help.

We must not be simplistic about trouble. There are times when trouble is an indication that we are being faithful and confronting evil. Other times, trouble comes our way with little explanation or purpose. We wonder why we are not exempt from difficulty. Then, often after the frustrating perplexity, we look back and see that through it we grew in God's grace. There are also times when trouble is a call of alarm to start running back to God, making us question the purpose and priorities of our life. Sometimes when things fall apart we realize that they were never intended to be together. We were forcing something out of self-will.

For Jonah, the run to God for help required a new theology and a changed attitude. He could not escape the presence of God. There was no place to which he could run that God would not be there waiting for him.

When Jonah was cast out on the shore, God was ready to go back to square-one planning again. The Lord's command was unchanged. The rebellious prophet dried off and began his journey to Nineveh. For a brief time *he ran with his Lord.* The results were alarming and shocking to Jonah. When he arrived at Nineveh he was given a message which matched his judgmental heart. What he did not anticipate was the repentance and revival it would immediately produce. The fiery Hebrew strode through the streets of the Assyrian capital shouting words of doom with undeniable clarity: "Yet forty days and Nineveh will be overthrown."

We can imagine that the people responded, "Who says so?" and Jonah told them about the judgment of Yahweh on the sin of their lives and the wickedness of their city. Reading between the lines of the fast-moving account in the third chapter, we can perceive the mighty stirring of God's Spirit in the pagan metropolis. When the king of Nineveh heard the message, he led a national movement of repentance. The whole city put on sackcloth and ashes of anguished contrition.

What follows is a twofold act of repentance that presses us deeper into our understanding of the Lord of the impossible. The people repented, and so did God! "When God saw their deeds, that they turned from their wicked way, then God relented concerning the calamity which He had declared He would bring upon them. And He did not do it" (Jon. 3:10 NASB). The same Hebrew word is used for the people's repentance and God's repentance. The Lord changed his mind in response to the people's confession. That's very significant for us. God is against sin and for us. We cannot fly in the face of his righteousness and justice. The judgment of sin is separation from God, now and forever. But the moment we turn to him, he is waiting with forgiveness and grace. And a new beginning!

That's what Jonah had suspected all along and that was the reason he didn't want to obey the Lord's command to go to Nineveh in the first place. Now the runner who had run with God so effectively in proclaiming his word to Nineveh, *ran way out ahead of him in anger.* Why was he angry? Because of God's gracious turning from judgment. The power struggle was on again in full fury. The thing Jonah wanted least was to have Nineveh forgiven. It meant he would have to change his attitude toward his enemies. He was more committed to his petulant, negative judgments than he was to God. His "prayer," if we can call it that, expresses the condition of his revengeful heart. "Please Lord, was not this what I said while I was still in my own country? Therefore, in order to forestall this I fled to Tarshish, for I knew that Thou art a gracious and compassionate God, slow to anger and abundant in lovingkindness, and one who relents concerning calamity" (Jon. 4:2 NASB).

Jonah could not give up the power struggle. He battled on to the last fatal round in which he questioned God's nature and purpose. He would rather die than give in. Do we ever get so committed to our predictions of what should happen to people and situations that displease us that not even the mind of God can change our minds? It is easy to be so bent on the destruction of the people and situations we've written off that the destructiveness turns on ourselves. To get our own ego involved in assuring the failure of something or someone we've predicted will never make it produces frightening results. The bittersweet "You see, I told you so!" or "I was right all along!" is a sure sign that we're running ahead of God in nursing our cherished anger. Do you ever feel an inner stisfaction when someone you dislike fulfills your worst expectations? Have you ever been shocked by your own delight when a competitor failed as you prognosticated he or she would? So many of our power struggles with people are an extension of our power struggle with God.

When God bypasses our negativism and blesses others, what can we do? Jonah had two choices: join the people of Nineveh in confessing his own sin, or take into his own hands the judgment of himself. The ultimate battle of wills with God comes when we play God over our own fate with self-condemnation. Jonah wanted to die because he couldn't get God to march to his cadences. Some people are more subtle: they kill off the special person inside their own skins by the slow death of anger turned in on themselves.

Jonah was running ahead of God as he sat east of Nineveh overlooking the city awaiting its destruction. The scorching sun and the oven-hot winds beat down upon his head, exceeded only by the furnace of anger raging in his soul. Once again, the Lord tried to reach him with unqualified love and care. He raised up a giant plant to shade him. That pleased his narcissistic self-interest. But not for long. The Lord wanted to heal his turbulent heart. He withered the plant with a worm to remind Jonah that as he gives, he can take away, if his blessings do not turn hearts to him. The Lord is gentle in his final struggle for Jonah's will. "Do you have good reason to be angry about the plant?" is a gracious way of asking who really has the right to be angry. If any anger was justified, the Lord had the right to be angry with his petulant prophet. Instead, he persisted in offering pity. But it's difficult to stop someone who is running at high speed in front of the Lord and is trying to tell him at the same time how to run the universe.

The Book of Jonah ends abruptly. What happened to Jonah? We do not know. Perhaps that's a good thing. We can write the ending for ourselves. How would we like it to end? Or more personally, how do we want to write the end of our own story? Be sure of this, in a power struggle with God the only way to win is to allow him to win. The final words God speaks to Jonah are filled with his grace which he longs for the prophet to share. "And should I not have compassion on Nineveh, the great city in which there are more than 120,000 persons who do not know the difference between their right and left hand?" (Jon. 4:11 NASB). What Nineveh needed, Jonah needed more. His judgmentalism, issuing in anger, was the result of not realizing that he too would be judged by God. God's forgiveness of him should have produced the precious pity he lacked so much. The Book of Jonah ends abruptly without that crucial response from the unwilling prophet.

The story of Jonah's power struggle with God unsettles us as individuals and as the church. God is up to a magnificent thing in the world. Exclusivism and judgmentalism are luxuries we cannot afford. The same God who struggled with Jonah and his people Israel to get them moving in his strategy of loving all people came in the "greater than Jonah," Jesus Christ, to reveal his pity and grace. When we give up our power struggle and accept his forgiving, enabling power in Christ, we can run with him to our Nineveh.

The secret of the abundant life is that when we know we have power, the power struggle ends. An experience of Christ's indwelling power sets us free from grasping for power with him or with other people. And when we realize that the power we have been given is to know and do his will, then our struggles are turned into a sublime peace. We know that we are loved and accepted. We no longer have to battle for leverage or jockey for authority. All power in heaven and earth is ours!

A final twist to our consideration of Jonah comes not from Scripture but from Michelangelo's painting on the ceiling of the Sistine Chapel at the Vatican. Of all the prophets, apostles, and patriarchs portrayed by the great artist, none has a more radiant countenance than Jonah! Did Michelangelo know something we don't? Or could it be that he longed for Jonah to know the grace the prophet so persistently struggled to resist? Perhaps he imagined that Jonah gave up the power struggle and became a communicator of love instead of anger.

The exciting thing is that we can paint our own countenance into the ceiling of now and eternity. The power struggle can end, and a flow of God's gracious inclusive power can begin in and through us. The portrait is not finished. Your last chapter has not been written. Praise God for that!

# CHAPTER SEVENTEEN

# The Loneliness of God

## ——Hosea——

Have you ever thought of the loneliness of God? We talk so often about his glory and power. Let us not miss the loneliness of his heart. We can identify with that loneliness from our own experience.

There is a loneliness which is more than the absence of others. It is a longing for things to be right between us and those we love. Broken or estranged relationships cause our most excruciating loneliness. We can be with a person and not be in touch with him or her. Distance between people is more than geographical; it is psychological, stemming from the breakdown of communication. People often talk to me about the loneliness they feel in marriage, within the family, or among their friends.

There is an ache of separateness when dreams are not shared, intimacy is not experienced, and deepest feelings are not exchanged. Erich Fromm once said, "The deepest need of man is the need to overcome his separateness, to leave the prison of aloneness." To leave that prison and build bridges instead of walls is not always easy. Especially if the people we love do things which necessitate our judgment and we must search to find creative, remedial ways of assisting them to achieve their maximum.

We've all felt it—the loneliness of profound concern which we cannot express because of the resistance of another. When we see a person we love mess up his or her life, we yearn to know how to reach out to help without negating the person's freedom or robbing him or her of the character fibre that grows through difficulty. Our temptation as spouses, parents, brothers and sisters, and friends is to step in and take charge. We want to solve everything, smooth out life's difficulties, and run people's lives more capably than we perceive they can.

I remember standing on the sideline of a soccer field while one of my sons was a goalie on the home team. He was being roughed up by the visiting team and was doing his best not to lose his temper in the persistent harassment and unfair decisions of the referee. The conflict ended in a wrestling match between my son and the bullies of the opposing team. When I could no longer stand there watching my boy being mistreated, I made the first step to intercede. A friend grasped me by the shoulder. "Don't do that! The lad must fight his own battles. Don't step in if you want that boy to become a man." Good advice, but painful! There is a loneliness of wanting to help a loved one and knowing it is best not to interfere.

Or I think of a friend who was deeply concerned about the drift of the life of someone he loved very much. He had tried to help and his concern was rebuffed. "What can I do?" he cried. "When I try to straighten him out, I am rejected. He is intent on destroying his life. Whenever I offer insight or a gentle corrective, it excavates a growing gulf between us. It is painful to stand by and watch him pour his life down the drain, but efforts to help have strained our relationship. I'm lonesome inside. I can't reach him!"

And then consider the feeling of the loneliness of estrangement a wife felt for her husband. She wanted to comfort him in his problems but could not condone his life-style which was responsible for the collision course with failure he was taking. She felt alone in her grief. She told me that anything she says is misconstrued as interference. She is shut up in a prison of aloneness with her righteous judgments which he needs to hear and the realization that the more she tries to help untangle her husband's twisted values and confused goals, the farther he runs from her.

The heart of every parent can identify with this loneliness. A man told me that he is shocked by the fact that both his faith and commitment to excellence and integrity are not shared by his son. He feels he has failed miserably in communicating love. "I love my

son very much," he said, "but how can I communicate that love
without affirming the things he's doing which I know are going to
scuttle his ship of life? I feel trapped by my own convictions which
I cannot surrender, but I have to resist living my son's life for him.
What can I do? I feel lonely without the friendship I once had with
him."

When we empathize with these people and get in touch with
similar feelings of frustration inside ourselves, we are approaching
the depths of the heart of God. His problem with you and me, as
with millions of his people, is no different. It is the complex
relationship of righteousness and grace. He created us for himself
and for the spiritual companionship of knowing and loving him
and allowing him to love us. But the wrestling we observed in
Jacob and the struggle we chronicled in Jonah is in all of us. We do
things which break his heart. Often we are determined to turn
away from him and do things our way. We do not always put him in
first place. We give ourselves to pursuits he has not willed for us.
We worship false gods erected by our pride. We resist his
guidance and close off the flow of his healing love.

The result is that our relationships with others are starved for
forgiving love and gracious encouragement. We break his
commandments and the essential commandment of love. What
can he do with us?

Sometimes blatant, inconspicuous skirmishes with his will for
us make us uncomfortable in his presence. Prayer becomes less
intimate, then formal, and finally ineffective. We try to use God to
meet our agenda and selfish desires. Often what we want is not
best for us. We evade honesty with him by carefully worded
theories about unanswered prayer. We drift farther apart. A
homesickness for God develops in our souls. But we cannot go
home because of what we've been or because of our arrogant
judgments leveled on the Almighty for the way he's failed to meet
our expectations. Our lack of creative self-love keeps us from
allowing God to fill our emptiness. We endure the estrangement
because of the demanding qualifications of reconciliation. Others,
fate, circumstances, even God himself, are to blame—we think.
And God, who will not negate us by obliterating our freedom,
seeks a way to make us willing to be willing. In response to our
guilt-motivated independence, God is lonely. Lonely for the

rapture of reconciliation. Righteousness. The intimacy for which we were created—his heart and our heart at one again.

Most of us cannot identify with the loneliness of estrangement in God's heart until we have experienced it with someone we love. It is a magnificent gift of Providence when we suddenly empathize with God's loneliness for us. We are in tune with his anguish when we feel the poignant aloofness and assertive resistance of a friend or loved one who has evoked our indignation as well as our concern when we want to help. When a person we love deeply holds us at arm's length because of resistant hostility to our desire to become involved, we have a sacred opportunity to know how God deals with loneliness with us.

We think of heaven as continual bliss and beatific joy. Surely there is uninterrupted praise as angels and archangels and the saints of the ages sing praises around the throne of God. And God is pleased. But I think God's heart is constantly drifting off—to the petulant planet earth, to his children for whom he longs with fatherly love—to you and me. God's primary attention is with the people who say they belong to him but are denying their family likeness with rebellious pride; or with those who make no pretense of knowing him and pretend they don't care. Think of that when you suffer painful loneliness, when people you love suffer because of their own willfulness and you must stand by and watch. Feel what God feels as you come to realize that judging them will push them farther from you. Identify with his problem when you know cheap grace or marked down, solicitous approval will make you a co-conspirator in what you know will eventually render the person less than what he or she was meant to be. All you can do is wait, it seems. And hurt for the person. Loneliness!

The prophet Hosea discovered the lonely heart of God through his own marriage. His wife left him to become an adulteress in the sexual fertility orgies of Baal worship. What could he do? He could not condone the sacrilege and his condemnation drove her farther away. Then, by God's inspiration, he saw the startling parallel between his anguish over his wife and God's disappointment over his people. In the crucible of his own personal crisis the prophet was prepared to speak the truth to Israel in love. Some have said that a bad wife made a good prophet. Perhaps. But in a deeper way, Hosea marks a departure from uninvolved prophetic proclamation because his own life and experience became his message. In a sense, God wrote the script from Hosea's pain and then preached through the prophet!

Hosea was to the spiritual discovery of the true nature of God's forgiving, relentless love what Copernicus was to the realization of the truth of cosmology. His prophecy of God's judgment was coupled with the message of his experience of God's grace. Out of his own experience with Gomer, his wife, and the loneliness he felt because of her sin, Hosea caught the pulsebeat of God's yearning over his people. The Lord's message to Ephraim (the corporate name used for the whole of God's people) was a combination of the delicate balance of righteous judgment and the anguish of finding a way to reestablish a new and a right relationship between him and his rebellious children. The message Hosea wrote and spoke to the Northern Kingdom between 750 and 725 B.C. came burning and flaming out of the caldron of his own domestic difficulties. What he proclaimed was much more than anthropomorphic transference of his own struggle onto God. Hosea did not go through the pain of his loneliness because of Gomer's sin and separation and then suddenly say, "That's how God must feel about Ephraim." Rather, in the depth of communion with God the prophet received startling, unexpected commands from God which exposed new truth about his nature and showed Hosea how to be reconciled with his wife. He then uttered his prophecy to God's people with personal urgency.

What God said to Hosea and the prophet relayed to Israel is worthy of a whole book of expositions. For our purposes here, we can get at the essence of Hosea's book by considering God's guidance for the prophet concerning Gomer in the third chapter, and then spell out the dilemma of authentic love with a passage from the fourth chapter and one from the eleventh chapter.

*First, God exposes his unlimited love in unqualified grace.* Feel with Hosea the perplexity of knowing what to do about Gomer. For a Hebrew no sin could have been more despicable than Baal worship. Gomer was drawn into the pagan fertility rites of fornication in Baal worship and then became a slave of the cult. The righteous thing to do was to judge her and have nothing further to do with her. But the separation resulted in the inexplicable anguish of loneliness. His heart yearned for his estranged wife. Then God told him to do something which seemed to contradict all propriety and integrity. "Then the Lord said to me, 'Go again, love a woman who is loved by her husband, yet an adulteress, even as the Lord loves the sons of Israel, though they turn to other gods' " (Hos. 3:1 NASB). Note the uses of the word *love*. It is as if the Lord said, "You love your wife, now go and love her with a deeper quality of love like my love for Israel."

What did the Lord mean? We are tempted to be simplistic. God always forgives—that's his business—we say, so we can forget our standards and offer forgiveness. Not so! The rest of the Book of Hosea grapples with the costliness of that forgiveness. The deeper Hosea penetrated into God's heart, the more he realized that God understood the struggle he would face in reconciling his wife.

That leads us to what seems to be an unresolvable paradox—God's love versus his judgment. The judgment of God on his people is stated in chapter four. "Ephraim is joined to idols; / Let him alone" (Hos. 4:17 NASB). That sounds like the end of God's patience. *A part of the loneliness of God is that there are times, out of sublime wisdom, when he must leave us alone.* He loves us so much that he refuses to band-aid our sin with bargain-sale grace.

We all know what it is like to feel that God has left us. There are days, weeks, sometimes months, when we feel that he is absent, his care nonexistent. He becomes a shadowed memory of better days.

David knew the feeling. Read Psalm 13 and catch the frustration of a man who wonders where God is: "How long, O Lord? Wilt Thou forget me forever? / How long wilt Thou hide Thy face from me? / How long shall I take counsel in my soul, / Having sorrow in my heart all the day? / How long will my enemy be exalted over me?" (Ps. 13:1-2 NASB). We are not exempt from what most of the great saints have felt many times in their lives.

We say with Isaiah, "Truly, Thou art a God who hides Himself." We pray and our prayers seem to return like boomerangs, returning unanswered or unheeded. We see no sign of his loving care, no whisper of his guidance, no sounding in our souls. He leaves us alone in our rebellion, like a father who must deal with a tantrum. We wish he would head us off at the pass and keep us from doing what will denigrate our dignity. Like a frightened criminal who leaves traces, in effect writing on the walls

of the places of his crimes, "Somebody, please stop me!" we wish
God would intervene. Nothing but silence! Or, in the grief of our
self-inflicted mistakes we want a father's arms to assure us that it's
all okay, that it didn't really make any difference. Silence again. Or
we pray for quick answers to problems we've spent years creating
and we are petulant as we stomp our feet, "God, where are you?"
Where does God go when we need him? We say with the prophet
Habakkuk, "How long shall I cry, and You will not hear?" (Hab.
1:2 NKJV). The question asked in the shallows of our
manipulative efforts to get God to do our bidding must be
answered in the deeps of a loneliness of God which matches his
loneliness for us!

That's the other side of it. God knows profound loneliness as he
waits for us to come to the end of our resource. How easy it would
be to shortcut the time in the blast furnace which is necessary to
create truly tempered persons. He loves us too much for that. In
the eleventh chapter, we discover what pathos that costs.

Hosea expresses God's heart at the time when he seems to be
most unreachable, most distant. Listen to what God said about
Ephraim. He says it about you and me. And the people we love so
desperately. "Yet it is I who taught Ephraim to walk, / I took them
in My arms; / But they did not know that I healed them. / I led
them with cords of a man, with bonds of love. . . . / How can I
give you up, O Ephraim? / How can I surrender you, O
Israel? . . . / My heart is turned over within Me, / All My
compassions are kindled. / I will not execute My fierce anger; / I
will not destroy Ephraim again" (Hos. 11:3-4a, 8-9a NASB).
God's seeming aloofness is balanced by his compassionate
involvement. He cannot do otherwise; his forgiving grace
outdistances his righteous judgment.

In Hosea's writing we are given a picture of God with hands
clasped behind his back, biting his lips in self-imposed restraint,
unwilling to invade our lives with anything which will deny us the
privilege to grow up through our mistakes. Then we see those
arms outstretched as he runs toward us. The stern look of
displeasure is replaced with a compassionate smile of acceptance
when we express the least inclination to turn from our sin and run
toward his outstretched arms. God is lonely for you and me. He
wants us back in his heart where we belong!

George Matheson experienced the depth of God's loneliness

for him when he felt the loneliness of a broken engagement coupled with the onset of peripheral blindness. His heart ached and then began to beat with God's heart. Greater than his hurt over human rejection was the dawning realization of God's faithfulness. He wrote:

> O Love that wilt not let me go,
> I rest my weary soul in thee;
> I give thee back the life I owe,
> That in thine ocean depths its flow
> May richer, fuller be.

When we have heard God say to us, "I cannot let you go!" we can say (and mean it) in our relationships with others, "Because God will never let me go, I will never let you go." We all need people in our lives whose love has that quality of endurance, people who consistently give us assurance and affirmation. They have earned the right to stand with us when we come to grips with life and do the things that are less than maximum for us. We can dare to be open with them knowing that they will not crush the tender plant of desire to be different. They will not blast us with harsh judgmentalism or transfer to us their own impatience with themselves. With patience they will wait until we are open, and multiply our desire to change with loving encouragement.

Then suddenly it dawns on us. If we need that kind of person in our lives, so do the others for whom God has made us responsible. When we ask God to help us know what to do and say, his guidance is not unlike what he gave to Hosea. We are to go to the person; be God's love to him or her; and then, confess our loneliness for the person and our longing to be of help. Love that is more than barter, a reward for change, will give the person the desire to change. If we can be the person with others we long for them to be, soon our example will get through to him or her.

That's not simple or easy. Condemnatory pronouncements and indignant judgments are so much more our inclination. But that has not been God's way with us, and our expression of authentic love can never be less.

The cross is the only place where love can be born and nurtured. The same lonely love which Hosea experienced and then was liberated to express is fully revealed on Calvary.

Judgment of sin, yes, but also inextinguishable love that exposes the true, eternal heart of God. "I cannot let you go! This is how much I love you. I am lonely for you!" May our response be to allow his love to fill our lonely hearts and then become his love to the people he's placed on our agendas.

# CHAPTER EIGHTEEN

# New Every Morning

## —*Jeremiah*—

Many of the letters I receive express a need for hope. Each week hundreds of people tell me in a variety of ways that they are running out of hope. One man's letter, however, was particularly pointed and pathetic.

"I've lost all hope!" he wrote. "A year ago life seemed to fall apart. A lot of it was my own fault. Some of it was caused by other people. Nothing seemed to go right. Friends told me that things are never so bad that they couldn't be worse. Well, they got worse! So I asked God to step in and straighten things out. What do you do when you ask for God to pull off some miracle and instead you get more problems? How can you hope when you ask God for help and nothing happens the way you expect?"

How would you have answered this man? He needed more than glib words of advice. Life had brought him to the threshold of a crucial discovery. I didn't want it to be wasted by telling him that he just needed to hang in there, mustering up more courage to keep hoping. He had lost his utilitarian, self-generated hope and was on the edge of receiving the gift of ultimate, God-infused hope.

When we talked face to face, I said something which startled and astounded the man. "You are a very blessed person." "A what?!" he said with consternation. "How can you say that with all that has happened to me? I've lost hope and all you do is congratulate me."

At least I had his attention for what I went on to say and, by God's grace, he was receptive.

"It is not possible to produce authentic hope. What you have lost is your yearning expectation, and wishful thinking. You have not lost hope. Perhaps you never have had real hope. True hope is not a humanly generated capacity you can gain by right attitudes or positive thoughts. Hope is a gift which is inextricably, inseparably related to the Giver. You need God more than his answers to your problems. When you experience an intimate relationship with him, hope will be one of the finest by-products. A hope which lasts is not a will-of-the-wisp, haphazard longing for God to act on your behalf. Rather it is an ultimate confidence that he is your life, now and forever, and that nothing in living or dying can separate you from him."

I am thankful that on the afternoon we talked, this hopeless man received hope as a result of truly making God the Lord of his life. He put first things first: God's kingdom, fellowship with God, and a willingness to do God's will. In the days that followed the gift of true hope began to grow.

The most painful discovery I have ever made, and must rediscover repeatedly, is that hope is a serendipity. We will be disappointed constantly when we search for hope as an end in itself. Dynamic hope comes from something or someone who is ultimately reliable. That's the rub. No friend or loved one, leader or institution, can qualify. They were never meant to. People, causes, movements, parties—or the frail longing that, given time, things will work out—always let us down.

"Is there any hope?" people are asking today, joining the chorus of others with depleted expectation. As I look out over my congregation each week, I see the question written on the faces of hundreds of people. Honesty and love must answer both yes and no. No, there is no hope from what we tell God we want; yes, there is hope in what God wants to be and do for us.

There are three levels of hope. The first two are facsimiles; the third is reliable. We all have an inner yearning for progress, success, and the fulfillment of our fondest dreams and plans. Some people who look for the best and expect it have been blessed with a sunny disposition. When even the most positive of personalities face problems and perplexities, they are forced to ask God for help in working things out according to their presuppositions. But it is when he doesn't meet our expectations or march to the beat of our drum, that we are blessed with the crisis of wanting God for God and not for what he will do as the enabler of our agenda. It is at this deeper level that hope is born.

This turbulent transition from utilitarian hope to ultimate hope is the story of the life of Jeremiah. He has been called the "weeping prophet." In fact, the word *jeremiad* meaning "tale of woe," "disappointment," "discouragement," was coined from a shallow understanding of Jeremiah's life and ministry. Actually, the prophet became a man of ultimate hope.

But he didn't experience that quality of hope initially or easily. It was the gift of his later years when prayers seemed unanswered, when his yearning for his people was unsatisfied, and when he was utterly depleted. That's why a consideration of Jeremiah is so crucial for our time. The experiences he went through in the forty years of his prophetic ministry in the Southern Kingdom leading up to the Babylonian capture and destruction of Jerusalem in 586 B.C. and the pitiful days which followed, with the exile of his countrymen to Babylonia, hammered out a man who speaks to our condition. Jeremiah did not live on the surface of the turbulent sea of Judah's history; he became a deep sea diver who descended into the depths and came up with a pearl of experienced truth. He received the gift of authentic hope and shared the secret.

Lamentations 3 charts Jeremiah's descent into the depths, and his ascent with sublime hope. The Book of Lamentations was written after the destruction of Jerusalem and the beginning of the exile. It is a compilation of elegies. The title of the book and the first word of the first chapter in Hebrew is *Ekah*, literally, "Ah, how?" or "Alas!" The ancient manuscripts had a heading which explains the title and the content. "And it came to pass, after Israel was led into captivity and Jerusalem was laid waste, that Jeremiah sat weeping and lamented with this lamentation over Jerusalem and said. . . ." And what he said is filled with sorrow and eventually indignation, which borders on blasphemy, over God's providence. How could God allow this to happen? The people had sinned, yes. They had been deaf to the prophet's most impassioned warnings, indeed. The chosen people had chosen false gods and faithless, disobedient political alliances, to be sure. But Jeremiah had prayed all through the treacherous demise. Did not God hear or care?

The anguished question, focused particularly in chapter 14, verse 8, pervades the Book of Jeremiah, "Thou hope of Israel, / Its Savior in time of distress, / Why art Thou like a stranger in the land / Or like a traveler who has pitched his tent in the night?" (NASB). Jeremiah could accept the judgment of God on the apostasy of his people, and both predicted and affirmed God's allowing the fall of Jerusalem and the exile of the city's finest citizens, but not without anguish, terrible suffering, and a serious question of the extent of God's punishment. It was when Jeremiah called out for personal sustenance to bear the pain that he felt bereft and forgotten. He thought he had been on the Lord's side through the anguish his people experienced. All that had earned him was rejection, hatred, and hostility from the very people he tried to help.

The first eighteen verses of Lamentations 3 capture the seeping away of utilitarian hope. The suffering of the people did not accomplish the end Jeremiah had hoped. Neither the means nor the end seemed beneficial. Like most of us who have been satisfied only with a hope that God would accomplish our vision, Jeremiah ended up questioning him. The images he uses to explain his plight are shockingly vivid. Jeremiah had seen affliction, but it was the rod of God's wrath he questioned. He felt alone in the darkness of seeming rejection from the Almighty. Didn't God appreciate his efforts over the years? Imprisoned by the captors, he felt alone and forsaken. When he prayed, there seemed to be no answer. "Even when I cry out and call for help, / He shuts out my prayer. / He has blocked my ways with hewn stone; / He has made my paths crooked. / He is to me like a bear lying in wait, / Like a lion in secret places. / He has turned aside my ways and torn me to pieces; / He has made me desolate" (Lam. 3:8-11, NASB). Note the personal pronouns of petulance. "My ways;" "my paths." His hope that God would do his bidding engulfed his soul. The ridicule and mocking of people was nothing in comparison to the silence of God. Jeremiah's lament reaches a crescendo of soul crisis when he cries, "My strength has perished, / And so has my hope from the Lord" (Lam. 3:18 NASB). He was nearing the breaking point. Good thing! He was being broken open to experience ultimate hope.

Repeatedly the prophet went back over what had happened. He

misused the gift of memory to refocus all the disappointments he'd been through. Did God remember? Jeremiah did! "Remember my affliction and my wandering, the wormwood and bitterness. / Surely my soul remembers / And is bowed down within me" (Lam. 3:19-20 NASB).

Then suddenly, a laser beam of truth penetrated the dungeon of Jeremiah's memory. Reaching bottom below bottom, he grappled with a remembrance that transformed his complex of consternations. In the depths of despair, the gift of hope was given. And the Giver was the gift. "This I recall to mind, therefore I have hope." Jeremiah's, "Ah, how?" becomes, "Ah, here is hope!"

So often we hear and repeat the frail words, "Well, here's hoping!" Jeremiah said the words with more than the thin and frayed thread of wishing. The impact of the next six verses exclaim with the emphasis of excited realization, "Here's hope, indeed!"

The prophet emerges from his dark night with three great convictions that lead to a liberating experience of indestructible hope.

The first is based on *the forebearance of God.* "The Lord's lovingkindnesses indeed never cease" (v. 22*a* NASB). The alternative translation of the Hebrew is: "It is because of the Lord's mercies that we are not consumed." Jeremiah was gripped with the realization that God's judgment had been coupled with the possibility of a new beginning. The exile of the people was actually more than they deserved. Total extinction might have happened. I've often wondered if the words God gave Jeremiah to send to the exiles became his own personal assurance as he wept over Jerusalem and his people. "For I know the plans I have for you, says the Lord. They are plans for good and not for evil, to give you a future and a hope" (Jer. 29:11 TLB). God was not finished with his chosen people or his appointed prophet. He had plans. What Jeremiah thought was the end was really a semicolon in preparation for a new beginning—all because of the patience of God.

When we feel that all hope is gone, our healing process begins when we remember how God persevered with us in spite of our resistance and rebellion. Because of God the "what might have beens" become a basis for praise and the first stirrings of hope. When I think back over my life and consider what could have happened if God had not brought me through the valleys, I am much more ready to trust him with the future. The contemplation of his nature of mercy prepares me for hope that is greater than wishful thinking. Think of the times you were spared the results of poor decisions, resistance to God's guidance, and blatant refusals to do his will.

Next, Jeremiah remembered *the compassions of the Lord* which do not fail. "For His compassions never fail." God's forebearance is expressed in his forgiveness and in his desire to reconcile us to himself. He will not go back on his word. What he said to Joshua, he says to us, "I will be with you; I will not fail you or forsake you" (Josh. 1:5 NASB). Much of what causes us to lose hope is the result of our own and other people's words and actions. We wonder why God doesn't short-circuit our human freedom and build a better world. And yet, his compassions persist, and he uses even our mistakes for our growth and his glory.

When we remember the past times of mercy, our willingness to take a different view of the future begins to grow. What else really matters?

And we know so much more of God's compassions than Jeremiah could muster in memory. We look back at the incarnation, the cross, the resurrection, and Pentecost. God does not give up. Christ was mercy incarnate in his ministry, unmerited grace in his death, and a source of ultimate hope in his resurrection. The mighty acts of God dispel hopelessness. He is the invading, intervening Lord of creation and human history. The cross and an open tomb remind us that the worst can be used by God for the best. Christ defeated the power of sin on the cross and death on Easter morning. Our meager hoping is replaced by a living hope.

Peter went through the same transition. His hopes were pinned on Jesus of Nazareth doing what he had presupposed he ought to do. Calvary dashed his utilitarian hope. The living Lord of the resurrection broke the chains of earth-bound expectations and opened heaven and abundant living for the apostle. Listen to his bracing word to the early church which had drifted back into using Christ as a means to accomplish its temporary hopes that he had mercifully allowed to be dashed in suffering. "Blessed be the God and Father of our Lord Jesus Christ, who according to His abundant mercy has begotten us *again* to a *living hope* through the resurrection of Jesus Christ from the dead, to an inheritance incorruptible and undefiled and that does not fade away, reserved in heaven for you, who are kept by the power of God through faith for salvation ready to be revealed in the last time" (I Pet. 1:3-5 NKJV, italics added). The resurrection of Christ is the basis of our growth in hope.

And not only Christ's resurrection, but our own! Hope is born when our false hopes of getting the Lord to do our bidding die. We are crucified in the death of temporary hope and resurrected to eternal hope. We are alive forever through being born again. Heaven has begun. Nothing can defeat that. God's compassionate mercy has saved us from despair—with ourselves, others, and our world.

But that has to be updated, refreshed, renewed each day. Jeremiah found God's mercies new every morning. His anticipation of God's forbearing and forgiveness led him to *the Lord's faithfulness*. "They are new every morning; / Great is Thy faithfulness" (Lam. 3:23 NASB). Hope is reborn daily, momentarily, in each new challenge and crisis; in each intervention when resurrection rehappens in and around us. The mercies of God not only are fresh every morning, they make mornings out of the night, what Keats called the "vale of soul making."

That's why, from our perspective on this side of Pentecost, the invasion of the Spirit of Christ with the baptism of his Spirit is so crucial. New mercies are not dependent on our perfection, or even our preparedness. They come when we least deserve them or are ready for them. And we are amazed.

The faithfulness of God astounded Jeremiah into awe and wonder. His mind was off himself and on to God's consistency and constancy. A time of hopelessness should not send us in a vain search of hope, but in search of God. And then we are amazed to realize that even the desire to pursue the Lord is because he is in hot pursuit of us. Even the realization of new mercies is a gift of the Lord. He enables us to enjoy the wonder of his daily breakthroughs into our depleted expectation. He gives the day and shows the way. Then we can sing,

> Great is Thy faithfulness, O God my Father,
> There is no shadow of turning with Thee;
> Thou changest not, Thy compassions, they fail not;

As Thou hast been Thou forever wilt be.
Great is Thy faithfulness! Great is Thy faithfulness!
Morning by morning new mercies I see:
All I have needed Thy hand hath provided,
Great is Thy faithfulness, Lord, unto me![2]

Jeremiah has gone deeper and deeper from self-condemnation and criticism of God to a realization far greater than his hopelessness. He thought about God and his goodness in spite of all he and Israel had done and been.

But that only prepared the prophet for the most crucial discovery about hope. *Ultimate hope is experienced in union with God himself.* The sublime source of hope is in consistent fellowship with the Lord who made us for himself and by his integrity must break any competitive source of hope. " 'The Lord is my portion,' says my soul, 'Therefore I have hope in Him' " (v. 24 NASB).

We have come with Jeremiah to the holy of holies. The heart of God. Nothing else can give us hope that lasts.

Some background on the idea of the Lord as our portion heightens the impact. When the promised land was divided among the tribes of Israel, no inheritance was given to the tribe of Levi. The tribe was distributed among the other tribes and each tribe became responsible for maintaining their part of the Levites, who were charged with care of the sanctuary and priestly duties. The Lord promised that instead of land he would be their portion. Jeremiah appropriates the language and idea. The Lord, not safety, prosperity, preservation of Jerusalem, or his own dignity and reputation, would be the prophet's portion. The loss of the land of Judah was on the sensitive preacher's heart. Jerusalem was empty of bygone glory. What was left? God! He alone was Jeremiah's portion. And hope. Newfound intimacy flowered in hope.

Jeremiah had moved from wanting hope *from* the Lord to experiencing hope *in* the Lord. The inadequate hope that had perished was replaced by an indefatigable hope that was imperishable.

The awesome thing is that the Lord will allow whatever it takes

---

for us to say and believe that he alone is our portion. He does not
send difficulties. He doesn't have to. There are enough to go
around in this fallen creation. But when tragedy strikes, losses
happen, grief breaks our hearts, or things don't work out as we had
planned, we can still experience hope.

Jeremiah wanted to share what he had been through. The
prophetic voice in him was released again, but now with the
loving-kindness of the Lord whom he met, not in the shallows but
in the deeps of a decisive encounter. What he has to say now is out
of the victory over hopelessness. He had waited on God, been
silent, and God gave him hope. He gave him an experience of his
Spirit.

"The Lord is good to those who wait for Him, to the person
who seeks Him. It is good that he waits silently for the salvation of
the Lord" (Lam. 3:25-26 NASB).

The same tumultuous transition from false to authentic hope is
one of the major themes of the apostle Paul in Romans. He uses
Abraham as an example as he develops his thesis. Abraham,
"contrary to hope, in hope believed, so that he became the father
of many nations" (Rom. 4:18a NKJV). As we have discovered in
our study of Abraham, it was when his own hopes were broken that
the gift of hope was given. Other translations render it, "In hope
against hope he believed." True hope always must combat
humanly generated hope.

In Romans 5 Paul goes on to tell us about *genuine* hope in
fellowship with God. "Therefore, having been justified by faith,
we have peace with God through our Lord Jesus Christ, through
whom also we have access by faith into this grace in which we
stand, and rejoice in hope of the glory of God. And not only that,
but we also glory in tribulations, knowing that tribulation produces
perseverance; and perseverance, character; and character, hope.
And hope does not disappoint, because the love of God has been
poured out in our hearts by the Holy Spirit who was given to us"
(Rom. 5:1-5 NKJV). The love of God, plus faith, equals hope. It is
a hope that does not disappoint us, as stable and secure as God
himself.

That prepares us for further *growth in hope.* In Romans 8, Paul
deals with the power of hope for the future. "For we are saved in
this hope, but hope that is seen is not hope; for why does one still
hope for what he sees?" (v. 24 NKJV). True hope helps us in our

daily problems and decisions. Paul tells us that the Spirit of God knows our hearts and inspires them with the specifics of what we can dare to hope for as a part of God's plan for us. "Now He who searches the hearts knows what the mind of the Spirit is, because He makes intercession for the saints according to the will of God" (v. 27 NKJV). In other words, we are told how to hope and for what to hope in God's unfolding will for us. When we pray for what God is willing and ready to give, our hopes are not a projection of our wish-dreams but his plan. When he is our hope, then hope for the accomplishment of his revealed will really works. And we can hope with confidence for, "We know that all things work together for good to those who love God, to those who are the called according to His purpose" (v. 28 NKJV). That's hoping!

Hope and the Spirit of God are one. When we are filled with the Spirit we have hope. When we close off the flow of the Spirit and demand his power for our plans, hope is diminished and lost. This is the impact of Paul's final word on hope to the Christians at Rome in Romans 15:13. "Now may the God of hope fill you with all joy and peace in believing, that you may abound in *hope by the power of the Holy Spirit*" (NKJV, italics mine).

Paul reminded the Ephesians that prior to their conversion they were bereft "having no hope and without God in the world" (Eph. 2:12 NKJV). To live in the world without God is to eventually face hopelessness.

But the sublime insight of the Apostle was given to the Colossians. The mystery of hope is revealed. "Christ in you, the hope of glory" (Col. 1:27 NKJV). There it is again: our hope is the result of the Spirit of Christ. The glory of being remade in Christ's likeness and living with him forever is the hope that pulls us forward in a deathless life which nothing can destroy.

Whatever life gives us or takes away is a blessing if it breaks the bind of utilitarian hope that constantly disappoints us, so that we can experience an ultimate hope that is as sure as the Lord himself. What Jeremiah found new every morning is ours every moment, for the Lord is not only our portion, he's our power—to hope!

CHAPTER NINETEEN

# A Fourth for Fire

## —Shadrach, Meshach, and Abednego—

My friend was facing a life-or-death operation. On the night before the operation, his wife tried to assure him with some comforting words. "Everything is going to work out," she said lovingly, "you're going to be just fine."

After she left the room the words kept tumbling about in my friend's mind. Sometime during the long night of waiting, he felt a profound inner calm. He said to himself, "And even if it doesn't, I'm going to be just fine!" He faced the possibility that he might not make it. And yet, he knew that nothing—further sickness, pain, even death—could separate him from God's gracious, loving care. In that moment of crisis he knew an eternal security and was convinced that he belonged to God whether he lived or died.

True freedom is found in that awesome territory beyond where we simply receive answers to our prayers for what we want or think is best. There is no lasting liberation from our fearful anxiety until we are able to say, "Even if it doesn't work out" as we planned or hoped, we will experience a greater victory. We are alive forever. Nothing in this life can defeat us.

So much of our faith is dependent on getting God to do what we think we need. We judge our Christianity, and that of others, on the basis of evident answers to our petitions. We remain faithful as long as there is a steady stream of miracles on our behalf. When we

205

face reversals or long periods of waiting for answers to prayer, immediately we think there must be something wrong with us. Sometimes, we even question God's faithfulness.

The account of Shadrach, Meshach, and Abednego in the Book of Daniel gives us four words of faith that introduce us to a Fourth for fire. Daniel's three Hebrew friends were overseers of the administration of the people of God during the Babylonian exile. They were faithful to Yahweh and would not worship the Babylonian gods. When Nebuchadnezzar, the king of the Babylonians, set up an image of gold ninety feet high and nine feet wide in the plain of Dura, they would not bow down and worship. The news reached the king and he was enraged. He gave orders that the three Hebrews be brought before him. "Is it true, Shadrach, Meshach and Abednego," he said, "that you do not serve my gods or worship the golden image that I have set up? Now if you are ready, at the moment you hear the sound of the horn, flute, lyre, trigon, psaltery, and bagpipe, and all kinds of music, to fall down and worship the image that I have made, very well. But if you will not worship, you will immediately be cast into the midst of a furnace of blazing fire; and what god is there who can deliver you out of my hands?" (Dan. 3:14-15 NASB).

The answer of the courageous Hebrews is filled with daring confidence. "O Nebuchadnezzar, we do not need to give you an answer concerning this. If it be so, our God whom we serve is able to deliver us from the furnace of blazing fire; and He will deliver us out of your hand, O king" (Dan. 3:16-17 NASB). What they said next expresses the secret of their courage. "But even if He does not, let it be known to you, O king, that we are not going to serve your gods or worship the golden image that you have set up" (v. 18 NASB).

*"Even if He does not!"* Five words for fire with which we can face anything or anyone. Shadrach, Meshach, and Abednego's faith was not dependent on deliverance, but on the knowledge that God would care for them beyond the furnace. Not until we can say those words can we live abundantly. The three Hebrews could not be coerced or cowed. They would not worship any god but Yahweh. Nor did they expect Yahweh to bow down to them! There was no quid pro quo of bartered allegiance. They did not trust God to get their way; they trusted him for a way through, and beyond, any trial.

There is no real power in the Christian life until we can say, "Even if he does not." They are the ultimate words of surrender that give us lasting strength. They express the maturity of postgraduate wisdom way beyond the sophomoric insistence that God march to our orders. We never really give God a problem of perplexity until we completely let go with an "even if he does not" quality of trust.

Disturbing? Yes! But sublimely liberating. We all have struggles that require God's power and help. Many of us live on the level of faith that asks and expects an answer. When we are faced with what seems to be unanswered prayer, we feel discouraged and neglected. But then we are given a blessed opportunity to grow. When we look beyond the answer to the assurance that God has even better plans, we discover a peace "that passes understanding."

We admire the courage of Shadrach, Meshach, and Abednego. But we know so much more about God and his power than they did. They stood firm with raw courage. We can stand boldly with enlightened courage. Through Jesus Christ we have "an inheritance which is imperishable and undefiled and will not fade away, reserved in heaven . . ." (I Pet. 1:4 NASB). All our prayers must be in the perspective of Christ's victory over evil and death. Nothing on this side of the grave can destroy the promise of what is on the other side of it. In that confident faith, we can relinquish our needs, know that God will respond in the way that is ultimately best for us. Even if he doesn't answer the way we would like or expect or think is most creative, we know that it is only a comma in the triumphant account of our spiritual adventure which has a sure and victorious conclusion.

So the first thing we can learn from Shadrach, Meshach, and Abednego is—*face the furnace.* Our own furnace is where our obedience meets the fires of evil in the world. Some of us get into trouble for the wrong reasons—pride, self-will, petulance. The three Hebrews were in trouble because they would not bow down to a pagan image. Erected around all of us are false gods which we are tempted to worship. Some of us face a furnace of difficulty because we won't bow down. There are golden images in our society which demand our worship—materialism, success, power, or popularity. When we refuse to bow down to them, we may experience rejection and criticism.

The furnace for others may be suffering physical or emotional problems. When life disappoints us, we are tempted to worship an image of frustration and futility.

The fieriest furnace, however, is to feel that God has forsaken us. This furnace is the result of the temptation to worship a god of our own making—a god who should do our bidding and answer our requests. He is common, not cosmic; an errand-boy, not the eternal Sovereign of all creation. But God won't be put on our agenda; he wants us on his!

The people around us often do not help. They tell us, when we pray and do not get our answer, "There must be something wrong with you! Something must be amiss in your spiritual life if you ask and answers are not given exactly the way you have requested." The unsettling suggestion prompts us to erect an even more pagan golden image—ourselves. We must be adequate or more perfect for God to hear and answer our prayers. As a result, when we face the furnaces of life, we are unsure of ourselves and also of God.

Facing our furnace means that we come to grips with reality. Whatever problems, perplexities, illness, or disappointment in human relationships we face in life, we can meet them head on with the knowledge that even if God does not extricate us from them according to our desires, he will see us through them. We face the fire when we commit it to his wise providence and trust him to strengthen us in it and get us beyond it.

When I am with people who are facing the furnace of life's difficulties, I try to empathize with them as they go through the process of finally surrendering their needs with an even-if-he-doesn't trust. The process forces them to see things in perspective. The problem is not all of life. They belong to God and are alive forever whatever the outcome of the problem. Frequently I visit people who are in hospital rooms facing the possibility of not getting well. In each case, I help them move into the investigation of what would happen to them if their prayer for recovery is not answered. Where would they be then? When that assurance of God's relentless grace becomes more important than the secondary answer of immediate healing, little else matters. They are given the freedom to say with Paul, "For if we live, we live to the Lord; and if we die, we die to the Lord. Therefore, whether we live or die, we are the Lord's" (Rom. 14:8 NKJV). The exciting thing is that the moment of relinquishment is often the beginning of healing or the resolution of a problem that seemed insoluble.

Martin Luther was asked where he would be when he faced the angry bishops, cardinals, and Pope before the Diet of Worms. His answer was one for all the furnaces of life we must face. "Then as now, I shall be in the hands of Almighty God!"

The second thing we learn from Shadrach, Meshach, and Abednego is to go into our furnace *leaving the results to the Lord.* When Nebuchadnezzar heard their courageous assurance of God's ultimate care, he was filled with wrath. His face was twisted by anger as he ordered the fire to be heated to seven times its usual temperature. The three vigilant Hebrews were tied up in their own clothing to make sure they could not move or stand. Then they were thrown into the blazing fire. But the flames did not match the radiance of faith on their faces. They trusted God for either his intervention or his strength through the pain of incineration.

Saying even if he doesn't leaves the results to God. We are not responsible for the outcome; we are responsible to be obedient. We can answer the taunting question thrown at Job, "Does Job love God for naught?" We can say firmly, "We love God for God!" No longer do we say, "God if you do this for me, I will do that for you," or, "I'll stop doing this or that, if you promise to do this for me!" We can say, "God, I leave the results in your hands."

That was the confidence of Shadrach, Meshach, and Abednego. And the results were astounding to them and astonishing to the king. Nebuchadnezzar looked into the furnace and saw the three Hebrews loosed and walking around in the midst of the fire—unharmed. That gives us the third thing we discover from this account. When we face our furnace and leave the results to God, *we can be sure of his presence with us in the fire.* Nebuchadnezzar not only saw the three men walking around free, he also saw a fourth person with them. "I see four men loosed and walking about in the midst of the fire without harm, and the appearance of the fourth is like a son of the gods!" (Dan. 3:25 NASB). The Lord was with them in the fire. He is the Fourth for fire!

The Lord always answers prayer. When his answer is not what we wanted or asked for, he gives us a far better gift—himself. He endures the fire with us. The incarnation is the sublime assurance of this. God lived among us in Jesus Christ and went through the fires of our humanity for us so that we might know that he will never depart when we need him. He is with each of us now. We can endure our fiery furnace when he is with us. The Fourth for fire was the one who got Shadrach, Meshach, and Abednego out of the fire. It is significant that Nebuchadnezzar recognized that the Fourth Person in the fire must have been a divine intervener. He said he was like a son of God. We know who that was! None other than the Logos, the Son of God, who later came as Jesus of Nazareth—Immanuel—God's presence in a pre-incarnation visitation to three men in trouble. Note that he did not extinguish the fire or lift the three sufferers out of the flame. Instead, it was the king's recognition of his presence that prompted him to call them out of the flames.

The intervening Lord comes to us on time and in time when we are willing to trust him even if he doesn't come. We can go into our furnace knowing that he will bring his results in his own way and according to his own time schedule.

And it will be done in a way that will convince others of his power. After he released the three from the furnace, the king gave glory to God. Look at what he said to all the high officials of his court. "Blessed be the God of Shadrach, Meshach and Abednego, who has sent His angel and delivered His servants who put their trust in Him, violating the king's command, and yielded up their bodies so as not to serve or worship any god except their own God. Therefore, I make a decree that any people, nation or tongue that speaks anything offensive against the God of Shadrach, Meshach, and Abednego shall be torn limb from limb and their houses reduced to a rubbish heap, inasmuch as there is no other god who is able to deliver in this way" (Dan. 3:28-29 NASB).

That's quite a statement from one who hours before wanted the three Hebrews punished by death in the fiery furnace. A cataclysmic event had to happen in the king's life to change his attitude toward God's people whom he had so ruthlessly deported from Jerusalem and Judah. Something also had to be done to reassure the people that Yahweh's power was not limited to Jerusalem and the promised land of Palestine. What happened in the fiery furnace caused a transformation not only in the king, but also in the Hebrew people. God was in charge, indeed! The intervention had earthquake proportions which changed the focus not only from the pagan gods to the Lord God, but also from fear and captivity to courage and hope.

Shadrach, Meshach, and Abednego were released and given property in the province of Babylonia. The king affirmed their faithful courage, and their witness in the fiery furnace converted him and his rulers to the worship of the "Most High God." The people of God had been exiled for their apostasy, and yet God used the exile to evangelize their captors. He does have the last word!

Don't miss the crucial point of it all. The three faithful Hebrews did not know what their obedience to the Lord would bring when they held fast to their beliefs. It would have been a good story if they had gone into the ordeal knowing what God would do. It is a great story because they did not. Their trust was not pinned to deliverance according to human specifications.

The final thing Shadrach, Meshach, and Abednego teach us is that *there is no limit to what God will do if we give the glory to him.* The result of their obedience was that God got the glory. So often we are willing to go through trials if we can be recognized for our gallantry. Not so with the three who met the Fourth for fire. The visitation by the Lord in the furnace was one phase of a greater plan. The three men fade out of the picture and the glory of the Lord remains. Our future prayer power is dependent on giving the Lord the glory for all that has happened in the past.

There are people watching what is happening to you and me. One may be the person who has caused our problems. What our trials do to us and what God does in us because of them will touch their lives in a significant way. And the issue is not that they become impressed with us, but that they are awestruck by what God did with our surrendered circumstances. Our most telling witness is that only God could have done what was accomplished, and that even if it had worked out differently we would still trust him.

A consistent theme has been woven through out studies of the heroes and heroines of the Old Testament. The Lord of the impossible called them all to risk; none of them knew how the trial or challenge would end. They didn't search for opportunities to be heroic; they simply obeyed God and trusted him to work out his purposes through them.

This all comes down to a personal question. Are we willing to let go of our fears of what might happen to us? Each of us is faced with some kind of challenge to be obedient to God in trying circumstances. The false gods are all around, tempting us to bow down in order to find an easy solution and avoid the pain or frustration. Most tempting of all is the "fix-it" god we've molded out of our own desire to control God. A sacred, blessed opportunity is before us. Can we say, "O world, my God is able to deliver me from the furnace of blazing fire, and he will deliver me out of your clutches. But even if he doesn't, I'm not going to serve your gods"? If we can declare our freedom from our other gods, we can surrender our needs to the only true God.

When we say and mean the four words for fire, "Even if he doesn't," the Fourth for fire will do more than we expect—and in a way better than we can imagine!

# CHAPTER TWENTY

# When All Else Fails

## ——*Ezekiel*——

A health food store where I often have lunch displayed a startling advertisement recently: "Fat Chance Diet." The play on words caught my attention, but it was the sentence beneath the title explaining the diet that arrested my interest. The words intrigued me and lingered on my mind for days afterward. "A last chance diet when all else has failed."

You guessed it. I began to think about a spiritual diet we might follow when all else has failed. Have you ever known a time in your life when all else seemed to fail? Some area of your life? A relationship or responsibility? Some problem that resists solution or challenge that you can't seem to meet? Ever get so low that you were disillusioned with life as a whole? What do we do when all else fails, when our best efforts and expenditures of energy only seem to make things worse?

Some have known this kind of failure in times of sickness. Others feel it with people they seek to love or help. Others have felt it about their jobs. Many feel it in their marriages. Still others know the frustration of it in trying to renew their churches. All of us have sensed it in the causes or programs in society that weigh heavily on our hearts. What can you do when all else has failed?

Ezekiel was called to be a prophet to the people of God at a time when everything else had failed. He was born about 621 B.C. In the first twenty-seven years of his life, he lived through the spiritual and political decline of Judah and Jerusalem. He saw the glory of the temple desecrated as the golden decorations and furnishings were stripped away in a last-ditch effort to avert defeat by paying tribute. The prophet witnessed the rise and fall of four of his kings. The Babylonians took over world domination and made Judah a vassal state. Finally, around 597, Ezekiel was carried off into exile in Babylonia along with King Jehoiachin and the leading citizens, princes, and craftsmen of Judah.

During the first year in exile, Ezekiel observed what happened to God's people and empathized with their spiritual plight. The discouraging reports from Jerusalem intensified their anguish.

Life in the Babylonian exile was not as bad as it had been for the people of the Northern Kingdom who had lost their identity when they were carried off to Assyria where they were scattered. The Babylonians allowed the Jews of Judah to live in communities and develop a semblance of normal existence. But the proud Hebrews could not forget their defeat and humiliation. Their limited conception of the providence of God fostered the belief that his sovereignty was limited to the promised land and Jerusalem. They felt alone and bereft in Babylonia. The universality and omnipotence of God was not a fortifying part of their theology. To be deported from Palestine was to be apart from the Lord. The ridicule and taunts of their captors only added to their anguish. Psalm 137:1-6 expresses their discouragement as well as their limited understanding of the Lord of all creation.

> By the rivers of Babylon,
> There we sat down and wept,
> When we remembered Zion.
> Upon the willows in the midst of it
> We hung our harps.
> For there our captors demanded of us songs,
> And our tormentors mirth, saying,
> "Sing us one of the songs of Zion."
>
> How can we sing the Lord's song
> In a foreign land?
> If I forget you, O Jerusalem,
> May my right hand forget her skill.
> May my tongue cleave to the roof of my mouth,
> If I do not remember you,
> If I do not exalt Jerusalem
> Above my chief joy. (NASB)

If we cannot sing the Lord's song in a strange and foreign land of adversity, chances are that we cannot sing it at all! But we've all had those times when our song of praise catches like a bone in our throats and there is no joy for singing. The melody of life seems lacking and we have no inclination to sing because all else has failed. It was during this time of songless depression that God raised up Ezekiel with a new song. And the song of hope he taught God's people to sing in the strange and foreign land was first taught to him by the Lord. What God wanted to have happen in his people, he first engendered in his prophet.

Ezekiel's call from the Lord contained three stirring admonitions. The first was to stand on his feet so that God could speak to him. It was as if the Lord commanded, "Attention!" and Ezekiel was brought to a salute of obedience with a ready, "Yes, sir!" The Lord wanted his prophet at full attention, on his feet, ready to move in faithfulness. "Son of man, stand on your feet that I may speak with you!" The second admonition was coupled with a gift. The Lord's Spirit entered the depleted soul of Ezekiel as he said, "You shall speak My words." And to fulfill the command the prophet was offered a scroll of the Word of God. The third command was, "Now you, son of man, listen to what I am speaking to you; do not be rebellious like that rebellious house. Open your mouth and eat what I am giving you." The scroll was given to Ezekiel with an urging, "Son of man, eat what you find; eat this scroll, and go, speak to the house of Israel" (Ezek. 2:1, 7, 8; 3:1 NASB).

There's a last chance diet, indeed! *Stand up, get going, eat and digest the Word of God.* When all else has failed, that's exactly what the Lord does for us. He gets our attention, gives us a challenge for his Spirit alone to sustain us, and nourishes us with his guidance as we chew on and digest the words of encouragement he gives us. The central theme of the Bible is the resurrection resiliency of the uplifting power of the Lord of the impossible. He can take dead people, churches, marriages, friendships, and projects, and resurrect them to new life by the infusion of his Spirit.

That was the liberating, hopeful message of Ezekiel to the people of God all through the twenty years of his ministry in Babylonia from around 592 to 570 B.C.

In that span of time he stood with the people as one hope after another collapsed. He spoke incisive truth about the seizure and destruction of Jerusalem. When the city fell in 586 B.C., he had a vision of what God could do with his people who felt that all had failed. Ezekiel became the prophet of the glory of God. His basic message was that God was omnipresent and ubiquitous among his people to resurrect them. He was a watershed for the people of God who marked the reversal of the flow of thought and expectation from death to life. Ezekiel was a prophet of the resurrection power of God.

The basis of Ezekiel's resiliency was a promise and a vision recorded for us in the twenty-sixth and twenty-seventh chapters of his prophecy. The prelude to the vision was a great hope. The Lord assured the prophet that he would bring his people out of exile and back to Jerusalem. But they would not be the same people who were carried out of their homeland. Exile would be like a death to all that had been and to their pride over it. And out of the graves of failure and apostasy, God would resurrect a new people. He would give them a new heart and place his Spirit within them—another assurance of a last-chance diet when all else has failed. The promise the Lord made is what we all need. "I will give you a new heart and put a new spirit within you; and I will remove the heart of stone from your flesh and give you a heart of flesh. And I will put My Spirit within you and cause you to walk in My statutes. . . . And you will live in the land that I gave your forefathers; so you will be My people, and I will be your God" (Ezek. 36:26-28 NASB).

Then the Lord gave Ezekiel an experience that revealed how this would happen. He took hold of the prophet, transfigured him, and gave him the vision of the valley of the dry bones. A combination of factors blended together to produce the vision.

The exiled Hebrews had a proverbial saying which pervaded their conversation. "Our bones are dried up, and our hope is perished. We are completely cut off." I wonder if that saying was tumbling about in Ezekiel's mind. Added to that was the report from Jerusalem of a final battle in which the fallen warriors had their flesh flayed from their bones and the bones were left to dry in the hot sun. But surely the strongest influence in preparation was the realization of the spiritual deadness of his people. They had become the dead among the living. What God wanted Ezekiel to witness was how he would make them the living among the dead!

We are told that the prophet was carried up by the Spirit. He was lifted out of himself and given an experience in which he was confronted with the real condition of his fellow Jews and with what God was going to do about it. What God put Ezekiel through must be understood in the context of the explanation after the vision. "Son of man, these bones are the whole house of Israel" (37:11 NASB). And they may be ours too—and our church's!

The Spirit of the Lord showed Ezekiel the valley of the dry bones and made him walk around in the midst of them. The bones were strewn about, unconnected and very dry. Then the Lord asked an incisive question. Like the question he asked Elijah, "Why are you here?" the Lord's question to Ezekiel was not asked because he did not know the answer, but because he wanted the prophet of the spiritually dead Israelites to experience his answer. "Son of man, can these bones live?" Note how the Lord picks up the proverbial saying of despair among the people, "Our bones are dried up." He wanted to know whether the prophet believed they could live again. Ezekiel responded with laudible humility and realism coupled with awe and wonder. "O Lord God, thou knowest" (37:3). It was a response of surrender and openness, as if to say, "O Lord, they cannot live without you. Only you could bring them to life!"

Ezekiel was commanded to prophesy to the bones and say, "O dry bones, hear the word of the Lord. . . . Behold I will cause breath to enter you that you may come to life. And I will put sinews on you, make flesh grow back on you, cover you with skin, and put breath in you that you may come alive; and you will know that I am the Lord" (Ezek. 37:4-6 NASB).

Ezekiel followed orders and did as the Lord told him. As he prophesied, there was a rattling noise, and the dry bones began to come together, bone to its appropriate connecting bone. Then sinews grew on them, followed by flesh and skin. The result was a valley of dead corpses lacking only breath to bring them fully alive again. For that the Lord told Ezekiel to command the breath to breathe on the slain. As he did so, the bodies came to life and stood on their feet like an exceeding great army. A resurrection from the dead had happened!

The Lord was quick to drive home in Ezekiel's mind the implications of the vision.

"Son of man, these bones are the whole house of Israel; behold they say, 'Our bones are dried up, and our hope has perished. We are completely cut off.' Therefore prophesy, and say to them, 'Thus says the Lord God, "Behold, I will open your graves and cause you to come up out of your graves, My people; and I will bring you into the land of Israel. Then you will know that I am the Lord, when I have opened your graves and caused you to come up out of your graves, My people. And I will put My Spirit within you, and you will come to life, and I will place you on your own land. Then you will know that I, the Lord, have spoken and done it," declares the Lord' " (Ezek. 37:11-14 NASB).

There are two crucial things this vision has to say to us when we think all else has failed. The first is—*own the bones!* The Lord wanted no ambiguity about the meaning of the vision. The bones were Israel. The meaning for us is that we too can be spiritually dead while physically alive. We are among the living dead whenever our capacity to hope is extinguished, whenever our love for God and others grows cold and perfunctory, and whenever our faith becomes a dull habit and duty. We are meant to be vibrant and radiant. Own the bones of drabness, grimness, and joylessness. There is nothing more ineffective than religion that has lost its zeal and zest. If we are not excited about life, expectant of what each day will bring, and aflame with enthusiasm, our lives are among the dry bones—fragmented and scattered. And the Lord says, "You are dead, dry, depleted, deadly dull. And I am going to give you new life!"

The church too often is like exiled Israel. When faith and life are separated, the thoughtlessly familiar repetition of rites and rituals can become boring and dull. Exciting truths can be preached with a joyless, parsimonious piety that hits wide of the mark of people's real needs. Pretense results and our confidence is placed in organization, programs, and buildings.

The more I talk with contemporary church members and leaders all over the country, the more I am convinced that the great need of American Christianity is for us to own the bones of dead institutionalism. All else has failed! We must admit, individually and corporately, our need for daily resurrection and the breath of the Holy Spirit to fill us. There are cycles of death and resurrection that take place in the lives of individual Christians as well as in churches. When we cherish our past more than our future, we begin to die. The experience of God in the past can never be a substitute for what he longs to be for us now and in the future.

I have gone through repeatedly the experience of having to own the bones of my own spiritual dryness. When secondary things block intimacy with the Lord, I begin to die. When I am shocked by the realization that I have joined the valley of dry bones among the host of dull church leaders, I must honestly own those bones. Every church I have served has gone through the experience of revival when the Spirit of the Lord led us to repent of our blandness or resistance to the new directions he was trying to give us. We've had to own the bones of programs that no longer worked, customs that perpetuated a past but did not help or heal people, or ingrown exclusivism that failed to fulfill the mandate of the Lord to reach those who don't know and love him. The Lord breaks churches as well as people. He allows them to come to the place where all else fails! He asks us what he asked Ezekiel, "Can these bones live?"

Before we can answer we have to admit that they are our own bones. God does not ask us to generalize about the dead bones of our churches. He wants more than endless theories and clever techniques of church renewal. We need something much more than a new program or fund-raising or membership drives. We must own the bones. "Lord we are dead. Dead in comparison to what you want your church to be. Dull when compared to the contagious Christianity we see spread across the pages of the Book of Acts. We want to come alive again. More alive than we've ever been. We long to be a center of new life, dynamic preaching, conversions, an inclusive beloved community where people are loved and set free to live the abundant life." Owning the bones, prayer like that will never go unanswered. The resurrection of the church can and will happen. The bones will live!

That requires a combination of ruthless honesty and a desire to live at maximum pitch for the Lord. It must begin with the pastor and the officers. Then, when they confess the dead bones of their efforts, God begins a resurrection in them individually and together. The things we long for in our churches cannot be produced by human effort alone. Only God can give verve and vitality to the preaching of his Word. He alone can enable people to respond. He is the instigator of conversion and the source of the gift of faith. He brings people to a church that's alive. He inspires leaders to develop the quality of program that really meets people's needs.

There's nothing worse than grinding out churchmanship with our own strength. But the moment God's people get honest with him and one another, he gives them innovative direction that they could not produce with their own cleverness. He creates a readiness and a responsiveness in his people that is nothing less than a miracle.

Most of us are so proud and self-justifying that we hold off at all costs the experience of owning the bones. Actually, the realization of what is dead in us or our churches is a sign of great maturity. The only thing worse than failure itself is the failure to admit it and to allow God to give the gift of resurrection. When we refuse, God must find ways to tell us how dead we are. His methods often are painful and alarming. It took exile for Israel. But the Lord was ready to begin again with his people the moment they repented. When all else has failed it is absolutely crucial to ask, "Why has all else failed?"

Criticism of other people does not help. "If onlys" targeted at friends or loved ones or leaders do not help in experiencing new life. The Lord says, "Own the bones—they are yours!" That's when the bones get new sinews, flesh, and skin. The resurrection is not far behind. Tennyson was right:

> Our little systems have their day;
>   They have their day and cease to be:
>   They are but broken lights of thee,
> And thou, O Lord, art more than they. . . .
>
> Let knowledge grow from more to more,
>   But more of reverence in us dwell;
>   That mind and soul, according well,
> May make one music as before, . . .
>
> I held it truth, with him who sings
>   To one clear harp in divers tones,
>   That men may rise on stepping-stones
> Of their dead selves to higher things.
>
> *In Memoriam,* Alfred Lord Tennyson

The second thing we discover from Ezekiel's vision is closely related to the first. After we own the bones *we must disown them.* The Lord gave Ezekiel a vivid picture of what was going to happen before he asked him to prophesy to the potential.

God's last-chance spiritual diet for Israel and for us is a new spirit and a heart that are capable of receiving and containing his own life-giving Spirit. The bones were brought together. The skeletons received sinews and flesh, but there was no new life until the Lord breathed breath into them. When everything else has failed to work for us, the Lord gives both a new spirit and his Spirit. I have always been intrigued by the fact that his promise to Israel was a new human spirit able to receive the Holy Spirit. My interpretation is that our new spirit is a new disposition, a different attitude, a liberated perspective. When Ezekiel was told to prophesy to the bones, he was given a new spirit of expectation and anticipation of what the Lord promised could happen. The point is that God prepares our hearts through confrontation and through our confession and confirmation of his love, before there is a readiness to receive his indwelling Spirit. His Spirit is the author of the preparation and then of the propitious infilling. Complete surrender is the prelude to resurrection of the dead bones of our broken dreams and unmet goals.

The secret of new, abundant life is offered us through Christ's death and resurrection and the power of the Holy Spirit. He died that we might be forgiven, he rose that death might no longer be our enemy, and he returns to each of us to be the source of our personal resurrection. "I am the resurrection and the life," he told us. He not only offers us the promise of a new life for our dead bones in our spiritual, self-imposed exile, but he also offers the power to make it happen. Our hope is not only that he was raised, but also that we are raised to a new life that will never end. Resurrection to a life filled with his Spirit promises the regeneration of our character and total being. He not only gets us out of our graves of impotence, he also gives us the power to live with freedom and joy as new people.

The disciples could not have made it without Pentecost. Nor can we. Being with Jesus during the three years of his ministry made the disciples the powerful new people who changed the world. The period between the resurrection and Pentecost was itself a valley of dry bones. What brought those depleted disciples to life was the infilling of the Holy Spirit. What happened to the dry bones in Ezekiel's vision is a prelude to what happened at Easter and Pentecost.

As I read history, each period of spiritual renaissance has

resulted from people who owned the bones and then disowned them through the experience of repentance and receiving the Lord's indwelling power. The time in which we are living is most exciting because God has allowed so many of his people, laity and clergy, to witness the failure of their plans and programs. Human effort, skill, and cleverness have been exhausted. But following repentance comes resurrection, and following resurrection comes regeneration. The dead bones come to life!

If you are at one of those times when all else is failing, thank God. If you feel that your heart has become cold and hard, believe that God will replace it with a heart of flesh—open, warm, receptive. You are ready to receive the breath of life, the Spirit of the Lord himself.

Recently, a young widow came to see me. Her husband had died a couple of years before. She had not allowed herself to feel the grief and go through the pain of loss. Instead, she filled her life with activity, hoping to avoid the sense of loss. Denying one feeling, she lost her capacity to feel anything else. She sensed a growing coldness inside and held people off at arm's length. Soon she felt rejected by God. She found it difficult to pray. "My heart is like a cold stone," she said, beginning to cry. "I feel dead inside. I've tried everything, and nothing seems to work."

After a long period of deep sobbing, the young woman was ready to accept what God had been trying to give her all along. The experience of recognizing and owning her spiritual and emotional deadness prepared a "heart of flesh" in the place of her "heart of stone." We prayed and the Holy Spirit invaded her total self—mind, emotions, will, and body—so that she left the valley of dry bones. That afternoon marked the beginning of a Spirit-empowered life that set her free to live and love again. When all else had failed, she took the last-chance diet. The same thing can happen to you and to me.